# TEACH
# A WOMAN
# TO FISH

Center Point
Large Print

**This Large Print Book carries the
Seal of Approval of N.A.V.H.**

# TEACH
# A WOMAN
# TO FISH

## OVERCOMING POVERTY
## AROUND THE GLOBE

## RITU SHARMA
WOMEN THRIVE WORLDWIDE

CENTER POINT LARGE PRINT
THORNDIKE, MAINE

This Center Point Large Print edition
is published in the year 2014 by arrangement with
St. Martin's Press.

The text of this Large Print edition is unabridged.
In other aspects, this book may vary
from the original edition.
Printed in the United States of America
on permanent paper.
Set in 16-point Times New Roman type.

ISBN: 978-1-62899-214-4

Publisher's Cataloging-In-Publication Data
(Prepared by The Donohue Group, Inc.)

Sharma, Ritu.
  Teach a woman to fish : overcoming poverty around the globe / Ritu
Sharma. — Center Point Large Print edition.
    pages ; cm
  "An insider's look at women in poverty, the inner workings of
Washington, and how change really happens"—Provided by publisher.
  ISBN: 978-1-62899-214-4 (library binding : alk. paper)
  1. Women—Developing countries—Economic conditions.
    2. Women—Developing countries—Social conditions.
    3. Poverty—Developing countries.
    4. Women in development—Developing countries.
    5. Large type books.  I. Title.
HQ1870.9.S53 2014b
305.409172/4—dc23

Give a man a fish and he eats for a day.
Teach a man to fish and he eats for a lifetime.
But teach a woman to fish,
and everyone eats for a lifetime.

# CONTENTS

# ACKNOWLEDGMENTS

*If you want to go fast, go alone. If you want to go far, go together.*
                                    —African Proverb

None of the things you will read in this book could have been achieved by working alone. Women Thrive Worldwide is a coalition fueled by deep collaboration—with more than 60 US-based allies, nearly 100 global partners in 35 countries, 10,000 caring American women and men in an action network, a passionate and gifted staff, an active board of directors, and hundreds of generous donors. For your sake, I am not going to name them all here.

I would, however, like to name the people who believed in this book long before I did: Leslie Levine, Joelle Delbourgo, and Jason Rohn. Joelle not only believed in it, she shepherded it from concept to the publisher's house. Thank you all for pushing me over the cliff. I flew, thank goodness.

To those who put up with my spending months away followed by endless hours at my laptop: my two wonderful boys and my bighearted partner, Rob DeFriese. Thank you for hanging in there with me. I'm back now.

To the extraordinary team at Women Thrive Worldwide, past and present, who accomplished all of the victories contained in these pages: Thank you with my whole heart. My gratitude to the team that took the organization forward while I was focused on writing: Melanie Richardson, Lauren Supina, Christopher Burley, Elise Young, Laura Henderson, Lara Pukatch, Mei Powers, Erin Kelly, Jillian Holzer, and Christine Hart. And my appreciation to our board of directors: Joe Keefe, Trevor Tomkins, Eileen Mancera, Eugenia McGill, Mark Blackden, Alonzo Fulgham, Suzanne Lerner, and Asif Shaikh. Women and girls around the world are blessed to have you on their side. My deepest thanks go to Elise Fiber Smith, our founding chair, for walking this long road with me.

Huge thanks and appreciation to Molly Lyons, who patiently waited for drafts and then edited them with a surgeon's skill, and to Hilary Flowers, who researched numerous topics down Internet rabbit holes for free. I am indebted to Julie Dixon, who left her comfortable home in North Carolina to go to Burkina Faso with me to photograph and record video of women in the 115-degree heat. I also express my gratitude to Martha Martinez, who fell in love with the women of Honduras as she translated their stories. Big thanks to all those who provided comments on the manuscript: Alberto Begue, Carol Bilzi, Gib

Brown, Christopher Burley, Christine Hart, Laura Henderson, George Ingram, Seema Jalan, Joe Keefe, Emily Martin, Mei Powers, Lara Pukatch, Melanie Richardson, Elizabeth Stanley, Lauren Supina, and Elise Young.

My gratitude to Karen Wolny and the team at Palgrave Macmillan for turning the idea into the book you now hold in your hands.

I also want to acknowledge and thank the Howard G. Buffett Foundation, which underwrote the travel and time necessary to complete the manuscript.

And above all, to the many women and men who let me glimpse into their lives for a moment so that you might be inspired by their courage, grace, and joy in the face of extreme poverty, violence, and injustice. I dedicate this book to them.

# TEACH
# A WOMAN
# TO FISH

# INTRODUCTION

The very first time I went up to Capitol Hill, I was not dressed for the part. It was a sticky day in June 1990. I was 21 years old and just out of college. I felt so lucky to have landed an internship at Friends of the Earth, an environmental advocacy group, and was excited to be tasked with a "Hill drop." This is the lowliest duty on the advocacy totem pole, delegated to interns and assistants, in which a flyer, pamphlet, or letter is hand delivered to every office in Congress. These were the days before 9/11 and anthrax letters, and anyone could walk onto the Hill and into any office in the spirit of open democracy.

I practically bounced up the steps to the Cannon House Office Building in my cute, airy, sleeveless dress and summer sandals. I entered the Cannon rotunda and gazed up at the majestic Greek columns and gilded domed ceiling, my mouth gaping open. The coolness of the marble floors and walls soothed my feet and face, which were hot from my walk to the building. I could not believe I was actually standing in the House of Representatives of the United States of America. The place seemed as grand as the momentous decisions that were made there.

I strolled into the first office on the first floor,

clearly marked by the US and state flags on either side of the doorway, and cheerily handed the receptionist a flyer as I said, "Hello. How are you today? Could you please give this to your environment legislative assistant? Thank you so very much!"

The Cannon building is one of the easiest for Hill drops. It's an open rhombus with a courtyard in the middle and a staircase at each corner. Once one floor is circumnavigated, it's easy to hop down to the next one and run another circle. I had great momentum and was feeling a rush of pride for my contributions to the democratic process.

I passed important-looking staffers in suits and ties, and my friendly smiles were met with dead-eyed stares or nothing at all. Occasionally, I would pass an older, gray-haired gentleman with a gold and red pin on his lapel and a young person trying to keep up behind while carrying lots of files. *Wow,* I thought. *That must be a real congressman. I wonder who that was?*

I finished Cannon still feeling elated and excited by the tall stately ceilings, grandiose murals of revolutionary battles, and significant-looking people. I took a quick break to rest my feet and down a Diet Coke and then headed over to the Longworth House Office Building, which is set up much the same as Cannon. About halfway through Longworth, my feet started aching from pounding hard marble floors that seemed to get harder with every step in cushionless sandals. I was getting tired, and the initially soothing coolness had turned to an unfriendly chill. My drop-off speech had gone from a sociable song to an artless "Please give this to your environment LA."

I entered the Rayburn House Office Building thinking it was my final stretch, but what awaited me was the largest (2.365 million square feet) and most terribly designed shape: a hollow square with huge L-shaped wings off every corner that do not connect to anything else. The only way to do Rayburn is to venture down every L and retrace your steps back, four times on each floor for six floors.

I learned my first important Washington lessons that day. First: Congress is an unforgiving place—even the floors don't give, so dress the part and wear Dr. Scholl's. Second: Attempting to get anything done in Congress is like being in a maze; your journey is so much longer and more winding than you can possibly imagine at the start. Third: Despite all this, don't ever stop feeling awed by the fact that regular people just like me can walk these halls and make change happen.

In the fall, I got hired on at Friends of the Earth as an entry-level administrative assistant. In between filing, copying, and standing for interminable amounts of time at the fax machine, I'd eavesdrop on the program directors' conversations and then offer to help them with this or that piece of follow-up to their meetings or phone calls. Pretty soon they were letting me accompany them to some of their meetings on the Hill or around town.

I had always thought political dealings in Washington happened in dark, wood-trimmed back rooms with cigar-smoking lobbyists shaking hands with silver-haired, plastic-faced politicians. But that's not what I saw. What I saw was smart people making little money, holding meetings in church basements or coffee shops, and taking nothing but their best ideas and most incisive arguments to the staffs of Congress' members. Their ideas would make no one rich, but they would improve our environment, or make our jobs safer, or contribute to solving the planet's grand challenges. I felt like I was walking through an Oz of good ideas, a world I didn't know existed: a place in which solid analysis and persuasive presentation, backed by Americans speaking out, made Congress take positive action. No big money, no fancy lunches, and no junkets for congressional staff—just good ideas and a lot of footwork.

I knew I'd found my place in the world.

I spent almost nine years walking around Capitol Hill promoting women's access to health care and family planning in developing countries and basic primary school education for children unlucky enough to be born into poverty around the world. In those years—1990 to 1998—we were living in the dot-com bubble, the US treasury was in the black, and our country was a little more willing to help people who scraped out a living on less than a dollar a day.

One thing I noticed during those years was that beyond the reproductive organs of women in developing countries, Congress paid no real attention to the issues that mattered most to women and girls overseas: violence, education, economic opportunity, and political voice. Every now and then a gruesome story about a child bride or acid-burn survivor would hit the front pages and a few members of Congress would push out a resolution condemning the violence in a spasm of care. By the next week it would all be forgotten. Every time it happened, it made me madder.

I became part of a little cabal of women advocates that would meet a couple times a year and go up to Capitol Hill to get Congress to mandate through law that our US aid agency throw a few crumbs to women's priorities. We called ourselves the Coalition for Women in Development and were led by Elise Fiber Smith, who was an advocate for women in developing countries at the same time Gloria Steinem was fomenting the revolution within American women's minds. I was by far the youngest member of the clutch and pretty much volun-teered to do any legwork needed. They saw it as a welcome freebie; I saw it as the chance of a lifetime. One day in 1997, Elise invited me to coffee and asked if I might help keep the group going after her retirement. I said yes before her coffee stopped steaming.

Within six months, our cabal became the founding board of directors of the Coalition for Women's Economic Development and Global Equality (Women's EDGE). I was incredibly lucky to become its executive director, getting to represent women's voices on Capitol Hill 24/7. In 2008, we changed our name to Women Thrive Worldwide.

I still walk through the halls of Congress—though now, I'm in better footwear and am armed with a tight grasp on the way things work in the offices I popped into years ago. I've also walked on dusty paths around the world, speaking to women who face vast barriers to feed, clothe, and educate their families.

We American and European women have more in common with women who live on less than a dollar a day than we think. They—like us—worry about their kids. They think about how to better their homes. And just as we do, they do their best to make ends meet no matter how long or short their shoestring may be. I carry this thought with me all the time when I'm on Capitol Hill or at meetings in the White House, but it hits home most intensely when I talk with women. It struck me particularly hard as I sat under a mango tree in a small village in Burkina Faso with my friend Mariam, a subsistence farmer. On the surface, Mariam and I couldn't be more different, but our conversation that day kept returning to our boys (she has four and I have two) and how tiring they can be. We are both in the mothers of brothers club, and we wear that badge with pride and joy.

Studies conducted in places as diverse as Timbuktu and Tegucigalpa show again and again that women are not only primary caregivers for the family but also important breadwinners. Women tend to put a larger share of their earnings into their family's basic needs—food, clothing, shelter, health care, and schooling—than men do. That's not to say men don't care for their families; they do. But research has found that women reinvest about 90 percent of their income in their children rather than in themselves, whereas men put 30 to 40 percent of their money into their household.[1] That is why I say, "When you teach a woman to fish, everyone eats." Development aid projects that overlook women miss their *best* opportunity to end the cycle of poverty. But what we want are programs that work effectively with *both men and women,* leaving no one behind. It's also important to note that women's empowerment—economic, social, and political—is a worthy end goal in and of itself, even if it doesn't have exponential benefits for families and society.

As an advocate for almost 25 years, I have seen

heartbreaking setbacks and watched the best intentions go bad. But more often I've seen how government actions, including those of the United States, have saved lives, eliminated hunger, created stability, and empowered families. What's more, I've seen how women in America, and around the globe, can use their voices to make these good things happen. In these pages, I'll show you how you can add yours to this critical chorus.

This book chronicles my travels through four countries where Women Thrive has worked with grassroots groups of women—in Sri Lanka, Honduras, Nicaragua, and Burkina Faso—and shows what it means to live in poverty through the eyes of real women. Together, these different countries, on three different continents, tell the full story of how women can—and do—overcome the forces that keep them poor.

My goal is also to take you one step further than others books that have popularized global poverty issues. I hope to bring into clearer view the broader systems that prevent women from leaving poverty behind. These systems can be highly visible, such as the cultural norms that prevent women from leaving their homes without a male chaperone. Or they can be almost imperceptible, such as regressive tax hikes on food staples that women must buy for the family. I hope that you will come away with a deep understanding that poverty is not a natural phenomenon, a stroke of bad luck, or something that will be solved by a few hardworking charities. Historical legacies, intentional exclusion, and powerlessness are at the root of poverty. And while history cannot be amended, exclusion and powerlessness are imminently changeable. In fact, women are breaking down those barriers every single day. I can't wait for you to meet some of them in these pages.

I hope you will also come to believe that our own governments can be powerful agents of change when it comes to the larger environments that keep women in poverty. My country, the United States, is the largest international donor, the most influential diplomatic force, and the most coveted trading partner on the planet. The aid it provides to poor countries does work, but you only hear about the debacles. You never hear how aid pays *us* back, or how it's a long-term investment toward the world you want your grandchildren to live in. When US aid takes into account women's roles and views, it is highly effective in transforming societies and lives. Corporate and private charities are only a piece of the puzzle. Charities can provide microloans, but governments create frameworks for banking systems. Nonprofits can help women understand their basic human rights, but only functioning governments can make domestic violence illegal and punish perpetrators. We need our government to engage those of poor developing countries.

The best news I have to share with you is that women in developed countries—such as the United States, Canada, the United Kingdom, and others in Europe—are uniquely positioned to create change for their counterparts in poor, developing countries. We can push our governments to act, and to act better. We can shop differently to reward companies doing good for their workers and producers. We can raise our voices together with those of women living in poverty to collectively demand that no woman or girl live in fear of violence or face a life of deprivation. The reality is, Western women *can* effect change by demanding that something be done.

And what about men? If you are a man, I warmly welcome you. Despite the stereotyping that sometimes happens in my field of work, men are not the enemy. In fact, we women love men, and it's a good thing because you are a big part of the solution. You have the power to change the way other men think and act. Wherever I go, the women I talk to consistently ask that the programs designed to help them don't exclude the men in their lives. This request is particularly poignant coming from women in Muslim-majority countries, whose men are so often vilified. Think about it:

When a woman's husband is unemployed and disenfranchised, offering her help and ignoring her husband means you've still only addressed half the problem. I'll illustrate for you how well-designed interventions that integrate men and are developed by local women have the potential to transform lives, and perhaps even our world.

We have the solutions to help hundreds of millions of people lift themselves out of poverty in one generation. We can teach a billion women to "fish."

It starts with their story.

# PART ONE

═══════

# SRI LANKA

From left: Malini, Dilki, Rushani (Malini's sister), Sanduni, and Malki look on while Upali performs a funny dance in the garden. Source: Women Thrive.

Upali and Ira relax in the morning sun outside of Malini's house. Source: Women Thrive.

Malini makes roti on her wood stove. Source: Chinthaka Magedaragamage.

# 1

## TSUNAMI MORNING

On December 26, 2004, as many of us were happily recycling holiday wrapping paper and breaking down boxes, the tectonic plates under the Indian Ocean shifted, setting off a massive earthquake off the coast of Indonesia. The jolt created a 100-foot wall of water that devoured the unsuspecting coastlines of countries in a matter of minutes.

In Sri Lanka there is an ancient folktale about a village that gets "attacked" by the ocean, but the story had been pushed to the edges of the country's memory. Though the island is surrounded by ocean, the people of Sri Lanka were utterly unprepared for the Boxing Day tsunami. They had no early-warning system. They had no disaster plan. Children did not practice safety drills in class. The waves crushed them mercilessly.

In Hambantota, a small Sri Lankan village with mud, stick, and thatch houses poised on the shore of the Indian Ocean, that early December morning was quite unremarkable.

Amanthi had just finished making breakfast for her husband and four children. The littlest one was contentedly playing at Amanthi's feet while she washed the breakfast dishes. The gentle morning sun was shining on the road beside her house, creating a perfect pathway of light.

Chandrika was feeding her baby while her husband hurriedly readied himself for work.

Nayana heard a rumble but thought it was just the grumbling of a truck's engine trying to free its wheels from the sand.

But then Rushani heard someone shouting, "Water! Water!" but couldn't figure out why.

Malki, washing clothes at the well, noticed people running and crying, "Water is coming! Run! Water is coming!"

Chandrika grabbed the baby, and her husband took their son in his arms, and they ran into the street. She didn't even take a moment to look back over her shoulder and see how close the churning water was to her heels. She didn't have to; the thunder of the waves was deafening as it ate houses, bicycles, and people.

Manisha was pregnant with her sixth child, and her husband had left for work a half hour before. She told her children to run up the hill. "Go! Fast! Run!" she screamed at their confused faces, and thank God they did as they were told. But her five-year-old daughter was just coming out of the latrine and didn't hear her mother's panicked orders. Manisha saw the first wave approaching and grabbed hold of a small tree with both arms, leaving her pregnant belly to face the onslaught. Her daughter couldn't reach her in time. Manisha watched powerlessly as her little girl was swept away like a small twig in the roaring rapids. The indiscriminate ocean took children and chairs as if they were equally satisfying to its appetite.

Shoba had delivered her twin boys by caesarean in the hospital just the day before. They were so small and still fragile. "The doctors left us and ran away to save themselves," she told me. "The nurse carried one baby down to the street. I couldn't run. My husband finally came with the motorbike and I got on. I held my babies, one in each arm. I wouldn't let them go. We wove in and out of heavy traffic. We somehow got away." One of the "tsunami twins," as they are now called, hung around his mom as she told me this story, pretending not to be curious. I asked him if he remembered the tsunami and he nodded. His mom burst out, "Ha! You were only one day old! You don't remember anything." I think the body remembers, even the body of a newborn child. But, like most of our childhood memories, his "memory" is probably constructed from grown-ups telling the same story over and over, each time adding a different color to the picture, and somehow the memory starts walking and talking on its own.

It's not that life was easy before the tsunami. Sri Lanka's devastating civil war, yet another senseless conflict rooted in the false belief that there is not enough to go around, had been raging for years. This yours-versus-mine way of thinking was evangelized by the Portuguese and Dutch, who colonized the island and sliced it into a game board in the sixteenth century. In the 1790s, the British took over, eager to benefit from the plentiful treasures of tea, coffee, and spices. They brought Hindu Tamils from the south of British India to labor in the plantations for little more than a loincloth and a few coconuts.

These Hindu Tamils were not welcomed by the resident Sri Lankans, who themselves had migrated from India's tip thousands of years before, had converted to Buddhism, and developed their own language—and culture—of Sinhalese. In 1948, when the island became an independent nation, the tensions between the Tamils and native Lankans became even more taut. The Sinhalese stripped the Tamil plantation workers of any citizenship rights, made Sinhalese the sole official language, and held a tight grip on the government. What followed was a predictable reaction: riots, assassinations, and uprisings. In the late 1970s and early 1980s, politics became nasty and vituperative as parties vied for control of parliament. Rhetoric became so divisive, racist, and hysteria-inducing that, in 1983, shortsighted and selfish men pulled their country over the cliff into a bloody and senseless war that lasted more than 26 years and claimed more than 70,000 lives.

Sri Lanka should not be poor. It is filled to the brim with treasure. One of every three diamonds that adorn our modern-girl fingers comes from this little island. Some of the world's biggest sapphires, including the one in the Royal British Crown, were formed when the island was born. Sri Lanka's teas, better known as Ceylon teas, have been legendary from the time the British planted the first bush in the high, moist Hill Country. Your pumpkin pie would be tasteless without Sri Lanka: clove, cinnamon, cardamom, nutmeg, and mace are all native to Sri Lanka. The coastlines are exquisitely lined with deep, white-sand beaches, and Caribbean-blue water laps the shore. The fish are plentiful and delicious. But colonialism, then the war and corruption, sucked the lifeblood out of Sri Lanka's land and people like bloodthirsty vampires.

Even on a good day in this war-ravaged, impoverished land, women experience discrimination. On a day like that of the tsunami, when chaos prevails, they are thoroughly abused. First, they didn't stand much of a chance against the monstrous waves. Most women were wearing traditional clothing—skirts, dresses, and saris—that didn't allow them to run very fast, particularly when wet and clinging to their legs. Their long hair, normally a treasure to be proud of, became tangled in debris and pulled them underwater.

Women had children, sometimes many of them, in tow. And they may have been responsible for elderly parents or sick family members, who could not miraculously rise from their beds and run. Women are not as strong as men and couldn't hold on to a tree or telephone pole as the tidal wave crashed in and then sucked back out to sea. Girls didn't learn to swim or climb trees, because that is unladylike; many were home taking care of younger siblings. Boys were at school or out to play. Men were at work.

The first wave ripped the clothes off people as it returned to sea. Naked women refused to stand up, or run, for fear of exposing themselves. Men were not so prudish. The women who crouched in shame stayed in place and were hit by the second wave, which was much stronger than the first.

For thousands of women who did survive, the men who might have protected them were lost, already dead from the long civil war or drowned that morning. Some monstrous men who survived picked at women like turkey vultures on roadkill. One girl was "rescued" from the ocean by a man who pushed her to the ground and raped her. Women gave hundreds of similar reports to organizations and local police stations that day.

Many pregnant women who managed to get away gave spontaneous birth in horrible conditions: on the street, in the mud, or behind a sheet of plastic. As if losing everything around them wasn't enough, they also lost what they nurtured inside themselves, the place that should be the safest of all.

Far more women than men died that day. A survey of villages in Indonesia, Thailand, and Sri Lanka by the advocacy organization Asia Pacific Forum on Women, Law and Development confirmed that almost 80 percent of the dead were women.[1] In the district of Batticaloa in Sri Lanka, a survey by a grassroots women's organization found that 64 percent of the children that died were girls and 91 percent of the adults were women.[2]

By sunset more than 35,000 Sri Lankan men, women, and children were dead, and 826,000 were homeless.

Since that tsunami I sometimes have a recurring dream. My two sons are too young to swim yet, but they are too heavy for me to carry both of them. I can only swim with one. Whom do I hold on to, and whom do I let go? I can feel his little hand slipping away from mine, hear his scream, and see his panicked, disbelieving eyes. I vomit guilt and grief into the putrid, churning water. Then I wake up covered in a cold, salty sweat, as if I just crawled out of the waves into my bed.

Like everyone, I was sickened by the reports of dead, bloated bodies washed upon the shores and distraught by the images of children climbing over rubble looking for their parents. To many people it was just another disaster in the stream of cataclysms that befall poor tropical countries. Unfortunately, I knew exactly what it meant to the millions of people whose lives were torn apart.

It is my job to know about all the horrors that stalk and kill women and girls in the poorest places on the planet, including natural disasters like the Boxing Day tsunami. It sounds like a terrible profession when I put it that way, but it's actually a privilege and joy to help women overcome violence, poverty, and powerlessness. Women accomplish that every day. The organization for which I work—Women Thrive Worldwide—is a small but feisty group that advocates for the priorities of women and families who live on less than a dollar a day. One of the important things that Women Thrive does is get information in real time about what is happening for women on the ground, listen to the solutions that *they* want, take those ideas to the US government and other powerful donors, and push those institutions until they take action.

Six years before the tsunami, when I first started Women Thrive, I had worked to address the impact Hurricane Mitch had on women and families in Central America. So I didn't need to wait for the body count from Sri Lanka to know that more women than men had died, that rape awaited the surviving women as they stumbled out of the mud into camps, and that within a week little girls would be married to old men who had lost wives. I knew the poor were most devastated, because they live in scrabbly little shacks on land they can't prove is theirs. For them, things would never go back to normal because they had no money to rebuild, no insurance to rely on, and no sway with their government. All these things are predictable, standard disaster fare.

And sadly, I could also predict that the billions of dollars that would flood in from generous people and rich country governments to assist tsunami survivors would not reach the local women's organizations that are best positioned to help women in their communities. The day of the tsunami I knew what we needed to do: gather and amplify the voices of women to make sure that the people directing the US response would pay attention to women.

In the tsunami's wake, we reached out to women's organizations in countries bordering the Indian Ocean, especially those hardest hit: Indonesia, Sumatra, Thailand, and Sri Lanka. We did it as sensitively as we could, knowing that women's hearts were heavy and their hands were more than full. But the window of opportunity to shape the tsunami aid package would not be open for very long; we had a brief moment to get women's priorities into the mix.

We received numerous responses from women's organizations across the region. Some let us know that the damage in their country was minimal. Some, especially those from Sri Lanka and Indonesia, described a world churned up with broken bricks, distended bodies, rotting garbage, twisted wood, and people's most private and prized possessions jumbled and tossed across the landscape.

One of the most in-depth and extraordinary responses we received was from Irangani Magedaragamage, chairperson of the National Women's Collective of Sri Lanka (NWCSL). I know. I didn't think I could ever pronounce her name either. But I broke it down: Ear-ahn-GA-nee Mah-GAY-dar-ah-GA-mah-gay, and then said it faster and faster until it became a melody. Now I think it's one of the most beautiful names I've ever heard.

Irangani's organization, which is an association of hundreds of local village women's organizations, conducts action research, excellent leadership training for village women, and national-level advocacy with the government. So Irangani was well positioned to tell us what was really going on. She sent a comprehensive twenty-page report. I felt sick as I read it. Waves of anger, then frustration, and then resolve moved through me.

Even with all that I knew and expected, things were much worse than I thought. We needed to get this information into the hands of US policy makers, especially members of Congress, as fast as possible.

# 2

# AFTER THE WAVES

In late 2012, I sat talking with Silverasa, a woman whose gorgeous golden eyes belied her name, about her experience with the tsunami. Before the disaster she worked a ring-spinner, spinning fine cotton threads onto spools for the cloth factories in town.

Her family survived. She, her son, daughter, and husband all managed to climb to safety in time, but the roof of their brick home was ripped to pieces. They took the label given to millions of people in the same situation: internally displaced persons (IDPs). It's such a ridiculous euphemism for people who have been uprooted, torn, or expelled from their homes due to disaster or war, or both. To me, it sounds like a pseudo-psychological term for somebody who has lost his or her ego. But you're only a "refugee" if you're in someone else's country.

"We were displaced and stayed in a government

school twenty kilometers away from here," she told me. "The local villagers helped us a lot those first three days. They brought us food until the government rations began." After three days, with massive and immediate international relief, the Sri Lankan government started to provide rations of water, rice, flour, canned fish, oil, and sugar. Not much, but enough to stay alive.

Silverasa and her family stayed in the IDP camp for about six months. I heard over and over from many women I met with after the tsunami that they were too afraid to return to their homes, even if they could. They imagined the sea's fury would rise again, maybe this time in the night when their families were sleeping, and no one would escape. But living in a camp is a specific kind of hell. I can understand why Silverasa and her clan overcame their fears of the ocean and went home.

UN agencies like UNICEF and the High Commissioner for Refugees, independent aid groups such as CARE and Oxfam, and local and foreign governments from the Sri Lankans to the Chinese create IDP camps. These camps come in all shapes, sizes, and levels of "luxury." Let me describe for you what I will call the average two-star camp.

First, there are the canvas tents, about ten feet long by ten feet wide if you're lucky. They are hot and small, and there's just one for you, your four children, your husband's brother, and his wife.

Sometimes there are cots, sometimes only plastic sheets on which to lie. Of course there is no lock on the tent, just a few cords that can be tied in a neat little bow for no real purpose, except perhaps to reduce the size of the hole through which mosquitoes, dirt, and camp flotsam blow inside. It goes without saying that there is no privacy whatsoever.

There is also no kitchen, and at most camps the mess halls, if there are any, are reserved only for the camp workers. So you have to build a small open fire between your tent and the next one with sticks that your daughter walked far away from the camp, risking rape, to gather. You choke on the smoke as you cook and hope a spark doesn't torch your tent or your neighbor's.

There are a few latrines—open pits in the ground—a ten-minute walk from your tent. There is no lighting anywhere, not even in the latrines. These are not marked with the cartoon women and men signs either; everybody shits the same, everybody uses the same latrines. The latrines are separated from one another with plywood sheets, but the boys have worn peeping holes straight through. You can't stand to use them, especially at night, so you dig your own hole near your tent, cover it with a few branches, and pray that small children do not fall in and the camp officials don't find it.

There is a fence made of sticks and rusty barbed

wire circling the camp, but the two-foot gaps between the wires render it useless for keeping marauders out or children in. There is no camp security force per se, just one guy in green khakis with a gun (which most likely contains no bullets) stationed at the entrance to keep new entrants calm and under control.

Though the conditions of these camps were familiar to me, I was horrified about what I heard was happening to Sri Lankan women who lived in IDP camps around the country. The abuses were so many, some so blatant, some that could so easily be addressed, that sometimes I felt like a few men in camps sat around coming up with new ways to slowly torture women and kids to death. Generally, inside camps, a committee made up of residents is typically the only way to make requests of the camp officials, and too often there are no women on these committees. Even if women were allowed to advocate for themselves, there is not enough official oversight of the camps by the UN, government, or foreign donors to ensure that women's needs will get addressed.

There were an overwhelming number of reports from local women's organizations that visited the camps that men in charge of supplies would only give items to male heads of household or demand that women perform sex acts in exchange for food, water, and basic necessities. This is hardly unusual, even though it is officially forbidden.

Many talk about the Boxing Day tsunami as the "second tsunami"—the first one being the brutal civil war that created countless widows. So at the time of the tsunami, thousands of households had no male head, a simple fact that the government and some camp workers couldn't get their heads around.

The NWCSL report relayed that "in one camp, which was served by a temporary electricity connection, women complained that at night someone would disconnect the electricity. In the dark, men would enter the areas of the camp where women were sleeping and fondle their bodies."[3]

The report went on: "It was revealed that in many of these [camps], the grief-stricken and distressed women have become easy prey for sex vultures. . . . To worsen the situation in a crisis, the mechanisms that are usually in place to prevent rape, violence, and molestation disappear. There are no family members to protect women and girls, no homes in which to hide, and fewer police and armed forces to dissuade would-be criminals. In one camp, a mother tearfully said that she could not have a proper rest as she was keeping an eye on her two young daughters, especially in the night."[4]

At night a mother must worry about rape; in the day she must worry about trafficking. We know that IDP camps are playgrounds for criminals that traffic in human beings for cheap labor and sex slavery. Where there is chaos, lost children, separated families, people without identification, hunger, and hopelessness, there are traffickers. Post-tsunami Sri Lanka was no different. We received numerous reports from camps that women and girls were being lured away by people promising them work in factories or as house-keepers. In desperation they followed, only to find themselves being exported as sex slaves to brothels in the Middle East or Thailand.[5]

Women's specific needs became acute after the first week—they were desperate for intact clothing, sanitary napkins, and underwear. Even this became a way to torment women. Reports like NWCSL's came to us from several women's organizations. "In some camps, when women's underwear was distributed publicly, especially brassieres and panties, the men made embarrassing comments, such as which size is for whom, et cetera," the report said. "Young women in one camp said that the distribution of sanitary napkins was kept under the control of male camp officials who handed out two napkins at a time forcing women to go back to them each time they needed a fresh one."[6]

Women found no refuge in their own tents. The lack of privacy didn't stop men from demanding sex even if it had to be done in front of the family.

NWCSL's report continued: "If they are kept for long in the camps, they will suffer from more mental pains than other diseases. One woman said when interviewed, 'I will go mad if I stay here longer. I have lost most of my family members. Lost our incomes. Now I have to look after the children. If I do not re-start my life soon, I will go insane.' "

We heard calls from women and their organizations over and over: help women restart their small enterprises, not only to help them begin generating an income again, but also to support them in restructuring their lives and maintaining their dignity.

Given that about 44 million people are refugees and IDPs due to war and conflict[7] (the population of California and Washington states *combined*)[8] and more than 75 percent of them are women and their children, these massive problems are not going to be solved by only putting women on camp steering committees. That step would help a lot, but we need a solution that addresses the whole system. And lucky for us, there is one: the Guidelines for Gender-Based Violence Interventions in Humanitarian Settings. Yes, it's a mouthful. So I'll just call them the Guidelines from here on out.

In response to the staggering rates of violence against women and girls in disaster, war, and humanitarian crises, including the Boxing Day tsunami, a group of leaders from the same international agencies responsible for delivering the bulk of help to refugees and IDPs got together in 2005 to create the Guidelines in order to have some basic standards for their own work. The document includes a number of commonsense recommendations, such as, "Do not hire any person with a history of perpetrating any type of gender-based violence, including sexual exploitation, sexual abuse, or domestic violence," and "Design communal bathing and washing facilities in consultation with women and girls to ensure that users have privacy and maintain dignity."[9] Pretty basic stuff.

They also require organizations that publicly sign on to the standards to do some thoughtful planning and monitoring to make sure violence doesn't start, and if it does, to ensure that they are ready to respond and shut it down. Some of the important suggestions here include immediately setting up a gender-based violence working group that includes all the various organizations—private aid organizations, UN agencies, and government bureaus—that come into contact with refugees and IDPs. The Guidelines also push these organizations to "compile a resource list of organisations, focal points, and services for prevention and response to sexual violence. Distribute to all actors, including the community, and update regularly."

It's sad that the Guidelines had not yet been written before the tsunami and were unable to help women in Sri Lanka. But even in the wake of the Pakistan earthquake later in 2005, the 2010

Haiti earthquake, and in many other war-ravaged places, we saw the same problems over and over again. What gives?

My friend and colleague Joan Timoney at the Women's Commission for Refugee Women and Children, an independent advocacy group representing the needs of displaced women with the UN and US government, says, "We have made progress since 2005. There is broad awareness of the Guidelines as the standard to which we all should aim, but thorough implementation is still a challenge, especially in the initial months of a crisis. In too many cases, people are still doing the work the way they always have."

Joan argues that the international community needs to get to the point—and quickly—where humanitarian organizations are implementing programs in accordance with the Guidelines. These should be seen as standard operating procedure, not as an optional activity as time allows. "What's needed now," Joan says, "is real and measurable accountability from humanitarian organizations and donors for quality implementation of the Guidelines. We have to make sure services for survivors are put in place immediately. We have to consider it unacceptable when basic prevention steps are not being taken—when there aren't separate latrines with locks for women and men, when camps are poorly lit at night, when women and girls cannot collect water or firewood safely. And if there are some barriers that are keeping dedicated people from setting things up the right way, let's find out what they are and get them addressed."

She and others are updating the Guidelines right now to add what they've learned and to better address new realities, like the fact that the majority of refugees and IDPs are *outside* of camps. That fact makes protecting women considerably more difficult.

# 3

# FAIR SHARE FOR WOMEN

President George W. Bush originally pledged $15 million to the global response to the tsunami. By the time Bush made that announcement, the US government had already spent about $13 million of that in emergency supplies of food, water, medicine, and other necessities. His pledge was a ridiculous response to a disaster of incredible proportions.[10]

By New Year's Eve, he upped that pledge to $350 million. Though it was a substantial amount, Bush was hardly the most generous. By January 5, Japan had pledged $500 million, Germany had promised $674 million, and Australia put a whopping $765 million on the table.[11] So on

February 9, 2005, President Bush said he'd throw in another $600 million for a total of $950 million ($1 billion, anyone?). Now *that* was a serious load of money! And it was a huge opportunity to get some of it—even a few million—to the small, locally based women's organizations like Irangani's NWCSL.

Women Thrive had been advocating for years to get the US Agency for International Development (USAID) to fund more local women's groups. USAID is the primary branch of the federal government responsible for delivering aid of all types to developing countries. While the individual staff members within USAID were friendly and sympathetic, they always told us that USAID has to abide by the restrictions Congress has put on them, which pretty much make it impossible to fund little organizations no matter how effective they may be. They were referring to the maze of procedures USAID had invented in an effort to protect itself from any possible accusations of misuse of funds, consequent scandal, angry questioning from Congress, and the inevitable budget cuts that would follow. The truth of the matter was that Congress *didn't* put all this red tape in place. There were no laws mandating these requirements. So the only way to "skin the cat" was to go to Congress and have them *order* USAID to figure out a way to get funds to local groups.

We knew the legislative process to pass the

bill providing tsunami aid was going to move incredibly fast, so we had to as well. We decided to go straight to a person who could make it happen. I called Beth Tritter, the lead staff person for Representative Nita Lowey (D-NY), who sat on the House Subcommittee for State and Foreign Operations of the House Appropriations Committee—a long name for the subcommittee that decides how much aid the United States will give other countries and how that aid will be spent.

The first time I met Beth, she had actually called me to come meet with her. Representative Lowey is a Democrat who represents the Lower Hudson Valley of New York, a progressive district with lots of diversity, from executives commuting to Manhattan to local mom-and-pop business owners to young families struggling to stay in the middle class. With all her grandmotherly charm, you might not guess that she had worked her way into one of the most powerful positions in Congress as the highest-ranking Democrat on the House Foreign Operations Appropriations Subcommittee (she later became chair of that subcommittee in 2009 when the Democrats won the majority in the House).

At the time, I had been working closely with Representative Connie Morella, a progressive Republican from Maryland, to create a holistic and comprehensive bill on women's priorities called the Global Actions and Investments for Women and Girls Act (GAINS). That bill covered ten areas critical to women and girls in developing countries, from education and health to peace and security. The idea was never to pass the whole GAINS Act, but instead to use it to educate Congress on the priorities of women from around the world and put forward a blueprint for what the US government could do to be most helpful. Parts of the GAINS Act were added to other pieces of legislation that did become law.

Beth heard about the bill's creation and wanted her boss to be the lead Democratic sponsor of the GAINS Act. It was the first time a congressional office had called me to say they wanted in on a bill I was working on. Up until that meeting I had spent about a decade begging, convincing, and persuading members of Congress to please-oh-please put their support and their name behind something. The only thing I could say to Beth was, "Of course, it's yours."

In January, a few weeks after the tsunami, we went to meet with Beth and brief her on what we were hearing from women's organizations across the region. We told her about the problems women faced in the camps—the rapes, the lack of access to appropriate help—and about the excellent women's organizations that were standing ready to help survivors if they could just get some financial support. Beth was as frustrated and mad as we were.

We worked with her over the next few days to

create a plan. There was likely to be a piece of legislation coming up soon in Congress to provide extra money for the military and aid operations in Afghanistan and Iraq. Beth was pretty sure that bill would be expanded to include money for the tsunami recovery as well. Our goal was to get some wording in the bill that would mandate USAID to allocate a portion of the $950 million in tsunami aid to small local women's groups.

Getting what's called "language" in a bill is the best scenario. If the bill passes and becomes law, whatever wording you got into it has the full force of law—there's no ambiguity about it. Each bill also comes with a corresponding report from the committee that drafted and introduced the bill. The report is like operating instructions for how to implement what is in the actual bill that becomes law.

A report is to a law what a mom's commentary is to an order given to children. That is, if the bill says, "You will wash your hands before dinner," the report says, "Use soap (wet your hands first). Keep scrubbing while you sing the alphabet (the whole alphabet at normal speed). Rinse with warm water. Dry hands (not with Mommy's good towels; use the white one next to the sink)." The report doesn't have the force of law; it's guidance. But just like Mom and her directions, Congress does not like it when its guidance is ignored. So it's definitely worth something.

Beth talked to the other staff on the Foreign Ops subcommittee, particularly to the lead staff person for the Republican chair of the subcommittee, to see if there would be enough support for—or at least no opposition to—carving out some money for women's organizations. She let us know there was enough backing to get a little bit of bill language, but it would have to be extremely short and not allocate a lot of money. She thought we had a pretty good chance of getting report language since she could just submit that herself.

We narrowed our proposal to the bare minimum: We wanted just $10 million to go directly to small local organizations in tsunami-affected countries to help women restart their lives economically. We knew that $10 million was nothing out of almost a billion but could still go a very long way with small grassroots organizations where the salary for a full-time person can be $5,000. We sent our draft language to Beth:

Draft bill language:

THE GLOBAL OPPORTUNITY FOR WOMEN FUND

Of the funds provided in this Act for relief and reconstruction in tsunami-affected countries, not less than $10,000,000 shall be made available for local nongovernmental organizations working to enhance women's economic opportunities.

Draft report language:

The Committee recognizes that women's economic activity is critically important to the development of nations, communities, and families. Local nongovernmental organizations in country have some of the most innovative and locally appropriate programs to enhance women's economic well-being. This Act requires that not less than $10,000,000 of the funds provided for by this Act be channeled into special projects to make grants and provide capacity-building technical assistance to local nongovernmental organizations conducting programs to improve women's economic activities.

Beth was able to get some of our language into the report, but the bill as it passed the House of Representatives didn't have any language with the force of law. Here's what we got:

HOUSE REPORT 109–16
TITLE IV—INDIAN OCEAN TSUNAMI RELIEF
Finally, in addition to other efforts to promote economic opportunities, the Committee recommends $10,000,000 be used for small grants to support training

and equipment for women-led local non-governmental organizations in tsunami-affected areas.

We still had one more shot at it. The House bill had passed, and the Senate bill had passed, but as you will recall from *Schoolhouse Rock*'s "I'm Just a Bill," the two bills had to be reconciled with one another, and then both houses of Congress needed to pass an identical bill.

We took our proposal to the Senate offices to get their support to take the House's report language and put it into the final bill in what's called a "manager's amendment," a legislative maneuver that allows members of Congress to add something new that wasn't in the version of the bill that passed the full Senate or House. These amendments are reserved for small clarifications and changes only, and we argued that direction on how to spend $10 million out of $1 billion was a "small clarification." We were making some headway, but in the interim, USAID caught wind of what we were trying to do and were very unhappy about it because it would create a lot of extra work in their system.

When the final bill was passed—with the total amount President Bush pledged, by the way—its accompanying report simply said, "Provided further, That of the funds appropriated under this heading, $10,000,000 should be made available for programs and activities which create new economic opportunities for women."[12]

I was seriously unhappy. The most important part of what we wanted—resources for local women's organizations—was taken out. Of course, USAID was going to do at least $10 million in economic programs for women out of almost $1 billion in aid. They would get that done in a month, working through their multimillion dollar contracts with US firms. Just addressing women's economic opportunity was not the point. The point was to get some US funds to the local women's groups that were doing incredible work yet were always shut out, sidelined, and passed over. The final report language didn't help us at all, but the House report still counted for something. We would have to *make* them show us the money.

# 4

# UPALI

He's a thin man with a long name—Upali Sisil Chandra Magedaragamage. You could wrap his name around him twice and still have letters leftover. But there is no name long enough to circle the size of his heart and his love for his country.

I came to know Upali through his wife, Irangani,

chair of the NWCSL. Upali is the organization's translator-in-chief and biggest champion. He was born among the cool, cloudy tea plantations in Sri Lanka's central Hill Country. His father was a trader by profession and also a practicing Buddhist—two things that sort of canceled each other out. "His mindset was not for business," as Upali put it. His mother was from a very rich and well-known Hill Country family. It was she who molded Upali into the tenacious but jovial, grounded but idealistic, and savvy but dreamy activist that he is. "She was the chairperson of the Lanka Mahila Samithi, the women's village organization," he told me, and I instantly understood where his fiery commitment to feminism emanates from. "I used to hold her finger and go with her to her meetings. I used to question her, 'What were you discussing?' And she would tell me about all the troubles of the village people."

These collective and collegial women's meetings punctuated his childhood. He remembers one meeting in particular where he studied the "auntie" who held the position of secretary. He asked her why she was writing everything in a notebook, and she patiently explained, "I'm writing the decisions down that get everyone's approval. Once they are included in the minutes, these decisions go into action. Nobody can change them. We know what we have decided and what we have agreed upon." From a young age, Upali was inspired by the women's consensus-driven and democratic approach.

He was born to be a community organizer. "My brothers and I, we played with organizations even at home. We had a government in our house. We held elections. The first time household president went to Father, but the second time it was Mother—Father even voted for her," he recalled with a chuckle.

"We had ministers—finance minister was Mother, of course. But once I was minister of finance. We were playing at home and my youngest brother was using calendar pages with a rubber stamp for money. He made some fraudulent bills and I had to take action. I abolished all the bills and reprinted all the money." He looked particularly pleased with himself telling me this. "And later, this was really done by Dr. N. M. Perera, finance minister of Sri Lanka from 1970 to 1975. He did the exact same thing! He wanted to pull out all the counterfeit money people had hidden away in jars and mattresses, so he banned 100 and 50 rupee notes and told people to change them or lose them."

He went on: "What is the first government you have seen? The first government is the family. We have everything in the family—health, education, finance—and two ministers—Mother and Father. The family is where we first learn about governance, about budgeting, about exploitation, about empowerment or disempowerment. Even now when I go and dialogue with people, I talk about family budgeting and politics. Inside the house, who is the exploiter? How is women's work taken for granted, never seen, or valued? My mother's views—looking from the Buddhist perspective on governance and management, life and family—molded me a lot. She helped me a great deal in my personal work."

Upali's personal work, his life's work, is to help villagers in Sri Lanka discover the sources of their own poverty, in their own way and in their own time, and then remove these sources one by one, leaving poverty and powerlessness behind them. This approach is the true way to end poverty because poverty is not about having no money; it's about having no power to change your own circumstances.

Often, we think that people living in poverty just need education, health care, and small loans of $50 or $100, and if we provide these things, poverty will naturally come to an end. But it doesn't work that way. These ingredients, as well as others, are important, no doubt about it. However, basic education, health care, and access to economic opportunities are goods that *governments* should provide (or work with the private sector to provide) to their citizens.

International aid groups jump in and deliver these services because the government is too poor or too selfish to do it, and we aren't going to stand by and watch people die or live without hope for the future. However, empowering people to demand these services from their own government, and working with governments to help them meet these demands, is the way it should work. Life stays the same because people in poverty too often don't know what their government's responsibilities are, and even if they do know it, they don't have the power to make their governments do their jobs. Even in places where corruption is endemic, it's still possible to make government accountable, particularly at the local level because those politicians are closest to the people they supposedly serve. They are not in a far-away capital city; they are right down the dirt road.

Of course, where government doesn't exist at all and where guns, not votes, decide who wins elections, it is extremely difficult and dangerous for people in poverty to simply demand their due. But I have still seen women make it happen in places as dangerous as Afghanistan and as war-weary as the Congo.

Upali is a dedicated practitioner of Participatory Rural Appraisal (PRA), sometimes also called participatory learning and action. PRA is both a philosophy and a methodology. From a philosophical perspective, PRA is grounded in the simple belief that people in poverty are more than capable of analyzing why they are poor and creating their own solutions to end poverty in their communities. The PRA methodology basically consists of building a high degree of trust between the community and a PRA facilitator. The facilitator then uses a wide range of tools and techniques to guide a community through a period of inquiry about its current circumstances and its causes, first assisting community members in defining and employing their own solutions. This way of going about helping people was captured and popularized by Robert Chambers at the Institute of Development Studies at Sussex University in the United Kingdom, among others.

There are hundreds of derivatives and adaptations, and the labels matter less than the ethos of the approach:

1. If we want to really help people, we need to live with them. Live like they do, eat what they eat, sleep how they sleep. We can't come in from the outside saying that we have the solution to their troubles, because in truth, we don't—they do. This helps to build a high degree of trust, which is important because what unfolds is intended to shake up the power dynamics within the home, village, town, and perhaps even nation.

2. The most precious thing we can bring is not a thing, but rather a process. PRA facilitators are conveners and catalysts. They do not insert their own opinions into the process, and they refuse to provide answers. What they bring are a plentitude of techniques, tricks, and tools to help communities gather data, analyze, draw conclusions, decide what to do, and then carry out the actions they have decided upon. Sometimes PRA practitioners teach conflict management, leadership, information gathering and sharing, agenda setting, and how to engage with powerful people in the community, government, or international donors to get what the community wants and needs. Most of all, they pay close attention to what a group needs in order to move forward in their process, and then they provide it.

3. The highest virtues of PRA are being patient, relaxed, and adaptable. This approach may take time, years perhaps, or maybe only hours. Every group of people is different, and their comfort levels with engaging difficult topics will vary. Sometimes one tool will fail, but another will work. PRA cannot be pushed, scheduled, or put into a checklist. If it is, it's not PRA anymore.

4. Most importantly, PRA deliberately draws those most marginalized—women, people with disabilities, the elderly, children, whoever stands outside the power circle—into the mix to take part in the collective journey.

If you think PRA sounds a lot like Mahatma Gandhi, Martin Luther King Jr., or even like our founding fathers—who believed in the ability of citizens to understand their world, claim their rights, and self-direct their futures—you'd be right. It's based on the very same principles.

As you can imagine, getting community participation in development projects is very appealing. Nobody working on poverty wants to appear unparticipatory. But don't be fooled. "Participation" is used by many international actors to describe everything from inviting people to a meeting so you can tell them, not ask them, what you're going to do in their community, all the way to true-blue PRA.

Before Upali started doing community empowerment work, he tried the corporate route for a while. That was a predetermined misadventure. "I was having money troubles, so I got an executive position at the Ceylon Glass Company, where my uncle was the general manager," he said. "The heat was high in the factory so the workers sweated a lot. Salt tablets were to be provided, along with gloves, protective clothing, and masks. But the management wouldn't provide those necessary items. The workers decided to strike. I saw how unprotected these workers were. The heated silica, blown by a machine and then put onto conveyor belt to cool slowly, could explode. When the glass cracked or split, the pieces would fly into workers' eyes. Nobody would talk about this. I was in an executive position, but when the workers protested against the management, I took the workers' side. I convinced some of the staff members to join us. The management didn't like it at all. Before they sacked me, I resigned."

One night, I just came straight out and asked him: "Upali, you're not afraid, given all the politically charged development work you do?"

"Let them come for me," he said. "I am not afraid of death."

"Maybe you're not," I replied. "But *I* am afraid of your death."

He tempts death every day by calling out the latest injustice of the corrupt government or by lighting up another cigarette. I hate smelling the smoke, not only because it's putrid, but also because every cigarette is another ten minutes off his life. Every day means two less hours of Upali's force in this world.

Upali started to tell me a story that illustrated exactly what I was worried about. "One night after the election, in 2010, we were informed that our house was to be bombed. We got the information from my son's friends who are in the army. They informed us to quickly move out. I said, 'I am not going. As soon as I go, this will be a closed place and they can do anything they want. No, we are not going out.'

"Kill? That they can. But if there are five people or more in the house, they cannot attack, according to the international code. We sent the children next door and kept the place lit; we got ready for petrol bombs. Irangani slept on the other side of the house. The boys and I stayed up. Everyone in the village had heard the news and they were keeping vigilant."

*"And?"* I gasped.

"They did nothing to us. You see, Ritu," Upali continued, rolling right over my momentary relief, "I am afraid more—more than my death or torture or whatever—of a government that continues like this, that is destroying the entire nation. They will torture me and they will kill me and they will finish me, but what will happen to the future generations and our great country? This is what I am worried about. One or two people dying? It's irrelevant. We cannot afford to get afraid." I was in awe and still afraid for him.

# 5

# IRANGANI

Irangani is the heart, brain, and hands of the NWCSL, which, as I mentioned before, organizes hundreds of small, local women's village groups to decide how they want to address their challenges, and then helps them do it.

Irangani and Upali are like two sides of the same coin. Distinctive, but inseparable. Upali is loud and boisterous, always kicking up a conversation and looking for people to organize and liberate from oppression. Irangani is quiet and steady. She will wait until you come to her for help, listen intently, and then show you the way with only a few words, like a lighthouse flashing every now and again to keep you moving in the right direction.

They are beautiful together. Before I met them, I had never really seen a marriage with such tender sweetness, firm respect, and unity of purpose. Don't get me wrong; they have been through their own hell and back together, but it has not seemed to harden their relationship. There is still the stolen touch on the shoulder that conveys so much appreciation, and the glance held just that extra moment that says, "I still love you."

Her mother's name was Beatrice; her father was Solomon. Beatrice studied in a convent to be a nurse but later became a Buddhist when she was moved by the lecture of a famous monk who stopped in her village. Solomon was a soldier during World War II and traveled the world with the army. They fell in love in Colombo. Their relatives were against the marriage. As Irangani said, "Love was just not appreciated back then." They settled in Solomon's village and Beatrice stopped working to raise their eight children, the second of which was Irangani.

Irangani has such happy memories of her childhood in the Hills. She smiled as she remembered the April New Year celebrations when she "wore special dresses, played with friends, went from house to house eating, and caught the tail of a calf and ran free. There were no restrictions, no congestion. Everybody was looking after the children."

It didn't last that way. Her father was generous to a fault. She recalls the day when a man came to their house and collapsed at their doorstep. He had no place to go, no place to live, and no one to turn to. Her father took off his gold ring and said, "Here, go build a house." Her dad was also a political figure, a liberal politician, and spent a lot financing his party. Solomon used what was left, and sold a lot of property, to try to save one of his sons from polio, but the child died anyway.

"We had money up until about eighth grade. Then we lost everything," Irangani said. "But I didn't learn stinginess. I learned both generosity and thrift." When she was thirteen, she started putting one handful of rice into a saving pot every day, and she never stopped the habit. She had to be frugal with everything, including the ink for her fountain pen. She would pay five cents to fill it in the morning and would be discerning about what she wrote in her notebook to make it last the whole day. There were no teenage daydream drawings, notes passed to girlfriends, or bubble letters on the corners of her notebook pages. Her family couldn't afford the shoe polish to keep their white school shoes white, so they used lime and water, but it dissolved Irangani's toenails and her toes got infected.

Irangani's parents knew she had huge potential. They made so many sacrifices, big and small, to make sure Irangani did well in school. "My mother would stay up late as I did my homework to make sure the kerosene lamps didn't catch fire. My father would stash some bread for me to eat if I got too hungry to go on with my homework. Mother would excuse me from chores around the house," Irangani remembered. Her mother didn't even tell her about the breast cancer until Irangani's exams were over; she wanted her daughter to stay focused on doing well.

She did extremely well. The day the scores came

out, Irangani ran the whole two kilometers home, laughing and crying all the way, to tell her waiting mother that not only did she pass, she placed number one! Her mother died not long after that.

Irangani went to the top university in Colombo to study economics, banking, and insurance. This was no small feat for a girl from the Hill Country in 1973. She would be able to make excellent money, have a comfortable life, and support her ailing parents and unemployed siblings. Irangani could be rich, be a minister in the government, or become a member of parliament.

But in the big city she was drawn to politics, social work, and a bigger world beyond the shores of small Sri Lanka. In 1975, when she was twenty, she went to Moscow for five days of meetings with young women leaders from around the world. For her, the travel was lavish; she used a fork and knife and took a bath with hot water for the first time.

Irangani graduated with honors and quickly got a great junior executive position in the government-owned Insurance Corporation of Sri Lanka. But her heart was pulled toward service work and leadership again and again. "I just kept becoming the leader. The others pushed me there. They expected me to take a leadership role." She finally succumbed to her calling and decided to leave to work for the National Heritage Organization, one of the prominent community development organizations in Sri Lanka at the time. There, Irangani created the women's program to put more focus and resources toward women's self-determination and development. It was the very beginnings of what much later became the NWCSL.

Down the hallway, Upali was working in the research division and he asked Irangani to join him because, he says, of her "excellent research abilities." They clearly liked each other from the moment they met. One day, he just casually asked her if she would marry him. Irangani had turned down many suitors along the way before Upali, and she figured he would just be another pearl on the string of forgotten proposals. She said she would think about it.

A few days later Irangani came back and said no. She had to take care of her whole family—father, brothers, sisters, and all their children—scattered around the countryside at that point. She felt that "no man would want this burden." To which Upali replied without hesitation, "You are pulling the cart alone. Why don't we pull the cart together?" And so they did and still do today, every day.

Irangani was determined that her family would have a proper house, so she started saving, unbeknownst to Upali because, like her father, Solomon, if he knew there was extra money around, he would give it away. "I am careful, he is not," she said bluntly, looking Upali right in the eyes. He just grinned back at her.

She took the secret savings, pawned her gold necklace, and bought a small piece of land. When Upali found out, he demanded the land be in Irangani's name only. "Everything is in Irangani's name," he affirmed. "She is the money."

The Magedaragamage household is, as Upali says, "a refugee camp." People come, family or not, and stay there until they are strong enough to fly on their own. The last time I stayed with them in Colombo, the household included Irangani and Upali's two twenty-something sons, Irangani's widowed sister and her two daughters—also in their twenties—and the sister's son, who is now a pastry chef. Also under the roof were Upali's brother, who used to work in the government but now suffers from mental illness and cannot work, and a Tamil man whom Upali took in and helped get permanent employment. The welcome mat is also rolled out for temporary residents, from village women to international guests (myself included), who might be in Colombo for leadership training or other matters. Irangani and Upali's daughter often visits with their two-year-old granddaughter. All business comes to a complete halt when the little one is in the house; she is a welcome break from the ongoing, heady discussions on politics and poverty.

It seems that at some point, everyone comes to

Irangani for her steady and wise helping hand, including the government. A few years ago, the Asian Development Bank and some other donors gave the Sri Lankan government a loan to build the country's first modern highway between the southern port city of Galle and the capital, Colombo. The government and donors thought people would be happy about it because it would open up commerce between Galle and the capital, create new businesses all along the way, and reduce travel time for tourists heading down to the beautiful beaches of the southern coast. But when the bulldozers started, people threw rocks at the trucks and even attacked the construction crews. So the government turned to Irangani to help them calm the villagers. Irangani wanted full authority to conduct her work as she wanted with absolutely no interference; they had to trust her or no deal. The desperate government officials agreed, not knowing what was about to hit them.

Irangani went to the villages along the planned route and just listened and listened and listened, for a long time. She did not lecture them about why they should love the shining new band of asphalt. She wrote down their complaints and problems, and she validated them.

"There was a whole heap of problems," she said. "Some people's land was cut in half by the road and they couldn't get to their fields on the other side. Their coconut trees were cut down and they only got 500 rupees ($3) in compensation. Houses with ancient architectural value were being bulldozed. There were no entrances and exits to the highway so that villagers could use it. It was ridiculous."

Irangani took the authorities to go see the problems they were creating. I can picture her holding those government bureaucrats by their ears and dragging them to see the mess they had made. Governments make this mistake again and again all over the world. They fear community input or simply don't care to hear it, which leads to complete ineffectiveness. Irangani ordered the technical officers to verify the complaints. She showed the local people the master plan and got the communities' input into where the off- and on-ramps should be, and where the bridges should go. She explained to the villagers that their land values would go up, that they were getting something out of it as well.

"The government people realized they should have just done all this upfront," Irangani said, stating the obvious. I would have been apoplectic, but not Irangani. She was cool, calm, and completely confident.

The day we drove back from Galle, where we were meeting with the Tsunami Women's Network for Development, was Irangani's first time driving on the new highway. Like classic Irangani, she didn't say a word about it. I heard about it all from Upali.

The thing about Irangani is this: She's wicked smart, she understands how people really work, and she's divinely patient, which means she is unstoppable.

# 6

# HOME MADE

It's not as though life in Sri Lanka was grand before the tsunami. But at least it was stable—"survivable" was the word the women in Ampara used a lot. The women all were weavers before the disaster. They made colorful cotton saris, sarongs, and *lungis* (men's pants like Gandhi wore). Between their weaving and their husbands' work, they made enough to live simply. They sent their kids to school. They could occasionally buy some sweets. They saved for their daughters' dowries.

Some of them lived in wattle-and-daub houses, with walls constructed from sticks and mud and roofs made of dried banana leaves. Some had proper brick-and-mortar homes. A lot of them built on land that wasn't really theirs, just steps from the beach. While technically they had oceanfront property, it was the poorest of the poor who squatted in meager housing on the government land on the coastline. With the Coast Conservation Law of 1981, the government made the first 100 meters from the beach a buffer zone, but it had never been enforced.[13] So that's where people would go to piece together a shack built of wood bits, rusted pieces of corrugated iron, and tree branches held together with plastic bags fashioned into rope. Laughable to the oncoming tsunami.

Even the real houses were badly built. There were lax building codes, and inspections were easily substituted with bribes. One day I was in Galle, standing on a balcony overlooking the ocean and talking with Upali. He pointed out a small Buddhist shrine across the street.

"People here think that shrine is magical," Upali said, "because it came through the tsunami completely unharmed. Not even the glass was broken." I could imagine the Buddha sitting on his meditation stool and serenely watching the world wash away. "But it's not magic, Ritu. It's just that the guy who built it was too afraid to do his usual shoddy job for fear of being cursed. Most of the homes and buildings around here should not have collapsed and killed people. More people here died of corruption than anything else."

And yet these dwellings were more than shelters for these women. They were their homes, the heart and hearth of their families. In fact, when I asked the women why they weave, they answered almost in unison: because we can stay at home. The ability to work from home might just be the strongest factor in a mother's selection of occupation, wherever she is. For me, it still dominates my career choice, and I know it does for a lot of my girlfriends, too. For women with little or no education it's an imperative, because they can't afford child care or they just aren't allowed to work outside the home because their culture would consider it offensive. I know that working from home sounds kind of appealing, but for these women, it comes with a lot of liabilities.

Actually, most women in the world work at home or on farms near their homes, and I mean beyond housewifely duties, which are not insubstantial. "Home-based work," as economists officially call it, makes up 25 to 60 percent of the work force in garments and textiles alone. More than 100 million people, mostly women, weave, sew, manufacture, or craft while balancing the duties of raising children, caring for the sick and elderly, cooking for their families, and cleaning house.[14] They exist outside of any legal or regulatory system, and they are exploited in many ways.

For one, many home-based workers don't know who else is making the same thing or what price they are getting for it. Knowing that the women are unaware of the prices in the marketplace, the middleman who collects the goods and delivers them up the retail chain can make a killing off these women by buying low from them and selling high to retailers. No one is watching to see if women are being paid a fair price for their work.

Even if the government wanted to try, they could never inspect millions of households to ensure the working conditions are healthy and safe. Women—and their children—can be exposed to hazardous materials and environmental toxins meant for use in a controlled setting, not a living room.

While it might be self-inflicted, women in their shacks, huts, and cinderblock houses will put in excessively long hours to earn the absolute maximum they can while the orders are coming. Who wouldn't? Sometimes, in desperation to meet a production deadline, they may engage their kids in doing whatever part of the work they can—cutting this piece, gluing on that bling, or packing up the final product. When a family is trying to survive, child labor is often just a fact of life. I don't vilify these women. I would probably do the same thing. If my eight-year-old was capable of reducing my production time by 20 percent and that extra 20 percent meant I could buy him milk to drink, I might just do it too. But in my reality, my eight-year-old wouldn't add that much value.

The most important thing to know is that in

developing countries, between 60 and 90 percent of working women are in this "invisible" economy. This is how the vast majority of people are making a living. It is not a phenomenon on the edge of normal life, it *is* normal life. This is not an accident. Lots of companies benefit from this system. Keeping things out of factories and in houses is extremely cost-effective.

Take, for example, our beloved blue jeans. The factories that make them usually belong to local companies because the big brand names don't want to own the physical plants or be completely responsible for the workers in them. They want to stay nimble, be able to move around, and expand or contract production within days. Low operating overhead means bigger profits.

When every fourteen-year-old decides they need to have those jeans before the middle-school dance, factories often don't buy more sewing machines and hire more people. They go out and pay women with sewing machines at home to start making kids size-fourteen jeans. These home-based workers are the last hired and the first fired. They are a flexible and expendable work force with no benefits, no contracts to protect their jobs, and no unemployment insurance.

Many major brands have been discouraging this kind of sourcing because the scandal liability is huge. All it takes are a few pictures of children sitting next to their mums sewing a company's logo onto shirts to wreak havoc on the bottom line. But the economics of it make it hard to change. Women who simply cannot work outside of the home for cultural, physical, or familial reasons are ready and willing to take the jobs; it's way better than nothing. The companies selling these products can increase their profits exponentially when they don't have to keep the factory lights on and pay the workers when consumers stop buying.

When our financial system melted down in 2008, that's exactly what happened: shoppers stopped shopping, and it was home-based workers, like these women, that fell off the ride first. They will be the last to get back on too.

A wonderful group called Women in Informal Employment: Globalizing and Organizing (WIEGO, and yes, the shorter name is much better), led by Marty Chen at Harvard University, partnered with the Inclusive Cities Project to survey workers in the informal economy in January 2009, about six months into the most recent global economic crisis.[15] These were all people already in the informal sector—that is, not laid-off factory workers—but they saw and felt the raw effects of massive retrenchment in their economies.

Over two-thirds of the home-based workers surveyed said they felt increased competition from women who used to work in factories but who now do piecework at home. One woman in Thailand reported that she used to sell her products at 199 baht ($6), but after the influx of new home workers, women are willing to sell their products as low as 50 baht ($1.70). That represents a 75 percent decrease in her income, a cut that probably put her back into poverty, if she had managed to climb out of it to begin with. Another Thai woman said to the researchers, "About twenty women who were laid off from the factories, including a woman with a newborn baby, came to ask for piecework, but I have no work to give them."

When the crisis hit, the costs of food and fuel had already risen due to the agricultural downturn in 2008. This just compounded the effects of the economic crisis for many people living on the edge of the poverty line. In focus groups done by WIEGO and Inclusive Cities, respondents shared that their budgets were at the breaking point. The majority of the people in the survey said they were eating less food and of lower quality in the first six months of 2009 compared to 2008. A quarter of the workers surveyed in Latin America had stopped eating breakfast. In Pakistan, home-based workers could provide only one meal a day, whereas they were able to give their families two meals before. A respondent talked about her situation at home: "When the work was good the children had all of their vitamins. They had cereal, milk. Not anymore."

There is a solution to the problems women face in the informal economy: organizing.

What do I mean by that? The daily life of a home-based worker is stressful and solitary. It's lonely to sit for hours every day at a sewing machine in the heat of a damp cement home with children tugging at your skirt out of hunger and boredom. You have no idea how much other women are being paid for sewing the same dresses or who you can turn to when the guy who told you to make the dresses never shows up to collect them and pay you.

Now imagine if you could attend a meeting once a week where you could talk with other women doing the same work as you, compare how much you're each getting paid, find out which buyers are trustworthy, learn how to create a simple contract with buyers, and maybe even find ways to pool child care so you can be more productive at your sewing machine. Not to mention enjoy some companionable conversation.

This group might even join similar groups in other villages, and pretty soon you and all the other women are able to agree on a fair price for your work and demand that price from the buyers. Being hundreds strong, you might even be able to create a savings pool to assist women like you when times are lean.

Forming associations of home-based workers, street vendors, and even garbage pickers, like the Self-Employed Women's Association of India has done, helps people access the resources and support they need. What respondents in the Inclusive Cities survey wanted most were community kitchens to enable them to pool resources and feed their families, and low-interest-rate loans to tide them over. They also wanted to band together and get the government and police to stop bulldozing their shanties, harassing them, and engaging in extortion. From there, they wanted to see their governments become part of the solution by waiving school fees for children during crises and by extending them benefits like social security and health care.

A vendor in South Africa hit the nail on the head when she said, "I know that if we were more organized as women and formed a group, we could mobilize ourselves and challenge the government to engage with us. We would be speaking with one voice."

The informal economy is part of the system that keeps people poor and caught in a cycle of working hard but never being able to get ahead. The tsunami survivors I spoke with that day in Ampara wanted more than that for their children. Despite having their lives turned upside down by the tsunami, all of the women I shared that afternoon with had big hopes for the future. One wanted to get another a loom and hire someone to weave with her, and maybe open a small shop in the market herself. Another mother spoke with great determination about how she weaves late into the night to earn enough to pay her children's school fees because, as she said with a smile on her delicate face, "They must not become weavers like me. They must move away from here. Far away. Where there are no tsunamis." Earning more money and having better jobs would certainly help the women weavers of Ampara. But that's really only half of the equation. Another thing my conversation came back to again and again was how much they have seen the basic costs of food and household items increase over the last eight years. Their explanation was that the government needed to raise revenue to cover the costs of reconstruction after the tsunami. Makes sense. But taxing basic necessities like food is a cruel way for a government to get resources, especially when a couple billion dollars are coming in from wealthier donor countries. It is the most regressive kind of tax.

Everybody has to buy food, soap, clothes, and bedding—the really bare necessities outside of shelter and water. As a percentage of their income, the poorest people in the world spend between 50 and 80 percent of their money on these necessities. It's a big, painful bite out of their earnings. When taxes on these products rise, even a little bit, it hurts the poor far more than it hurts the people who spend 10 or 20 percent of their cash on the basics.

So why not tax people's income and investment gains, like we do here in the United States? Lots of reasons. First and foremost, the people deciding who and what to tax in poor countries are the rich. It's unlikely they are going to raise taxes on themselves. Second, collecting and checking taxes from individuals and businesses takes a massive infrastructure that is expensive to run and also requires honesty from the bottom to the top of the hierarchy. It's much easier to collect the tax from a smaller pool of wholesale and retail businesses. Sri Lanka and most other countries also collect income and investment taxes, but too often it's an honor system. Figure 6.1 pretty much says it all. In the United States, the lion's share of 2011 tax revenue came from income and investment gains. Brazil and Bangladesh have been getting a little less regressive over time, and in 2011, it was a pretty even split between goods and income taxes. Sri Lanka really stands out among these and other countries as a highly regressive place.

Consumption taxes are inherently discriminatory against women, especially in developing countries. In many traditional societies it is the woman's income that covers the costs of household necessities, not the man's income. Sure, a consumption tax might hit men harder when they spend more income on alcohol and tobacco, but

FIGURE 6.1   TAX REVENUE SOURCES BY COUNTRY, 2011

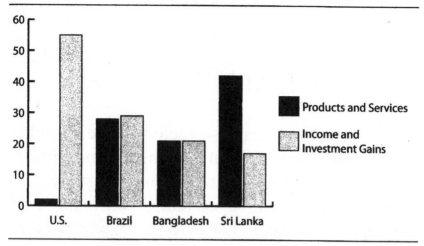

Source: World Bank, World Development Indicators, 2013

if higher taxes on these goods mean less consumption, that's a good thing by me. I can't say the same thing about food and clothing. If higher taxes on these items mean less consumption, that means kids are going without because their moms can't afford as much as before.

When most of us think about why people are poor, we usually think about the lack of education, health care, or food. Regressive taxation isn't at the top of that list. But it's not hard to see how rising prices on basic goods—whether from inflation, taxes, or anything else—burn through the budgets of people struggling to get by on a dollar a day or less.

Once again, things stay the same because people do not have the power to make things change. And once again, it doesn't have to be this way.

# 7

# THE MAID TRADE

Most of the tsunami-affected women I talked with that afternoon in Ampara had gone to school up to fifth or at most seventh grade. One with gorgeous, dark eyes and a red head scarf, Shakti, told me about her twin sister, who went all the way through school and now is the manager of a small bank—a good and precious job in this employment-scarce country.

Shakti's parents were weavers, and at thirteen she left school and began threading the loom. Her earnings supported her twin sister's education. At fourteen, she forged her passport to say she was twenty and went to Kuwait to be a housemaid until she really did reach twenty years old. Her adolescence was spent swaddled in scarves and hidden away in a small apartment as she raised other people's children and ironed their underwear.

Shakti sent her earnings home to her mother, who used the money to build a real house of cement and brick, a house that washed away with the tsunami. All those years of Shakti's cash and childhood swept away in a morning.

What a different life than her twin! They were

the same in all ways except education. Like a control group and a trial group in a scientific experiment, these twin lives are clear evidence of how education separates those who have and those who don't. Education not only gives you the ability to read and write but also gives you the power to get a job, understand basic human rights, and be a part of a country's decision-making class.

Shakti's story made me feel heavy and tired for her. But she showed no sign of self-pity or regret. It just *was*. Like it was and is for tens of thousands of Sri Lankan girls and boys who give their teenage years to the Middle East. Every year, Sri Lanka sends 260,000 people to the Middle East as manual laborers, maids, nannies, or service workers. At any given time, about two million people—23 percent of the labor force of Sri Lanka—are working outside Sri Lanka.[16] And 85 percent of migrant workers departing in 2011 were female housemaids.[17] These facts are alarming. They mean that Sri Lanka's economy isn't generating the employment desperately needed by its people. Can you imagine the riots in the United States if that many households had to send one parent overseas for years at a time to make ends meet?

But from the government's perspective, exporting people is a win-win situation. First, it takes the pressure off of the government to get busy fixing its economy and creating jobs. Second, workers abroad are Sri Lanka's largest source of foreign currency. Sri Lankans working overseas send home 569 billion rupees ($4.4 billion) each year.[18] This benefits the government in two ways: It keeps poor families fed, clothed, and sheltered enough not to demand solutions to their poverty, and it brings in heaps of foreign exchange. Rich Sri Lankans can't buy things from overseas boutiques without changing their rupees into greenbacks, rials, or euros. The international marketplace might take Visa, but it doesn't take rupees. The only places that will buy these rupees are the government-backed banks, and they have to have foreign cash on hand to make the exchange. So the more foreign cash coming in as remittances from exported workers, the more Sri Lanka can shop at the global mall.

Horror stories of girls being raped regularly by their "host father," wages being withheld indefinitely from manual laborers, and many more abuses are common. In fact, the government of Sri Lanka keeps track of the formal complaints that are lodged against foreign employers. In 2011, the government received about 10,000 complaints, about 8,000 of those from women, the most common reasons being nonpayment of wages and sexual harassment.[19] These complaints are only the tip of the iceberg, because things have to get really bad before workers go through the cumbersome process of formally lodging a grievance. The statistics also show that most complaints are investigated and the workers receive compensation. Of the 10,000 filings from 2011, the government reports that a little more than 9,100 were settled.

The toll on Sri Lankan families is devastating and less documented. Children left behind without mothers are often neglected or abused by fathers, siblings are split up and sent to various family members to be cared for temporarily, and sometimes children are left to simply raise themselves.

The solution of course is to create jobs in Sri Lanka, and to do that, the government, the private sector, aid agencies, and, most importantly, citizens themselves need to get involved. Here is where the US government can play a vital role: in discouraging the corruption that suffocates businesses, by helping successful Sri Lankan enterprises grow and employ more people, and giving Sri Lanka access to the huge US consumer market, to name just a few.

Still, not every migrant's story ends in tragedy. I met Farida while visiting with women who got some loans and grants from the Women's Development Federation (WDF) to help them get up and going after the tsunami. WDF is a membership association made up of village women who want to end their poverty by using their own skills and talents. They also organize women into savings groups and conduct empowerment training. I kept getting distracted by Farida's ebullient, effusive, and bright spirit. Her round face was ensconced in a colorful head scarf, and she kept smiling at me from ear to ear, eager to talk. Farida is one of the coordinators of the Muslim ladies for WDF. There's always one like Farida in every community I go to—the woman who has survived unbelievable hardships herself, but whose heart never runs dry of generosity and loving help for other women who need it.

Born in Jaffna, the epicenter of the civil war, she was one of five girls and two boys. Her father worked in the salt fields, and they were one of only five Muslim families in the area. As the girls grew, Farida's uncle advised her father to get out of Jaffna since he needed to marry off his girls to good Muslim boys and their town offered slim pickings. Her father didn't want to leave the beautiful shores of Jaffna, but he finally relented. Farida was six when she moved to Hambantota. Her father continued in the salt industry there, and her mother, an excellent cook, worked in several restaurants, including the luxurious Peacock Hotel. On some days, Farida would go with her mother to play sous chef, especially as her mom got older and was often sick.

Like so many other underage girls who want to emigrate, she forged her age on her passport and left for Saudi Arabia in December 1981. A short Palestinian man 30 years older than she approached her in the airport there and kept asking her if she was Farida. She didn't even know how to say yes in Arabic. The man's wife embraced her when they arrived at the small apartment. It was the fortieth day after their baby was born and they had roasted a sheep in celebration.

"They asked me to come share in the feast," Farida said. "We all sat at one table. I had no appetite. I was about to burst into tears. I had no idea what would happen to me. I had heard horror stories about girls who go to the Middle East, that the men keep their housemaids and their wives in the same way. They showed me my room and said that I would be safe there. The next day, the woman gave me the formula powder and filtered water, left me with the baby, and said she would be back at 2 o'clock. I had no idea what to do!"

The children taught her Arabic by asking her for things like *maya* (water). The child would say "no, no," until Farida guessed it right. It took her only three months to decipher the code. From the children she learned to write Arabic. They came to love her so much, and she them. She smiled as she told me, "The children wouldn't sleep in their own rooms, they would come to my room to sleep. I would put them back in their beds, but in the early morning they would come back to my room."

She spoke lovingly of Madam, her boss. "I learned about giving in Saudi Arabia. During Ramadan, the family would collect food and money for the poor and they would send 10,000 rupees ($75) to Sri Lanka for my family." She worked for them for ten years until Madam lost her job.

Later that evening, as a surprise, Upali and I picked up Farida and her thirteen-year-old daughter and took them to dinner in the grand dining room of the Peacock Hotel, where she had stood by her mother helping in the kitchen. Farida giggled as the waiter tucked her chair in and placed the napkin in her lap. I smiled and squeezed her hand. It made me happy to give something special to someone who has so little yet gives so much to those around her.

# 8

# THE RULE OF MEN

Ramakrishnan was my first translator in Sri Lanka when I went there in November 2005, just shy of a year after the tsunami. His English was passable; his greatest asset was that he spoke both Tamil and Sinhala. However, his biggest liability was his flagrant editing of my questions and women's answers. He kept inserting his own point of view into the conversation, which is the exact opposite of what you want in a translator.

After a few days of this, we had a straightforward conversation while driving in our minivan to visit another tsunami-affected community. I was expecting he'd react with the usual women-should-know-their-place-and-stay-there line, but that's not the reason he gave for generously editing conversations about women's rights.

Ramakrishnan felt that women's rights were a gateway to a world where men are no longer needed or wanted. He felt not unlike a father might when he realizes that his daughter is now grown up and independent. I suspect he's not alone in that feeling. Many men fear not being needed anymore, not having a purpose in life defined by providing for women and children. If women can take care of themselves, then whom will men take care of?

Perhaps if we approached men's fears with more understanding and less dismissal, our women's movement could get a lot farther, faster. But I think in our own fear as women, particularly women who have been violated, abused, hurt, or abandoned by men, we cling to our own anger to drive us forward in our fight for rights. It's great jet fuel, but perhaps it propels us slightly off an optimal course.

I'm not saying we should excuse men's violations of our rights; that's a hard line we should not move or even bend. What I am saying is we should acknowledge the various facets of how the world of basically good men would change as a result of women's increased independence. We should offer them the same kind of empathy we so desperately seek from them.

I became a much better advocate for women when I began to forgive men, when I realized that depending on a man could feel good, when I started to see the world through a little boy's eyes, when I met men who became good friends and allies, and when I let go of anger long enough to see men as precious human beings. Women's rights were no longer just about women's lives to me anymore. They were also about taking down the walls that limit what men can be, do, say, or think. Millions of men want to be released from the prison of cruel masculinity as much as we want to close those prisons down for good. If we could join forces—women and men as allies— we would be truly unstoppable.

This is my theory about men: Lots of them are good and unshakable allies and vocal advocates for women and girls. I don't know how many men this is, but overall it's probably not the majority of men in the whole world right now.

I think a majority of men are deeply influenced by whatever the dominant paradigm is for how men should be. They adapt to the myriad pressures on them from the media, their friends and relatives, faith leaders, and even the women in their lives. Whether they like the framework of masculinity around them or not, they often just fit themselves into it. I can't blame them. It's hard, and sometimes dangerous, to swim against these powerful currents.

Then there are a very tiny number of men who are destructive to themselves and to people around them. Perhaps they were abused as little boys or imbibed a distorted version of masculinity from an influential male figure. These men tend to wreak more than their fair share of havoc on the world.

The problem is that when members of this tiny minority end up in positions of power, they create things like the Crusades, World War II, the Taliban, and mass rape in Congo. When they influence culture, politics, and religion, they shift the general masculinity framework in an unhealthy direction for the majority of men.

The solution is not to kill off the "bad" men. The solution is to help the white-hatted, women-loving, and healthy men set the dominant standard for society. We need to help life-supporting masculinity flourish and influence the majority of men to follow. The solution is in mothers teaching their boys to treat women with adoration and respect, starting with her. It's in giving the progressive religious leaders great big megaphones. It's in fathers supporting fathers in raising their boys into awesome men. And it's in women recognizing, thanking, and rallying support for all the wonderful men out there who are part of the vanguard.

# 9
# PROUD TO BE AN AMERICAN

Siti, married at seventeen, has one daughter who is 22 and who inherited the family house as her dowry when she married, which is Sri Lankan custom. Unlike India and most other traditional societies, in Sri Lanka the daughter stays with her family and the son leaves his behind. Siti now lives in one small room of her daughter's house. She also has two sons. The elder one lives far away, and her seventeen-year-old mopes about the house because he didn't pass his exams and cannot continue his education.

Before the tsunami, Siti's husband was a "coolie," or day laborer. It was a hard life, but they lived on his income and she didn't have to work. She didn't even leave the house. According to Muslim tradition, she didn't go to the market; her husband did all the shopping.

When the tsunami came, her sons were at the mosque. They called her on her cell phone and told her to run. Her husband had gone to the market, right by the water's edge. He never came back.

The house was partially damaged, but what was even worse was that the canal next to it was filled with dead bodies for days. In line with another Muslim custom, she stayed in the house mourning her dead husband for 40 days. She couldn't go out, not even to get help removing the bodies.

When I visited her, I am happy to say, she was doing much better.

One of the organizations that got support from the US government—the kind of assistance we were pushing for—was the WDF of Sri Lanka, the group that Farida works with. The US government had already been supporting its excellent work before the tsunami. In fact, USAID helped build a very modest training center and guesthouse in Hambantota where WDF has helped hundreds of women become community leaders and motivators, and where I was lucky enough to stay one night. It makes me so happy when I see US taxpayer dollars being put to such fantastic use! I fell asleep smiling that night.

After the tsunami, USAID provided WDF with a small grant to make special donations and loans to women. Siti is one of the women who benefited. With her WDF grant of 25,000 rupees (about $200), she bought dishes and serving ware for weddings. Her brother-in-law is a good cook who caters for big events like weddings. He used to rent the dishes from someone else, so it made more sense to rent dishes from Siti and keep that income in the family. Her profits vary—sometimes she'll rent three times in a month, sometimes none. Her goal now is to save enough to build a small, new house right next to her daughter's so they can each have a little privacy.

Siti is also part of WDF's savings society, which meets twice a month. This is a very typical community development program in which women each make a small contribution to the collective savings account and then, together, discuss and decide who will get a loan from their pool. Here, the minimum "ante" is 250 rupees (just $1.98) each month, and the WDF head office insures the loans in case something really awful happens to a woman while she has an outstanding debt. She is covered in the event of death, disability, fire, theft, or, most relevantly, disaster.

The society structure also enables women to share information and get support, as well as access all kinds of health, psychological, and educational programs. The women in the WDF societies even help each other take on really tough stuff, like a husband's drug use or incest within the family. It's a wonderful model I've seen work all over the world in wildly different places and cultures.

I also got to meet with another lovely woman

who is a part of WDF's societies. Before the tsunami, Prema's house was very small, with tin walls and a *cadjan*-leaf (coconut palm) roof. But her husband was earning good money by making bricks in a kiln they built next to their home. The morning of the tsunami, she was preparing to go to the market. Her son wanted to tag along, and she was waiting for him to get ready. Thank God he was lollygagging. They were headed for the same market as Siti's husband and would have been killed. It made me think of how many times my kids have dilly-dallied tying their shoelaces or finding their coats. Maybe one or two of those times they've saved us all from tragedy?

Prema turned out to be a godsend to several children. She found a six-year-old boy clinging to a tree, his jaw smashed terribly. She stopped a passing truck and pleaded with them to take him to the hospital. She found a sixteen-year-old girl in the water who had been carried inland by the waves. The girl lived with Prema for one month until Prema could find the girl's parents. She smiled as she told me that they are still friends; the girl is grown and married now.

The government did not help Prema's family at all because no one in it was killed, and their home had no real value before it was destroyed. She was able to join WDF and get a loan of 50,000 rupees (about $400), and she and her husband restarted their brick-making business. Their house is now made of bricks (of course). Her husband was in bed with an injured back when I visited with her. I could only imagine how many thousands of pounds of bricks he's lugged around and what that has done to his back. WDF was helping them with the funds for surgery and medicine. Prema shyly but proudly told me that, in the meantime, she and the children were keeping the business going, and keeping the income coming. WDF and the help from the United States were real blessings for her family. She won't forget it and neither will I.

Though USAID did not make special outreach to local groups, as we had wanted them to, I'm still very proud and grateful that they did work with the WDF and that the hope and resilience of Siti's and Prema's stories were repeated by many other women I met. USAID did get grants and loans to tens of thousands of Sri Lankans, $50 here and $200 there, that gave people back one thing above all others: the means of supporting themselves and their families again.

The evidence of US help for the people of Sri Lanka after the tsunami was visible everywhere I visited, even on the roads on which I drove. I could tell when a stretch of asphalt had been repaired or replaced with US support because for that mile or two it looked exactly like the roads at home, with two pretty yellow lines down the middle, neat white lines marking the shoulders, and shiny, stainless steel guardrails. For just a few minutes, I could have been in Florida.

However, I couldn't find much evidence of what I went to Sri Lanka to look for: locally based grassroots women's organizations that got support from the US government. Other than WDF, a few large Sri Lankan groups got some money to work with women, but mostly the aid came and the aid went. Our government passed over, once again, the plethora of women's groups that were helping village women before the disaster, through the disaster, and after everyone else had gone.

# 10

# THE TSUNAMI WOMEN'S NETWORK

There are really two kinds of development work. There's helping people, and then there's helping people get what is due to them from their own government.

We Americans are generous. We don't like seeing people suffer and die needlessly. Where a government fails to help its own people or, worse, is the source of their suffering, we will provide lifesaving help. It is a long tradition that makes me proud. And frankly, it's in our own self-interest. We can help countries build stability now, or we can send our troops there later to extricate al-Qaeda when they fill the void for poor and desperate people. A soldier costs many times more per day to send to a country than an aid worker. So take your pick. I vote for the latter not just because it's cheaper, but also because if we do it right we'll make more friends, not more enemies. I saw a great bumper sticker after the Iraq war began in 2003 that really summed up the futility of the military approach: "We are making enemies faster than we can kill them."

Still, I think we could do our aid work much smarter and cheaper by not just providing services like education and health care to help in acute situations, but also by helping people organize themselves to demand the education and health care that their own government should provide to them. This is truly the best way to make lifelong friends. Give people what they really long for— the power to get what they need themselves—and they'll defend you for forever.

When I met with the Tsunami Women's Network, a self-organized group of women who survived the tsunami and went on to turn the tragedy into a springboard for making their lives more prosperous than ever, I said to myself, "Now, *that's* what I'm talkin' about!" These female firecrackers are where we should be putting our money.

Karuna is a short, stout, and solid woman with a

warm smile and glowing heart. Her long, jet-black hair is braided all the way down her back and sways side to side as she talks. You can see on her face that she might be quiet, but she's fierce. Karuna comes from the village of Wilpotha, far to the north of Dadalla where I was visiting the Tsunami Women's Network. She started the Women's Savings Collective (WSC) of Wilpotha, and after the tsunami she decided to take her model to the south and see if women there wanted to replicate it. The most important part of her model, I think, is that she just kept going back to Dadalla to see how the women were doing after the tsunami and share news about her community's collective efforts. She didn't foist the savings scheme on the women of Dadalla; she just shared her own experience and let them decide what they wanted to do with it.

"We were poverty-stricken women and we stood up against it and we won," said Karuna, speaking of poverty as if it were an attacker. "Now we are helping other women in the country to fight back and win. Our motto is 'We take you with us on our journey.'"

"Before the tsunami, we never had any kind of opportunities to get together and work as a collective," said Ranjani, the chair of the Tsunami Women's Network. "There were many organizations that came here to help, but it was Karuna that kept coming back to help us all the time."

She continued the story through Upali's interpretation, who was translating for me that particular day. "All these charity groups came and then they withdrew. They did not have a long-term plan or program. Karuna suggested to us that the women's savings society wasn't the end of the journey, that we have to go further. At the initial stages she visited us several times, and she told us about how they organized themselves in Wilpotha. Karuna pointed out the value of organizing and getting together. She also invited us to go to Wilpotha; that gave us an insight as to how we could organize ourselves in Dadalla. We started with the savings scheme, and now we have four divisions of savings groups. We got ourselves all together and formed the Tsunami Women's Network. Karuna helped us get training to improve our management and financial skills, and as a result of this skills development, we were able to expand into new areas, do things we never did before—it was a new era for us. Now we can go anywhere, talk to anybody, and ask any question we want. We are powerful now."

Partway through the meeting, Upali said, "See this one over here. She is being too modest. Her name is Kadira and she's done something incredible, and I have to tell you about it. In her village there was no water to drink. So instead of doing nothing, she organized such a strong advocacy campaign. She said to the local politician, 'You provide the water, we'll provide the labor.' The village got the trenches ready, laid the pipes, and then told the guy, 'Now turn on our water.' The politician was so shocked, he went running and did it right then." That is power! The woman Upali spoke of, Kadira, was grinning ear to ear, and so was I.

What Upali told me next was even more interesting. Kadira's village is connected to another by a short causeway. During the rainy season the causeway is covered in water. One time when the entire area was flooded, they had to transfer food between the villages using ropes. "She pressured the government to build a bridge. And she did it so smartly. Her group became friendly with all the local politicians and then started agitating with them," Upali went on.

The government started to build the bridge, but it was too narrow and too low. Rather than confronting the government officials, the community approached them as friends and advised them to start over so as not to risk bigger problems down the road. By reaching out in conversation, they even got the contractor who was building the bridge on their side. They had built up enough trust that the government guy said, "OK, you design the bridge." And they did. "A bridge by the people, for the people," said Upali like a proud father.

Remind you of the highway Irangani had to

commandeer? I can't tell you how many development projects go so awry—building the wrong thing or putting it in the wrong place, giving a community something they already have enough of, or creating something way more expensive and complex than what's needed—because those at the helm don't consult with the community or, better yet, let the community design the project. This is a great example of a community saying, "Don't do something stupid, just give us what we really want and need. It would save so much money in the long run, and it would go so much further in making us new friends."

So why isn't the US government finding and investing in small groups like the Tsunami Women's Network? Yes, here we are again. This association, like the thousands of organizations like it, lacks the sophisticated and expensive management and accounting systems needed to satisfy the US government's auditors. American taxpayer funds must be accounted for; there is no argument with that. However, village women like these, some of whom are illiterate but still lead thousands of other women, can't navigate the 55 pages of the federal government's procedures for what costs it will and won't cover for nonprofit organizations. I get tired of hearing back in Washington when I show how effective these women's organizations are that "they don't have the absorptive capacity." That is not a reference to paper towels. It's another way of saying that they're too small, it's not worth it to train them, and if they can't handle the accounting system, we just can't do it.

I decided to give the group its first American donation of $100, right on the spot. No accounting forms required.

I asked the women how their husbands and families have reacted to their newfound power. They all giggled. Finally someone spoke up: "Actually, prior to the tsunami, we were just household women, only participating in the death aid societies (a community collection for a family when a death occurs). But not like this; this is totally different."

"Now the men are fully supporting our actions. Whatever we do, they come following behind us," said another member with a broad, bright smile. "Before, we couldn't go out of the house, and now we go away for two or three days for trainings."

Another chimed in: "In this village, when we have our meetings, it's the husbands that come and clean the building, set it up for us, and bring us water and food. All the heavy work is undertaken by them."

Best of all was this response: "Earlier our husbands were not taking care of the children. Now when we are out for trainings, they take care of the children, feed them, and cook. This is a surprising change. We're happy with that."

"At home, when we are together, I still give him a cup of tea and I don't mind," said another woman, just in case I was getting the wrong idea. "Now there is respect between us. We couldn't have moved so far and achieved so much without Karuna's support."

I was emboldened to ask them if their children viewed them differently now too.

"They are surprisingly changed also!" sang out one of the moms in the group. "The kids bring the phone immediately when I get a call from the association. They take it very seriously. They also understand that we are making progress towards development. Whenever we go to meetings, we learn new things, and we take it back to our homes and we share it. Sometimes, the children come with us and participate."

Karuna smiled and added, "I involved my son in everything I did from the time he could talk. I taught him how to cook, and one time I feigned being sick to see if he could really do it himself. He made me a meal, not perfect, but a meal. Now he's married and I heard he was cooking for his wife when she was sick. I felt so happy."

I had to tell them how incredible they were. "You're changing this country fundamentally by changing how your children are growing up, seeing their mothers as strong change agents, seeing their parents respecting one another," I said. "Even in the United States, the gender roles can be very traditional still. Even for us, it's hard to break out of traditional roles. You really are leading the world in a new way, not just your village." I pushed the words out of my mouth quickly to Upali to translate.

Just as Upali finished translating my burst of admiration, an ice cream truck rolled in playing "It's a Small World." I had to laugh at how sweet and hokey it was.

We broke for tea and I discovered my favorite food of Sri Lanka: *hallapa*. It's a delicious little package of millet and corn flour made into a pancake, stuffed with shredded coconut and honey, and then wrapped in a big green leaf and steamed. It's a very typical, low-cost, portable treat eaten by villagers. The earthy taste of the leaf mixed just right with the creamy texture of the millet and corn and the angelic blend of honey and coconut. *Now, this is heaven,* I thought, and smiled at the women of the tsunami network over the rim of my teacup.

# 11
# SHOW ME THE MONEY

Back in Washington, DC, a few years after the tsunami, I put one of our best and brightest associates on the case to find out exactly how much USAID had given to local women's organizations. From that moment on, we entered an *Alice in Wonderland* world as we were passed from one person "in charge" to another to another, only to find ourselves back again to the first person who was supposed to be in charge.

Many of the USAID program officers were very friendly; they are good people who do the work they do because they care about the world. Somehow, though, it seemed like all these good human beings had checked their common sense at the door and traded in their plain English-speaking ability for the "Guidelines for Ensuring and Maximizing the Objectivity, Utility, and Integrity of Information Disseminated by Federal Agencies." These outline USAID's procedures to ensure that information prepared and disclosed by the agency is accurate and safe for public consumption.

One midlevel person we found in the Asia and Near East Bureau was kind enough to tell us, "USAID intends to implement small grants programs to support training and equipment for women-led NGOs in tsunami-affected areas." (Does that sound familiar? Gee, it's a lot like the House Report language.) She said that activities in Sri Lanka would "strengthen the capacity of women-led NGOs" and in Indonesia would "provide organizational development assistance and programmatic support for women-led NGOs in Aceh, Indonesia." We were thrilled! And ready to give USAID praise for moving in the right direction.

A couple of days later, a short, terse e-mail from a higher-up came to us stating flatly, "Please disregard the information received from the Asia and Near East Bureau representative. She was not authorized to release the information. USAID will not be tracking support for local women-led NGOs and no further information will be forthcoming."

*That* was the wrong answer, and it just made us poke them harder. We did not cease asking questions, every couple of months, for two more years. We started following the money to the contractors that received USAID funds and went directly to them to ask what they did with local women's organizations after the tsunami. The answer was always "nothing," or "we did some stuff, but we don't have time to tell you about that." Then we called the Asia Foundation, which is a San Francisco–based nonprofit that implements US government projects across Asia and the Pacific. They had the only concrete project to help women's groups in Aceh, Indonesia, probably the one that staff person mentioned in her e-mail. They had been given a $500,000 grant from USAID. Whoop-de-doo, 500 grand. That's enough for women's groups to hire about 50 people for two years. That's pathetic. And I still wanted to know what happened to the other $9,500,000.

It was too late for Sri Lanka; we had come to the end of the USAID trail. But that three-year journey—listening to what women were saying, carrying their priorities to decision makers, trying to create change through legislation, seeing that women's groups didn't matter to the powers-that-be, and investigating every lead to a dead end—just made me feel bolder. The thing about me is that when it comes to women and girls, I really don't like to lose. Even more than that, I hate to be shut out. What started as a small campaign around tsunami aid became a major program at Women Thrive to fundamentally change the way US aid is distributed around the globe.

# 12

## TWO CUPS OF D

Nothing fits me as well as a Victoria's Secret bra. I've tried lots of others, but I keep reaching for those cups every morning when I get dressed. I always felt guilty about that, though. Victoria's Secret's advertising doesn't exactly promote women's empowerment, and so I assumed their manufacturing practices probably didn't either. But my time in Sri Lanka opened a window into the world of ethical manufacturing and made me feel a little better about my lingerie of choice.

Globally, manufacturing provides tens of millions of jobs, and each of those employees supports a family. Many millions of people are able to eat and have shelter as a result of the manufacturing sector. Millions of others are employed in industries that support manufacturing, from construction to cooking. The employment size and potential of manufacturing is hard to ignore.

But as you already know, there is a lot of exploitation and abuse in the manufacturing sector. Too many factory owners care less about their employees than they do about street dogs, and those are the ones we always hear about in the news. Can manufacturing be a solution for poverty, particularly for women?

Right now, the only way we ensure that manufacturing lifts families out of poverty is by pressuring brands like Gap, Marks & Spencer, Victoria's Secret, and others to buy from factories that treat people well. While this creates some positive competition between factories to lower their risk of scandal, it hasn't stopped slave-like conditions or rampant exploitation. Stories about factories that burned down with locked doors, and women forced to have sex with line managers to keep their jobs still appear in the headlines. The public cries out, and the brands run from the offending factory to others that may be no better. When they cut and run, all the factory workers at the abandoned plant lose their jobs. This only hurts the people we are trying to help; thousands are put out of work and pushed into poverty. There's got to be a better way.

The most worthy solution is making country governments do the job they're supposed to do: enforce the labor, health, and safety laws that they probably already have on the books. I'm going to talk about this a lot more in Chapter 14. Another approach is to reward the factories that are doing the right things and to buy from brands that favor good manufacturers rather than hissing and booing when things go wrong. There are people out there who care about their employees as much as they do about making money.

One exception to the race-to-the-bottom school of manufacturing is Mahesh Amalean, chairman of MAS Holdings, the largest manufacturer of textiles in Sri Lanka and one of the largest suppliers to Victoria's Secret. His factories are part of a growing social responsibility movement in this sector and stand as an example of how to do things better.

Mahesh didn't start out wanting to make bras and panties. He got there through exquisite patience and a keen eye for the modern textile marketplace. His ancestors were village tailors in Gujarat, India. In 1926, his grandfather decided to break away from the family, but not its trade, and start a small clothing factory in Sri Lanka.

Mahesh's father and his uncles grew up amid buzzing sewing machines, business transactions, and fashion. They naturally picked up the family business when they finished their educations. But Mahesh wanted something different, something more modern, fresher, and freer. Even so, he couldn't swim against the strong current of family expectations, at least not directly against it, and he spent about seven years at his grandfather's factory. He worked hard while he looked out the window at the changing world of fashion and manufacturing. He tried to steer the family factory toward more modern shores, but his uncles felt they knew what was right for the business they had helmed their whole lives. Like his grandfather two generations before, Mahesh decided to leave and start out on his own, but not without his uncles' blessings. It took him three months and many conversations to get that. Exquisite patience.

He pooled his money with that of his two younger brothers, Ajay and Sharad (hence M-A-S), and started up a small plant with 24 sewing machines and 60 employees to break into the synthetic textiles market. Their first lucky break came in a joint venture with MAST Industries out of Boston. (The similarity in names was only a synchronistic coincidence.) With an influx of capital, MAS scaled into a modern plant that could deliver high-quality synthetic clothing to top brands like Speedo and Victoria's Secret. By

2006, it was Victoria's Secret's largest supplier. Today, 60 percent of MAS's business is with Nike and Victoria's Secret. The other 40 percent is for lots of other brand names you know and love, including Lululemon, Marks & Spencer, H&M, and Athleta.

Over 25 years, MAS Holdings has grown to 34 factories in Sri Lanka, three in India, one in Bangladesh, and soon one in Indonesia. It employs more than 57,000 people. When the civil war ended, MAS opened two new factories in the northern part of Sri Lanka, an area that was off limits before because it was at the war's epicenter. The MAS factories provided critical employment to people throughout the country during all the years of civil war, and they still do.

What I found interesting about MAS is not its size, profits, or products, but its commitment to being socially responsible while simultaneously making money. "Very often we come to a crossroads between two business decisions," Mahesh told me, "and sometimes you really don't know which of two options is the right one. One option has a good economic benefit; the other one has a social benefit and an economic benefit, but probably isn't as profitable as the first. At that crossroads, you really have to ask yourself, 'What's the right thing to do here?' This one might be less profitable and more work, but it's probably the right thing to do, so let's do that."

Mahesh, Ajay, and Sharad did not set out to make MAS a beacon of good corporate practice. As Ajay Amalean said in an interview with the International Finance Corporation, "We had absolutely no idea that twenty years down the road things we were doing would be called corporate social responsibility."[20] In a way it's really sad that simple human kindness, treating people with dignity, and taking care of one another became so unusual in business that it needed its own special term: corporate social responsibility.

The things that MAS does are simple but important. It pays its employees at least the minimum wage, and often better than that. It provides safe transportation to and from the factory; one large meal a day; tea breaks; free health care in on-site medical centers; uniforms; and, importantly in this tropical nation, air conditioning. It does not conduct pregnancy exams to screen out workers. In fact, it provides free prenatal care and other special treatment for pregnant team members.

In 2006 and again in 2012, I visited several MAS factories. I could have been walking into state-of-the-art manufacturing facilities in California, except that every single person in there was Sri Lankan. Hundreds of women and a noticeable number of men, most of them in their early twenties, were organized into units of ten to twelve people. Each unit was responsible for making one bra, panty, or nightgown of one color and style from start to finish, including quality-control inspection and packaging. The team members in the unit could switch to different jobs in the process, helping them to avoid complete mind-maddening boredom (which isn't good for high-quality production) and to develop new skills. There were incentives for making the target number of items on schedule as well as for producing the lowest number of rejects. Most importantly, there were no penalties for missing targets, just incentives for reaching them.

I kept getting distracted by the cute nightie on one row or the pretty bra a team was sewing on another. I almost asked if I could shop right on the spot. What better way to know that what I'm buying was made ethically than by watching it actually happen? But I bit my tongue and made a note to myself: Look for that lovely bra-panty set when I'm back in the States.

Every now and then I saw a girl with a pink uniform on, so I asked what that meant. A pink frock means a woman is pregnant, and she gets a glass of milk every day with her meal, additional bathroom breaks (finally, someone understands!), and free prenatal care at the health clinic.

In 2003, MAS piloted a small program called "Women Go Beyond." The idea was to highlight remarkable women who work on their factory floors by recognizing them with the Empowered Woman award. Shevanthi Jayasuriya, head of human resources for MAS, put it this way: "It is not about rewarding good work. These women all come from very difficult economic backgrounds, so what we look for are people who have . . . true self-determination and strength; who have overcome major challenges. . . . The Empowered Woman is someone who has the strength to succeed in life." Every year, external judges select one person from each factory, and MAS throws an all-stops-out gala in honor of these Empowered Women.

Some of these truly incredible awardees have gone from living on the margins in abject poverty to being the engines of prosperity and positive change in their families and communities. Sujeewa was born right into poverty in a mud hut in a small village in Sri Lanka. When she was just six, her desperate mother left for the Middle East to make enough money to build a proper house, and Sujeewa went to live with her aunt. After two years, her mother came home to discover that her hard-earned revenue had been drunk away by her alcoholic husband. She left again for the Middle East, this time sending the money to her eldest son instead. Sujeewa decided then to stay at home and take care of her younger brother, who was just four at the time. She would rise before the sun, get herself and her little charge ready for school, and end the day after the sun had set when she finished her housework. Long days for a little girl of only nine. When she was fifteen, her older brother felt they had enough money saved to start building a house. The children made the bricks themselves, carrying water endless times back and forth from the village well 200 yards away. Soon after Sujeewa finished school at eighteen, she got a job working at an MAS factory. She started as a cutting helper and soon moved up to sewing machine operator. At nineteen, she married and moved into a tiny house she and her new husband built; it had a dirt floor, no power, and no furniture. She was starting from scratch again. The managers noticed her hard work and diligence and asked her to become a sample operator, which was much more challenging work. By 23, she and her husband turned their shell of a house into a comfortable home for themselves and their baby girl.[21]

Priyangani remembered being hungry throughout her childhood. She was one of nine children who often pieced together their daily meals from a single fish given to her brother, who helped fishermen bring in their nets, and a loaf of bread from a generous baker. "I remember some of our relatives would pretend they didn't know us, not wanting to be associated with this family who had to rely on charity to live," she said in an interview before receiving her Empowered Woman award. As the eldest girl in the family, she left school at sixteen to find a job, but the only thing she could find was an unpaid apprenticeship in a dentist's office. She stayed there hoping in vain to become a real employee. She eventually quit when she found a position at MAS as a sewing machine operator. "You can't imagine how much the meals that the factory provided meant to me," she recalled. "For the first time in my life, I didn't have to worry about my next meal." She worked hard, provided for her younger brothers and sisters with her earnings, and within two years got promoted to supervisor. She's been at MAS for 23 years now, is a garment technician helping to manage one of the company's mini-factories, and is the mother of two. To prevent other little ones from a hungry childhood, every Sunday she provides lunch to the children attending temple school in her community.[22]

I could go on and on with many similar stories. If ever you doubt that women have what it takes to end poverty in one generation, just remember these two women.

Women Go Beyond has grown to be much more than just the Empowered Woman awards. The program now includes four additional components:

1. Career Development, which includes English and information technology classes. This

is, by far, the most popular part of the program.

2. Work-Life Balance, which covers stress management, sexual and reproductive health, pre- and postnatal issues, and nutrition.

3. Skills Development, which helps women learn an income-generating activity they can rely on when they leave the factory, usually after they get married. These classes include making small crafts, doing beauty treatments and make-up application, creating bridal dressings, and the like.

4. Managing Personal Finance, which helps female employees improve their money management skills, from budgeting and banking to planning for long-term needs.

Last year MAS expanded the Women Go Beyond program to all its plants, including its fabric-making facilities. And yes, factory employees get paid time off to participate in these training programs.

MAS also has a long-standing tradition of encouraging women to play sports, even the ones normally reserved for boys and men. It's had two women actually go to the Olympics to represent Sri Lanka in—you won't believe this—boxing and sharpshooting. Remind me not get on the bad side of that production team!

Boxing and sharpshooting don't represent the

lives of most Sri Lankan women, who are not trained to kill. Rather, they are most often the targets of violence. I was about to bring up the touchy issue of violence against women, but Shevanthi beat me to it: "An outside group did a survey that showed 62 percent of our women were subject to violence in the home. Ninety-nine percent of these women are the sole bread-winners in their households, but they are still subjected to this kind of thing. Women would go to the nurse's office to rub make-up on their bruises before going onto the floor to work. I went to the chairman [Mahesh] and asked how do we as a company get involved in this?"

She continued, almost in a whisper, "We teach our women first that this is not right. We teach our people that there are laws against it; teach them that if it is happening to them, there are places they can go to get help. We started using our Empowered Woman past winners, and some men too, to be change agents, not to be counselors, but just a friend to someone who's looking down, encouraging them to go to the counselors we have put in the factories. We have been monitoring visits to the counselors; the numbers have increased, but that can be a good thing. The production managers are so happy we are doing this. They've said to me, 'We know these girls are going through this. Long before HR knows, we know. We can see it.' From a company point of view, it helps with absenteeism, productivity, and turnover overall."

In 2012, Shevanthi took on the big challenge of creating a gender-sensitive work environment, which is about more than just harassment training. "You have to teach people what it means to be gender-sensitive in all ways," she said. "We spend two days changing men's attitudes. I open these two-day trainings at the beginning and then I come back for the last evening. You see 35 men who have changed attitudes; men that have openly talked with one another about their beliefs and behaviors that harm women. At the very least, their wives at home and their children will have a better time. Now they [the men] are asking for more," she continued. "Some of the divisions decided themselves to have quotas to increase the number of women in their departments. It works because the men decide themselves what to do, they are not told to do it. One factory that I'm going to this afternoon—they decided that they had to stop the name-calling that happens in the office transport. There was no management involvement; they took it upon themselves because they learned that this isn't right, they spoke to their colleagues, they got together, and they stopped it. For me that's real empowerment."

Yes! Yes! Yes! I was practically levitating in my seat. This is the vital ingredient that our women's movement too often leaves out: men. Remember those guys from Chapter 8? (The majority of men who are good souls that follow the dominant culture.) They need to be retrained that there's a better way. MAS is showing that this, too, is possible.

# 13

## THE WOMEN'S EMPOWERMENT PRINCIPLES

Shevanthi had a road map for helping the women in her company. It's called the Women's Empowerment Principles, which are a set of seven business-centered voluntary principles that promote women's needs and priorities at work, in the marketplace, and within their communities. I'm really proud that Women Thrive provided key input to the Principles during their conception, and even more proud that Joe Keefe, president of Pax World Mutual Funds and our board chair, was one of the masterminds behind it. Joe headed the creation of the Calvert investment fund's Women's Principles as their senior adviser for strategic social policy. On the outside, Joe looks like the quintessential investor: preppy in khakis and button-down blue oxfords, sharp as a razor, politically astute, always on the lookout for a great new opportunity, and doesn't tolerate any BS. But on the inside he's a Peace Corps wannabe, adoring father of a daughter, and 1960s social crusader.

"As the World Wide Web and new global media took hold in the 1990s and 2000s, we started seeing all kinds of human rights and labor abuses all over the place, which were there before but weren't visible," Joe told me in his usual I-see-the-missing-piece, business-guy way. "People responded by creating codes of conduct for specific industries like the apparel sector, rug industry, and the like. But there was nothing that addressed the different abuses women were facing in workplaces around the world. There was nothing on how corporations should treat, empower, and protect women employees. There needed to be a global corporate code of conduct on how companies should interact with women."

Codes of conduct that were set up in the past to protect gender-neutral workers put the focus on standards like the right to collective bargaining and the obligations of employers to provide a safe work environment and to pay a minimum wage— all critical to both men and women. However, these codes did not shine a light on all the dark places women have to live that men don't: being forced to take monthly pregnancy tests against their will, supervisors sexually abusing and harassing them with no consequences, and getting paid a much lower wage for the exact same work because they're women, to just name a few.

"We knew that promoting women's rights standards was the right thing to do, but we also had a hunch that it would be good for the bottom line," said Joe, going right to the part that would get the attention of CEOs. "This was before we had all the evidence showing that there's a real business case for empowering women." The *Economist* estimates that increased women's employment in developing countries had added more to global economic growth than the emergence of China.[23]

At the same time that Calvert was incubating its Women's Principles, several key people within the United Nations were seeing the same missing piece from its almost opposite vantage point. Joan Libby Hawk was working at the United Nations Development Fund for Women (UNIFEM), the small UN agency charged with women's empowerment, political participation, addressing violence against women, and many other women's issues. (UNIFEM was later transformed into a larger agency for women, now called UN Women.) Joan was one of the few Americans at UNIFEM and was Women Thrive's lifeline, as well as our UN-to-real-world translator, whenever we wanted to get more money for UNIFEM from Congress. We spent many days together (in flat, comfortable shoes) walking the Hill to up the US contribution for UNIFEM's programs, first from $1 million to $2 million and ultimately to $6.5 million a year. "In 2000, when Kofi Annan was secretary-general, we were going full speed into globalization, and the UN really recognized the important role of the private sector in the world," Joan, our UN explainer, explained, "Annan wanted to create a way to link business with global norms and values on human rights. So he launched the UN Global Compact, which has ten principles from anticorruption, to human rights, to antitrafficking. Companies become members of the UN Global Compact and pledge to integrate the principles into their operations and report back each year on their progress. The reporting is a requirement, though the code of conduct itself is voluntary.

"In 2001, when I went to UNIFEM," she continued, "there were a lot of openings in many sectors to advance women. But there was very little going on with the private sector. Realizing that globalization had hit us full-square and considering the gender of the people taking the jobs at the lowest end of the chain, there was a giant vacuum on gender equality."

So Joan started talking to Calvert about their Women's Principles and developed a partnership with them. After a few years it became clear that the Women's Principles could be recast to reach a much bigger audience of corporations. And Joan recognized that the UN Global Compact needed (and wanted) to get a lot stronger on gender. With her partners at UNIFEM and the Global Compact, Joan reworked the principles based on extensive feedback from around the world. UNIFEM and the UN Global Compact relaunched them as the Women's Empowerment Principles for International Women's Day in March 2010.

I asked Joan if the voluntary nature of the Principles just let companies use them for "pink-washing" their public image. "We confronted this full on and recognized two things: first, our limited capacity to monitor and evaluate corporations. That's a whole other model the UN cannot replicate. We had to get companies to report back to us, just as the Global Compact does. Second, an incentive-based approach fit our strategy. From the get-go, we wanted to build this like a movement. A movement grows not because it's obligatory, but because it attracts people for a variety of reasons. We had to make compelling business *and* human rights cases.

"One thing we knew from the very beginning is that attracting the company CEO to publicly sign on to the Principles was a good way to go," Joan explained. "The truth of the matter is that when a CEO has to sign something public, it gets a lot of attention and sparks a lot of conversations among management, board members, and, of course, lawyers. We continue to hear that the Principles make conversations happen in the C suite and the boardroom. Almost every company that signs onto the Principles undertakes an internal assessment to figure out what they really are, and are not, doing on gender equality and women's empowerment. The seven Principles are a very helpful guide."

As of August 2013, 598 companies from all over the world and in all industries have signed on, and that number is growing every month. "Given that we started in 2010 with about 40 signers and that it's an initiative that has four or five part-time staff people, getting up to almost 600 is pretty impressive. It shows a lot about the Principles' attractiveness," said Joan.

While Joe loves the Principles, he feels that there's a long way to go: "I think the Principles are a straightforward, simple, and manageable list of commitments that a company can do and measure itself against. What we still struggle with is that not enough companies have endorsed them and taken them seriously yet. There's still reluctance on the part of companies. Their lawyers are telling them, 'Be careful, you might get sued.' The legal and risk management folks always say, 'Don't do it unless you have to.' Companies say they care, but they're not willing to sign on because they will potentially be held accountable and liable, which they'd just as soon avoid. In the end, companies will do it because it's in their best

# WOMEN'S EMPOWERMENT PRINCIPLES HIGHLIGHTS

*1. Leadership that promotes gender equality*
- Promote gender equality and human rights through top corporate leaders and company-wide policies
- Have goals and targets for gender equality and make progress part of managers' performance reviews

*2. Equal opportunity, inclusion, and nondiscrimination*
- Pay men and women equally, including benefits, for equal work; pay a living wage
- Ensure workplaces are free of gender-based discrimination
- Proactively recruit and appoint women to managerial and executive position, including boards (get to 30 percent or greater women in decision-making positions)
- Offer flexible work options and support access to dependent care

*3. Health, safety, and freedom from violence*
- Provide safe working conditions, protection from hazardous materials, and

disclose potential risks including reproductive health risks

- Have a zero-tolerance policy toward any form of violence at work, including verbal, physical, or sexual harassment or violence. Train managers and security staff about laws and company policies on human trafficking, labor, and sexual exploitation
- Strive to offer health insurance, and other important services like domestic violence assistance, to employees
- Respect time off for medical care or counseling for employees and their family members
- Identify and address potential safety issues, including for women traveling to/from work or for business
- Train security staff and managers to recognize signs of violence against women

4. *Education, training, and professional development for women*
   - Open avenues of advancement to women at all levels, and encourage women to enter nontraditional fields
   - Ensure equal access to company-supported training and education programs, including networking and mentoring

5. *Enterprise development, supply chain, and marketing practices*
   - Expand business relationships with women-owned enterprises
   - Support access to credit through gender-sensitive solutions
   - Ask business partners to respect the company's commitment to women and equality
   - Respect women's dignity in all marketing and corporate materials
   - Ensure that no company products, services, or facilities are used for trafficking, labor, or sexual exploitation

6. *Community leadership and engagement*
   - Showcase the company's commitment to equality and women's empowerment
   - Advocate for gender equality within the business community; encourage business partners to collaborate to promote women's empowerment
   - Help open opportunities for women and girls and eliminate discrimination in the wider community
   - Promote and recognize women's leadership and contributions in their communities
   - Use corporate philanthropy to support equality and human rights

> ### 7. *Transparency, measuring, and reporting*
> - Make public company policies and plans for gender equality
> - Establish benchmarks for inclusion of women at all levels
> - Measure progress and report on it internally and externally

interests to do it. And to get there, they need to be pressured by all sources—government, social movements, consumers, and shareholders. They have to respond to the people who buy their products and give them a license to operate. If they don't know it's a priority for their shareholders or consumers, why should they do it?" Yep, there's no BS with Joe.

As president of Pax World Mutual Funds, Joe is all about shareholders voting with their investment dollars. One of the first things he did when he got there was purchase the Women's Equity Fund, originally pioneered by Linda Pei and Leslie Christian. He relaunched it as Pax World's Global Women's Equality Fund, in which the Women's Empowerment Principles are used as a guideline to determine which companies belong in the fund. It's the only mutual fund out there that systematically focuses on gender equality and women's rights as a lens for investors. It's brilliant.

"Wherever I talk about the principles, and I talk

about them a lot, I get nothing but an extremely positive reception," Joe said. "People think that companies should conduct themselves this way. I think that the Principles are part of a larger mosaic that has taken shape the last five to ten years, which makes gender equality a much more important issue, not just generally, but in the business sector. All kinds of things have come together, but the Principles are an indication that the moment has arrived for really tackling gender equity in the workplace."[24]

MAS is one of the first companies to take the Principles and weave them throughout all aspects of its business. In 2011, they drew up a strategic plan to go beyond Women Go Beyond. Now the program is part and parcel of its core human resources program; it's no longer just a side corporate social responsibility project. Shevanthi was proud of the change that she's brought about at MAS: "It's not just something we do when we have the time and money, and it's something we do everyday."

# 14

## LIFE IN THE ZONE

I wanted to see where the girls working in the Export Processing Zone (EPZ) factories lived. EPZs are geographic areas set aside by a country where factories can manufacture goods and ship them out without tariffs or taxes. These areas can be large or small, with 10 to 100 or more factories. Workers often migrate from rural villages to work in the EPZs and stay in crowded boarding-houses or shantytowns. Sri Lanka is no different. Thousands of girls between 16 and 30 come to the Colombo area EPZ to find jobs.

We asked a local women's organization to take us to some dormitories or boardinghouses where the young women live. We entered a doorway, barely noticeable between a street café and an electronics shop, and walked up a dank cement staircase with a single bare light bulb, which provided just enough light for each stair to cast a shadow and for us to discern one step apart from the next. At the top of the stairs was a landing with two large rooms on either side. From the doorway, I could see the metal bunk beds lined up close to one another, starting right at the entrance to the room and surrounding every inch of the perimeter.

I entered the room to get a complete view. There were more metal bunk beds with old cotton mattresses worn down to the thickness of a crepe by countless petite bodies tossing and turning in the night. The metal was rusted, the paint worn off of the frames long ago, no better quality than the rickety shelves you can buy at Home Depot for your garage storage space. The smell of too many bodies and too little airflow hung in the room. A few girls who were not on their shift were asleep in their beds. My interpreter and host pointed to one girl in the corner, her eyes sunken in her bony skull, who was sick and not working at the moment. My stomach turned over.

"Is this how they all live?" I asked my guide.

"Some places are better, some are worse," she said. "But the girls find the cheapest places because they want to save as much money as possible for their dowries or to send home to their families."

We left that room and walked into the other, laid out in a mirror image of the first. A young woman with a round face and an inviting smile looked at me, and my host explained who I was and asked her if she would be willing to talk with us. She agreed as long as I wouldn't use her name.

She had been living in this hostel for six years. Her job was in an EPZ factory soldering computer parts together, for which she made 6,800 rupees a month ($50). With overtime she could make

8,000 rupees a month ($60), but there wasn't overtime every month. Her factory did pay for transportation and one meal, like MAS does, and I gathered this was standard procedure. Her goal was "to live in a nice way without troubling anyone and to get married." She expected she'd work in the factory a few more years to save up enough money to reach those humble goals.

Around the corner was a communal kitchen, where two girls were preparing their midday meal of coconut roti. They chatted happily, perhaps about their families back home or about the boys they hoped their parents had arranged for them to wed. A kerosene camp stove was on one old, chipped countertop, and the faucet to a deep cement sink dripped on the other.

"The girls really like to live together like this," my host volunteered, probably reading the sad, sullen look on my face. "They are like family to each other." *I'm sure they are,* I thought. There's nothing like shared misery to make mere acquaintances into sisters.

Some factories might provide housing for the girls, but most avoid the liability that comes with that. The boardinghouse I visited clearly paid no attention to safety laws for fire or health laws to prevent the spread of disease. I know that many women's organizations pound on factory owners to improve the living conditions for the women. There is no doubt they should play a role here since they directly benefit from women being able to live close by their work sites: lower transportation costs to bus them to and from the plant and the possibility of shift work and overtime.

When I visited with MAS's leadership, I specifically asked about how they approach this sensitive issue of living conditions. They have a two-pronged approach. First, they provide information to their employees about the importance of safe and hygienic housing. Second, and more usefully, they have placed their factories around the entire country; only two factories are in the Colombo area EPZs. This has huge benefits for young women. They can live at home with their families, which is both safer and free. Their families are much more comfortable allowing them to work in close-by factories (MAS invites families to tour the plants several times a year) than the far-away urban EPZs. Rural factories create more economic activity, as every factory needs a host of support services to keep it running.

It certainly costs MAS more to transport raw materials all around the country to their various factories and then truck the finished products to the ports for overseas shipping. The Sri Lankan Board of Industry, a government agency, has provided incentives for all manufacturers, not just MAS—such as tax breaks and good terms on long-term land leases—to spread the employment around the countryside. So it's not complete altruism here. It's common sense.

Living conditions are an important part of worker rights, but the most complex topics in manufacturing are unions and living wages; both are fundamental to ethical trade. I talked with Julia Kilbourne of the Ethical Trading Initiative (ETI) in London. ETI is a leading alliance of companies, trade unions, and nongovernmental organizations (NGOs) that promotes respect for workers' rights worldwide. They help bring together the resources, knowledge, and skills of their members to understand conditions in global supply chains, to identify rights abuses, to develop long-lasting solutions, and to put these solutions into practice. I figured if anyone could provide an unbiased view, it would be ETI.

I asked Julia how they work with unions. "The right to freedom of association and collective bargaining is a central tenet within ethical trade, which is enshrined in our ETI Base Code of labor practice," she said. "Freedom of association is the right for workers and employers to establish and join trade unions of their own choosing, without prior authorization and interference. So unions are incredibly important to ETI's work, and the work of our member companies." Julia added that from a business perspective, strong unions also make good sense. "A dialogue-based workplace empowers and engages its workers, enhancing

144

morale and leading to improvements in performance. By contrast, a subdued and disempowered work force will tend toward low engagement and underperformance. In our work, we witness all stages of organizing, from the mature trade unions of the UK through to the fledging trade unions of countries like China and Bangladesh, which are doing their best to advocate for issues such as a living wage in what can be a very challenging environment."

"What do you think about so-called employee associations like the ones MAS has?" I asked.

"The thing to look at is whether companies are willing to be transparent and show that workers take the lead on certain discussions, particularly wages. Open bargaining for a decent, fair, and living wage is indicative of whether workers have the ability to bargain collectively, as part of a union or not. Can workers bring up some of the sensitive issues like gender-based discrimination or harassment? The place to start is to see if workers feel comfortable enough to raise issues about how they are treated."

"What about living wages?" I inquired. "Manufacturers seem to always say that their profit margins are so small that they'd go under if they paid people more. Is that true or just smoke and mirrors?"

"Calculating a living wage can be complex, as there are a number of different formulas. What is certain is that you need to take a thorough look at the product chain, starting with the retailer's profit and ending with what a worker takes home as pay. You can then see where the profit is amassed. It could be the retailer that's making the most. Those retailers making large profits can probably share some of this value with the workers on the production line, without going out of business. It is possible for an industry to remain economically viable, while also sharing profits with the workers."

These are challenging issues, particularly given the complexity of global supply chains. Working together is the key. We have to get brands, factories, governments, workers, trade unions, and NGOs to come together and make sure that work actually lifts people out of poverty while workers' rights are respected and protected. "Consumers need to know that one company can't do it alone," Julia said. "We have to work collectively to harness the purchasing power to effect real change."

I do not believe that the factories bear all the responsibility for the lives of their workers. Instead, living conditions, wages, and working conditions are places where governments should and do have a role to play. One of the most basic jobs of a government is the social contract outlined by countless philosophers that sets limits on what human beings can do to one another. We understand that not all of us can rely on an internal moral compass to keep us on track. Greed, also known as the "maximization of profits," is the most common magnet that interferes with our compasses. Someone else has to say what is out of bounds in the pursuit of wealth and hold us to it. We all agree collectively that the government— as a neutral third party—should play referee.

As Americans, we can take for granted (I know I often do) all the health and safety regulations that stop us from hurting ourselves or others, from building codes to health inspections to licensing of qualified professionals. We complain about red tape, excessive regulation, and high taxes (which pay for all these services). Whenever someone says to me that we need to drastically reduce taxes I want to invite them to spend a month in a country with practically no taxes, and therefore little government services to protect citizens. The schools stink; the roads are falling apart or don't even exist; there is no fire department to save your house from burning down; and if someone jilts you in business, there's no functioning court system where you can go and get the money you're owed. If that's your cup of tea, then by all means, move to a low-tax or no-tax country.

The entity that should be pressured to set and enforce basic standards for how young women live and work in factories *is the government of that country.* The way I see it, there are three ways to go about this: the Carrot, the Stick, and the Shopping Trip.

First, the Carrot. The US government can provide incentives for manufacturers and foreign governments to do what's right. The US government determines which goods enter our country and which ones don't, so they can use this power for good. For example, fruit and vegetables must meet lots of health standards before they are cleared for your favorite grocery store's produce section and, eventually, your mouth. But the clothes we wear do not have hard standards around their production and import. If they did, we might not see the label "Made in China" anymore. Since the 1990s, our government has been giving a nod to labor and environmental concerns in trade agreements, but it has not established hard provisions that goods must meet. It just encourages positive movement in the general direction of labor rights and environmental protection. Until we can get binding requirements into trade agreements, we've got to find another way, and there is one.

The United States also gives merchandise from very poor countries access to our shores as a way of fighting poverty and supporting economic development. This program is called the Generalized System of Preferences (GSP). A limited set of products from poor countries can come into the United States if the country is "taking steps to afford internationally recognized worker rights."[25] The trick here is that human rights groups can petition the US government and formally challenge a country's participation in the program on the basis of poor labor rights enforcement. This has happened numerous times, and in 2013 the United States suspended Bangladesh from the GSP program because of the government's failure to address several petitions on worker rights violations.

The trouble is that GSP doesn't include *all* products from developing countries. The products that developing countries manufacture most, like apparel, are intentionally cut out to prevent competition with US textile manufacturers. That would make sense if these products really did displace goods from US factories, but our country doesn't produce many textile products at home anymore. Furthermore, the majority of firms making clothing in these developing countries— and that would benefit from importing them into America without big tariffs—are US retailers.

Let's take Sri Lanka. In 2012, Sri Lanka exported $158 million worth of nontextiles to the United States under the GSP program.[26] Every year Sri Lanka exports $1.05 billion worth of textiles. Almost seven times as much as the GSP products! Clearly, textiles is where the money is, and it would create a huge incentive for countries to get better about worker rights. Getting a few million here and there isn't enough to make it worthwhile for many foreign countries. Women Thrive, with a strange-bedfellow coalition that includes both Oxfam and Target, has been working on getting a proposal called "100 Percent Duty-Free Quota-Free" (I know, another sexy Washington name) passed by Congress. This would let in all products from poor countries if they uphold internationally recognized labor rights and environmental standards.

Then there's the Stick. We could use our diplomatic pressure to make our trading partners pay attention to the conditions of work and the living situations of workers in factories, especially in EPZs. A visit from the US secretary of state, or even the secretary of labor, to a developing country is a big deal for a small country like Sri Lanka. Given the difference in relative power, a nudge from our labor secretary can feel more like a hard push to some developing countries.

Finally, the Shopping Trip. We've got to change how we shop. Let's face it, women do the lion's share of the shopping in the United States and in most countries. We like to gather and bring home a full basket. It's in our DNA. I really like this method, not just because I like to shop too, but also because I think this is the most effective, long-term solution to the vexing problem of human rights abuses in manufacturing.

I believe we women don't fully understand the

power of our purses. There are thousands of people in corporations across America that spend every day worrying about what you think: of their products, of their ads, of their packaging, and on and on. They are listening very carefully to what you are saying when you buy this yogurt instead of that one or that shade of pink lipstick instead of the other one. But you and I have the right to know not only that the products we buy are safe but also that they were made ethically. Right now, we only get that information on a few products labeled "Fair Trade." You mostly see this on coffee, tea, and sugar, though it's coming for lots of other products too. So let's whisper something new in corporate ears. If enough of us shoppers asked about how corporations treat women, take care of the environment, and protect human rights, I guarantee you they will respond—and fast.

Would it really work? Well, some researchers decided to test it out in the real world, not just in a poll asking people what they'd do, but by actually seeing what people did. Straight from the study: "We find that a label providing information about fair labor standards in workplaces had a substantial positive effect on sales of labeled items. Sales of labeled brands rose by around 10% when the labels were applied; sales rose between 16–33% when the label was combined with price markups of 10–20%." That's right, sales rose *more* with the higher prices. The report continued:

"The market shares of the brands rose by 20–41% when they were labeled and offered at a price premium. . . . A label with information about fair labor standards in factories making manufactured goods appears to generate a substantial positive response to the brand among consumers in terms of actual sales at higher price points."[27] Another field experiment conducted in 2012 found that sales of an expensive women's item increased by 10 percent with a fair labor label. The researchers discovered that even in an outlet, where customers are concerned about price, a fair labor label raised sales by 14 percent.[28] So what's the downside here?

The alternative is what we have now: a broken system in which we wait until a fire kills hundreds of workers, or an investigative reporter uncovers the systematic assassination of labor rights advocates, and then American companies simply up and move to another country until a scandal hits there. This only creates a life-shaking disaster for the tens of thousands of people that lose their jobs. Read on and I'll show you exactly how you can help fix this system.

# 15

# MR. BUSH GOES TO WASHINGTON

No one expected President George W. Bush to be a great internationalist when he arrived in Washington in the winter of 2001. Surprisingly, however, by the time his helicopter lifted off from the White House lawn to go back home to Texas in 2009, international aid was at levels not seen since the late 1970s.[29]

One of Mr. Bush's flagship international programs, which continues today, is the Millennium Challenge Account (MCA). Administered by the Millennium Challenge Corporation, an executive branch organization, the MCA aims to eliminate global poverty. Rather than giving aid to countries solely based on neediness, this program requires countries to qualify in order to get the money by meeting a set of eligibility criteria, which range from respecting basic human rights to upholding contracts between parties to providing basic education and health care to citizens. Which means corrupt dictators who hoard their nation's wealth for themselves are off the list for MCA funds. Humanitarian aid to the people of those countries could still go through USAID.

In addition, the countries themselves create proposals for MCA projects, rather than bureaucrats in Washington, DC, developing grand plans. As you've already gathered, this solves a persistent problem.

Best of all, in creating their proposals, countries can't just rely on their bureaucrats. The purpose of the MCA is to reduce poverty, so logically, the government is required to consult with people living in poverty to develop its plan. This pushes the governments of poor countries in a new and healthier direction; they cannot just invite their business and political buddies to sit around a table, drink, and dream up ways they could use international aid to get richer. Instead, the voices of those in poverty can be truly heard to empower those who typically have no agency.

Finally, and most importantly, the MCA presents a chance to bake women into the cake from the very beginning, to make sure they are part of every single thing, and to get every dollar of the $10 billion to help *both* women and men.

When President Bush announced his intent to create the MCA at a conference in Mexico in March 2002, it took the aid community by surprise. More than a few aid advocates fought it, fearing it would undercut the US government's traditional aid-delivery arm, the USAID. Others worried that the MCA, whose slogan is "Poverty Reduction through Economic Growth," would forget about the poverty part and just grow the economies of rich people in poor countries.

But it intrigued me, if for nothing else than the amount of money President Bush was proposing: $10 billion over five years to help countries with good potential make a big leap into economic prosperity. I like to follow the money. Over the years, I have learned that as an advocate, it takes just as much time to influence a $1 million US government program as it does to impact a $10 billion program, so better to put my mouth where the money is.

For an international policy geek like me, the excitement of this once-in-a-lifetime opportunity was irresistible. The last time the United States created a new aid agency was when President John F. Kennedy started USAID in 1962, before I was even born. A chance like this might not come again in my lifetime. So while some folks were ignoring it and others were putting it down, Women Thrive reached out to the people in the White House and State Department with our interest and our willingness to roll up our sleeves and help the initiative be successful. I didn't expect a bunch of women's rights activists to get a warm welcome from the Bush administration, but the small group of people who were given the Herculean task of making the MCA happen were overjoyed to find some friends in the aid world.

We kept our case short, simple, and focused on

what they really cared about: getting Congress to pass legislation that would create the MCA. A president can do a lot of things, but he (or she) cannot create a whole new agency in the federal government without an act of Congress. Here was our proposal in a nutshell: You (MCA people) need friends in the aid community to support you in Congress because if lots of aid organizations oppose your idea, Congress might not approve it. We (Women Thrive) have friends in Congress from both parties. There are a few things that the MCA must include in order to have our support:

1. The criteria for qualifying countries must look at men and women and boys and girls separately, because when it comes to things like human rights, for example, men can have it pretty good while women are routinely abused. Countries shouldn't be able to get by on just how they treat the men.

2. Programs supported by the MCA need to do a gender analysis before they are designed. This is not the same as simply including women in a strategy. What gender analysis means is looking at the different roles, rights, responsibilities, and resources women and men have and then using that information to make sure both women and men participate fully in a project. For

example, if a farming project makes owning land a requirement to participate, only men will get access, because in most developing countries women don't get to own land, even though women do a lot of the farming. The other important thing about gender analysis is that it's not just about women and girls. If the analysis shows men or boys are at a disadvantage somehow, that should be addressed. Gender analysis benefits everyone.

3. As countries consult with their citizens to create their proposals to the MCA, a reasonable amount of local women's organizations must be included in the consultations to make sure the needs of women living in poverty are adequately considered.

4. Any data collected and reported must list women and men and boys and girls separately. Similar to the first item on this list, if a program proves to be good at helping men but bad at helping women, the MCA needs to know that and do something to fix it.

We thought these were pretty straightforward and simple requests. Nothing fancy. Nothing onerous. Just smart. The team developing the MCA actually thought so too. They immediately understood how doing these four simple things could make their programs much more impactful. But (and you knew it was coming) somewhere between the desks of the people doing the work and the people making the decisions, everything on gender got left out of the MCA legislation that was proposed by Senator Richard Lugar, a Republican from Indiana, on behalf of President Bush. Luckily for us, we had a pretty good relationship with one of Senator Lugar's key staff people. And, as backup, Senator Dick Durbin, a Democrat from Illinois, was ready and willing to offer an amendment for us that would put gender into the MCA bill everywhere we wanted it to be. Long (and winding) story short, we got women and gender into the bill that passed Congress and landed on the president's desk.

Excerpt from The Millennium Challenge Account Act of 2003[30]

SEC. 607. ELIGIBLE COUNTRIES.
(A) DETERMINATION BY THE BOARD.
The Board shall determine whether a candidate country is an eligible country for purposes of this section. Such determination shall be based, to the maximum extent possible, upon objective and quantifiable indicators of a country's demonstrated commitment to the criteria

in subsection **(b), and shall, where appropriate, take into account and assess the role of women and girls.**

(b) CRITERIA.—A candidate country should be considered to be an eligible country for purposes of this section if the Board determines that the country has demonstrated a commitment to—

(3) investments in the people of such country, **particularly women and children,** including programs that—

(A) promote broad-based primary education; and

(B) strengthen and build capacity to provide quality public health and reduce child mortality.

SEC. 609. MILLENNIUM CHALLENGE COMPACT.

(b) ELEMENTS.—

(1) The Compact should take into account the national development strategy of the eligible country and shall contain—

(D) an identification of the intended beneficiaries, disaggregated by income level, **gender,** and age, to the maximum extent practicable;

(d) LOCAL INPUT.—In entering into a Compact, the United States shall seek to ensure that the government of an eligible country—

(1) takes into account the local-level perspectives of the rural and urban poor, **including women,** in the eligible country; . . . [emphasis added]

We are only talking about 22 words. But as you will recall, words in a bill are *really* important: They have the full force of law. And as I will show you in the chapters ahead, these 22 words have made a world of difference for tens of thousands of women and girls.

# 16

# WHAT WOMEN WANT

Have you heard of the MCA?" I asked Upali during one of our conversations about the tsunami.

"The what?" he replied flatly.

"The Millennium Challenge Account," I said, annunciating each syllable of Mil-len-ni-um slowly.

"Whose account?" he asked.

"I'll take that as a no," I concluded.

Sri Lanka was one of the first countries to begin talking to the United States about a potential

MCA proposal soon after the new agency was created. I knew Upali would be interested in what his country was proposing. It was another opportunity to organize people living in poverty to induce their government to meet their needs— exactly the sort of thing Upali lived for. I had a hunch he had not heard about the MCA, even though Sri Lanka's government had already completed its consultation process with its citizens months before the tsunami. If Upali didn't know about it, I also knew right away that the consultation process must have been really pathetic. If the Sri Lankan government were asking for the people's input on something, Upali would know about it. Apparently, the MCC also thought the Sri Lankan government hadn't done a good enough job—this whole "talking to your citizens" thing being new to them—and in spring of 2005, just a few months after the tsunami, the agency asked for a revised proposal that would focus "on the key bottlenecks to poverty reduction" and underscored "the need for a broad consultative process."[31]

"I was really happy when I heard about the MCA supporting Sri Lanka," Irangani told me as she recalled the first time she heard about the agency. "Actually, we received the e-mail from you in the middle of the night. Upali and I were walking around the room; we couldn't sleep! I was excited because this was a huge project and could bring in a lot of support for rural villagers. We started dreaming about it. We started to visualize it.

"Later that night, when we got the government's proposal from you, I started asking questions. 'Will these activities really help the rural poor? Is this what they really need?' The government was proposing huge programs with export zones and road building. I thought about the village women I had worked with for 35 years. If I asked them if they want an export zone in their area, they would laugh at me. Their needs are very, very different than what the government put forward."

Upali added, "It looked like another trickle-down matter. Some people will get richer. The poor will just wait and wait. It will take years for marginalized rural women to see any results. There was no mention of how women, who are 52 percent of the population, could participate in the project and benefit. We thought it was extremely necessary to intervene and insert ways that women could directly benefit from this massive new program."

I was traveling to Sri Lanka in November 2005 to meet with women affected by the tsunami, and I suggested to Irangani and Upali that Women Thrive and the National Women's Collective of Sri Lanka work together to gather grassroots village women from around Sri Lanka while I was there. We could let them know about the

**Glossary of MCA Terms**

You'll be reading a lot about the MCA, and it has its own lexicon. Here are the most frequently used terms you'll see:

**MCA:** The Millennium Challenge Account program overall

**MCC:** The Millennium Challenge Corporation, the name of the United States government agency that runs the MCA program

**MCA [Country]:** Each country receiving funds from the MCA program must set up its own entity, which is related to but separate from its government. This entity implements the MCA program in that country. You will see MCA Sri Lanka, MCA Honduras, and so on.

**Compact:** The MCC and the government of the recipient country sign an agreement called a compact. This is a contract covering what the MCC will do and fund, and what the government of the country will do with those funds.

**Eligibility Criteria/Indicators:** A country is eligible for an MCA compact if its score on a set of indicators exceeds a minimum score. The criteria cover three major areas: ruling justly (human rights, corruption, democracy, and governance),

> investing in people (spending on health, education, and other social services), and economic openness (trade and fiscal policy, regulatory systems, ease of business development, and inflation). Third parties like Freedom House and the World Bank, with no connection to MCC, compile all indicators.

$590 million MCA program for Sri Lanka that was aimed at alleviating their poverty, get some of their input to take back with us to Washington, and then share it with the MCC staff. I didn't even finish the sentence before Irangani and Upali said, "Yes! We must do it!"

The room in the elegant colonial building turned NGO conference center was packed. This conference center, in the heart of Colombo, has played host to many of Sri Lanka's most vibrant movements from human rights to freedom of the press to women's empowerment. Women from all over Sri Lanka in their bright saris, with curious eyes and ears ready to hear about the MCA, crowded into the classroom-sized hall we rented for the day. Irangani warmly introduced me and the Women Thrive team to the congregants. I explained that I was not part of the US government (or the MCA) and that I was there simply as an American citizen who cared about how women and girls were treated by my government.

"My country spends about $25 billion a year on projects to help people who live in poverty around the world, and I'm happy about that," I shared. "It's actually less than one half of 1 percent of the US budget. Americans spend more than twice that each year on their pets."[32] A few smiles appeared and some chuckles cracked. "I think we ought to be able to do better.

"Nevertheless, these aid dollars are my tax dollars, and I believe that I have the right to know if they are, in fact, lifting people out of poverty or not. This new program Irangani will tell you about—the Millennium Challenge Account—is supposed to focus on reducing poverty. Everyone at Women Thrive has worked very hard in Washington to make sure that the MCA program pays close attention to women in poverty—to what women like you think the solutions are and then delivering those solutions. Based on what I know, no one has really asked Sri Lankan women in poverty what they think. So I asked Irangani and Upali if we could change that. And here we are together with you today to do just that."

I explained how countries had to qualify for the MCA by getting passing marks in three areas: democracy and good government, investing in people, and open economic policies. I talked about how the law creating the MCA mandated that countries have real, meaningful consultations with citizens, including women's organizations, and that the programs had to pay attention to gender. Then I faded into the beige cement wall, listened, and watched them for the rest of the day. It was a privilege.

Irangani laid out for them what their government had proposed to the United States so far. She talked in their native tongue, which I could not follow; I had no translator at that point. Every so often heads would shake in disapproval or eyebrows would rise in disbelief, so I was able to get the gist of it. The women conferred all morning and over a spicy Sri Lankan lunch. By late afternoon they had decided what they would do. I was floored.

First, they would pull together women from every district of the country for an intense 48-hour workshop to take a deep dive into each area of their government's proposal. There was no translation of the hefty proposal from English into Sinhala and Tamil, a telltale sign that the government was not serious about consultation, so the women would get that done themselves before their workshop. They would then create their own shadow proposal for the MCA. And, when the MCA started working in their country, they would set up local citizen monitoring committees to make sure that people in poverty were benefiting and that no funds got lost to corruption. These women were on fire!

I left Sri Lanka amid escalating violence

surrounding the impending election. Soldiers with AK-47s stood at every entrance to the hotel, and security checkpoints were set up all along the route to the airport. The previous president had taken a conciliatory approach toward the civil conflict between the northern Tamils and majority Sinhalese. His challenger, Mahinda Rajapaksa, came out with fiery rhetoric and plans to end the violent conflict through more violence. The Tamils in the north, hating both candidates, boycotted the election. Intimidation of the Tamils who did try to vote was rampant. Rajapaksa won with 50.4 percent of the vote.

Back in Washington, our Women Thrive team gave the MCC staff a full briefing on our trip and let them know that village women were organizing their own "consultation" on the government's proposal. The country leader for the MCC, Darius Nassiry, and his colleague, Eileen Burke, were thrilled to hear about it and planned to attend the gathering of Sri Lankan women. Irangani had invited all the Sri Lankan government representatives, up and down the food chain, but didn't get a single response.

The women, organized by the National Women's Collective of Sri Lanka (Irangani's organization), held their retreat just a few days before the first anniversary of the tsunami. Back in Washington, I eagerly awaited the report from Irangani and Upali.

Upali wrote to us, thoroughly exhausted but elated, at the end of the two-day discourse:

The MCA delegates came during lunch hour on the first day and were completely stunned at how many women were there seriously discussing each aspect of the proposal. They came back the next day with their interpreter and stayed the entire day. Darius Nassiry and Eileen Burke said this was the first time they had the opportunity to meet a group who organized a consultation on their own to scrutinize a proposal and make recommendations to the government. Darius told the gathering "not to underestimate their voice as it will be heard in Washington" and "there will be a chair for you at the government discussions with the MCC." Everyone was so inspired when he stated, "Do not think for a moment that your voice is small, your voice is heard very strongly in Washington now." Eileen stated that the MCC pays special attention to the participation of women in development activities. She said, "This consultation will be a model to other countries" and that "the recommendations of the consultation should be made to the government of Sri Lanka."

# GOVERNMENT'S PROPOSAL VERSUS THE WOMEN'S PROPOSAL TO THE MCC

## Irrigation
*Government wanted:*
- Three medium-scale water reservoirs for farm irrigation, locations to be determined by politics

*Women wanted:*
- Renovation of minor reservoir systems and irrigation channels that already exist to be used by small farmers and maintained by local populations thereafter

## Roads
*Government wanted:*
- Upgrade of 20,000 kilometers of existing roads, locations to be decided based on incidence of poverty

*Women wanted:*
- Priority upgrading of rural roads, especially small roads that help poor farmers get their produce to local markets
- Consulting of communities on exactly where roads should go and how they should be structured to make them safe for all types of travelers—trucks, cars, donkey carts, bicycles, mopeds, pedestrians, three-wheel taxis, etc.

## Industrial Development

*Government wanted:*

- New industrial townships in Ampara, Kegalle, and Hambantota, which were affected by the tsunami

*Women wanted:*

- These areas have gotten substantial support post-tsunami; there is greater poverty in the northern and eastern regions of Sri Lanka, and site selection should be in consultation with the people
- Create rural industrial development through access to information and training for farmer and village-level industries

## Rural Electrification

*Government wanted:*

- Provide electricity to large businesses outside of the capital city

*Women wanted:*

- Focus on renewable energy sources such as solar and mini-hydro
- Prioritize access to power for local small industries, rather than large businesses
- Pay careful attention to equity, cost, and affordability in electric supply
- Help local populations operate and maintain electrical infrastructure themselves

> **Small and Medium-Size Enterprise Development**
>
> *Government wanted:*
> - Nine regional market/shopping centers and 45 cyber cafés to create business opportunities in rural areas
>
> *Women wanted:*
> - Improve existing market/shopping areas, rather than building nine new ones
> - Focus on rural businesses that women are in and have the potential to really grow:
>   - Small-scale rice paddy mills for processing raw rice for sale
>   - Handloom weaving
>   - Local dairy production
>   - Local fish processing

These next lines from Upali brought tears to my eyes. "This was the first time ever that a group of citizens of Sri Lanka had the chance to look at a proposal of our government and give their input to it. This has never happened in our country. It was a moment of joy and a moment of victory especially for the women here in Sri Lanka that struggle for social justice and empowerment. All the participants were jubilant and elated! They all felt the power of togetherness."

So what did these women want? The best way to summarize it is this: What the government proposed to the MCC was "trickle-down development"—build big roads, get electricity to big companies, get big amounts of water to agribusinesses, and it will eventually trickle down to the poor. What the women proposed was "trickle-up" development—connect villages with no access to the outside world to roads, renovate the local irrigation systems that already exist and that small farmers can use, provide affordable electricity to microenterprises, and invest in businesses like weaving and fish processing where women in poverty make their living. The benefits of this kind of economic growth would start with the poor and eventually trickle up to help the whole country.

The women also put forward some pretty basic general principles for the Sri Lankan program with the MCC. They wanted their government to:

- Announce publicly the amount of the US contribution and its purposes.
- Identify locations for interventions and broadcast how communities could contribute and participate.
- Include Tamil women in the tea plantation sector (300,000 women) as well as people with disabilities, who are most often left out of development projects.
- Approach communities as collaborators, not as adversaries.
- Support local women's organizations to

monitor MCA projects on the ground.
- Be careful of discrimination on the basis on religion, political party, ethnicity, gender, and so on in selecting enterprises or other populations to target.
- Ensure transparency in all decisions.

I returned to Sri Lanka the following year, in September 2006, to do further research on MAS Holdings. Irangani and Upali used my trip to leverage a meeting with the minister and deputy minister of MCA plan implementation. We felt optimistic going into the meeting since the minister was a woman, though she was just appointed by the new and belligerent Rajapaksa administration. How bad could it possibly be?

It was bad. Really bad. I said my hello, introduced Women Thrive and myself, and thanked her profusely for the meeting. Then I handed the torch to Irangani to lead the way into the dark dead end of the encounter. Irangani graciously thanked the minister and her deputy for their kindness in taking the meeting and provided an overview of the women's ideas for the Sri Lanka MCA.

The minister wasted no time in getting right to the point. She asked us to "look after our affairs rather than trying to intervene in government," Irangani recalled. "She said to 'go to the village, make porridge, and feed the children.' This was how the top women officials estimated us. This only made us more strong and persistent. She made us determined to change the activities to make MCA assistance address the real needs and aspirations of our people. We expected that as a woman she would have a better attitude, but she was worse than many men in the government," Irangani added. "We see this with a lot of women in powerful positions; they think the same way as men do. They only have a woman's name."

# 17

## CEO, POVERTY REDUCTION, INC.

President Bush wanted the Millennium Challenge Account to run like a corporation, not like a government bureaucracy. It's designed so its head is a chief executive officer (CEO) who reports to a board of directors chaired by the secretary of state. The board of nine members is made up of five government people and four public members from the private sector and nongovernmental organizations. It's actually a great model because, unlike secretaries, who head departments like the State Department or Department of Education, the CEO answers not only to the president but also to the board. He or she must consider a wider set of interests, and more than just a few minds are giving input to decisions. That difference alone insulates the MCC from being pushed this way and that based on political winds. Most importantly, it means decisions have to be made in the bright, open light of day.

Given the business-type model of the MCA program, the president wanted a business-type guy to run the place. The first CEO came from the investment banking world. For its second CEO, Bush chose John Danilovich, a tall, silver-haired, chisel-faced international investor and shipping industry mogul. Danilovich was ambassador to Brazil at the time, a place with no small amount of poverty, but that didn't automatically make him an expert in reducing poverty. To be honest, I had low expectations for Ambassador Danilovich's entrance onto the Washington stage. I did not expect a shipping guy to understand much about global development, let alone gender. In addition to that, sometimes business leaders come to Washington with guns blazing, ready to take on this bastion of bureaucracy with straight talk and corporate efficiency. Then, a few months into their new jobs, they realize that they cannot maneuver the overt and covert politics of Washington if they approach it with disdain. But Danilovich's performance, especially under pressure, rescued the MCC and eventually won me over.

Years after he left the MCC, I asked him why in the world he took the job when he could have been the US ambassador to France next if he had wanted it. The MCC was still in start-up mode; its engine couldn't seem to stop spitting and move the program past first gear. Its bumpy start did not make the initiative well liked on Capitol Hill or in the aid world at the time.

"When we went to Brazil, after three years in Costa Rica, I was astonished by the vastness of the country and how complicated travel was," Danilovich said. "I set out on an extensive travel program immediately. I wanted to get to know the country and its peoples, not just the hot spots like Rio and São Paolo. I wanted people to have a chance to talk to the American ambassador. I traveled to very remote, obscure, and forgotten parts of Brazil—poor places and poor people, not starving, but with very basic infrastructure and subsistence living conditions. If a flood or drought came, it was over for them. Your heart hurts at the sight; it's just a human and compassionate response. It's not possible to turn away and not want to help.

"When the president asked me to take the MCC job, I saw it as an opportunity to help an organization that I knew would have, if I could get it to work, a transformative impact on the lives of millions of people. I understood the size of the challenge to reorganize and redirect the MCC. The professionals there were first-rate, but they needed to redirect their energies on the product and not obsess about the process. I saw it as a once-in-a-lifetime chance to really make a difference."

Congress originally liked the MCA model because it held out great promise, but support had lapsed and its slowness was frustrating people. Danilovich knew he had to reinvigorate the program and win them over. He spent enormous amounts of time on the Hill, on both sides of the aisle, trying to convince them that the program was worthwhile and to give it a second chance.

"It was tough," he said. "As a Bush initiative, Republicans were in favor of it. Democrats were annoyed because they thought that as an aid program, it should have been a Democratic initiative. But there was one leader in the House, who I won't name, that I had to work very hard to win over. One time we were left alone without our aides and she said, 'You know, I'm not sure about you. I think you're a Democrat.' And I said, 'I'm an American. This is an American aid program. It's not partisan.' She became a strong supporter, but she never gave me an easy time."

Danilovich was able to secure enough support from Congress to keep the MCA going. He restructured the agency to get money flowing to countries. And he created the space for the MCA to innovate on many things, including gender.

The truth is that many, many Republicans wholeheartedly support international aid programs.

They're logical about it: We can send assistance to countries now to help them be stable, prosperous, and safe, or we can send troops later to beat back the terrorists that have taken over because chaos and hopelessness reigned. This was Afghanistan before 2001. Many Republicans are closet aid enthusiasts because their constituencies back home couldn't care less about aid (at best) or hate it with a passion that borders on psychosis (at worst). At the very end of the Senate Foreign Relations Committee meeting to set up the MCA program, Senator Lugar said, "Every member of the committee is keenly aware that development assistance has garnered only modest support among the American public. It is one of the reasons that the committee has not passed a foreign aid bill in over a decade." Can you imagine what would happen if the American public threw their weight behind aid to the poor?

# 18

# THE GENDER POLICY

Like it or not, it was still a man's world. Many folks at MCC didn't get why it was important to look at men and women separately, and more than a few didn't *want* to get it. Women Thrive went to the MCC offices three times to train senior-level staff. The first two trainings were optional, but the third was made mandatory by upper management. Our goal was not to make the staff care about women's rights per se; it was to underscore how the MCA program was going to fail if it didn't think about gender and women. We brought with us two people who could speak the same language as the MCC team: Caren Grown, one of the top international economists and a professor at American University, and Mark Blackden, a Brit from the World Bank's Africa Division. Mark talked about a failed World Bank program to help families in Cameroon grow more rice and increase their incomes. But that program didn't look at the roles of men and women on the farm first. While women did most of the labor in the rice paddies, the men of the family controlled the income from that crop. After women finished working their husbands' land, they would tend to their own sorghum crops, the profit of which they controlled. So when the bank showed up and provided training and services just to men, they were missing the boat. The women weren't benefiting from the rice crops, so they had no incentive to work harder, longer, or differently on the rice crops. Even if they wanted to, they weren't being trained. Hence, rice production did not go up. When it comes to deciding whether to include gender in programmatic development, "it's simply about whether or not you'll be successful," Mark said matter-of-factly in his British accent.

Making the case that the MCA program pay attention to gender was only the first step. Even if the staff wanted to do it, they didn't have the expertise to know what to do, what questions to ask, or what to do with the answers even if they did ask the questions. Women Thrive did as much we could to provide information on gender as it intersects with a multitude of sectors, from infrastructure and land rights to farming and financial systems. But our role was not to provide free consulting services to the US government; our job was to make them do gender right. They desperately needed a full-time gender specialist.

Soon after its creation, we started pushing the MCC to hire a senior-level gender expert. After almost two years of making the case and pointing out that the country proposals in formation were completely devoid of any gender analysis, and hinting that it would lose our support, MCC finally brought in an extraordinary woman who was up to the task.

Virginia Seitz was something of a celebrity to me when I was in college. I read her work in my first class on women in development, and she was among the guides that pointed the way to my lifelong avocation. I was nervous meeting her for the first time, feeling as though I was back in school going to talk with a famous professor.

Would I be smart enough? Did I know my stuff well enough? God, I hope I pass the test!

As we sat down in a local coffee shop, she was warm and thanked Women Thrive for all we did to help create her position, putting me at ease momentarily. She goes by Ginny and is about five foot two, with gray streaks running through the strawberry blonde hair that falls in soft curls around her face. She wears professorial glasses and looks over their rim right into your eyes to emphasize her points. "You know I have an impossible task, right?" she said. "I've got no staff, no budget, no mandate, and a whole bunch of country proposals with no gender."

All I could say was, "Yes, believe me, I know. That's why we need you," while I was thinking, *Oh, man, I am so failing this test!* I filled her in on what we did to get gender into the original MCA legislation, what we were up to on Capitol Hill to encourage the MCC to dedicate more staff and budget to her shop, as well as the advocacy we'd been engaged in to get her new employer to create a gender policy, which would make integration of gender analysis and women's participation in projects mandatory. By the end of the meeting, she knew we'd have her back, and I knew the MCC had no idea what it was in for. We'd make an exquisitely synchronized inside-outside tandem.

Her first few years at the MCC were not easy.

The agency saw anything other than a laser focus on economic growth as frivolous. At that time, gender analysis was seen as a safeguard function, and Ginny was placed in the Environmental and Social Assessment (ESA) group with two tasks: develop MCC's approach on gender and help build the capacity of ESA to address gender. Until the Obama administration, Ginny struggled to get the MCC to understand that social inequality—especially gender—was an economic issue. Gender inequality and discrimination against women constrain growth and limit poverty reduction. "Sadly, environment, social assessment, and gender were seen as the people who came in after a project was designed to make sure it didn't cause harm, or to at least reduce those risks," Ginny told me years later. Her first major breakthrough was creating a training curriculum so that all MCA staff would get the basics without her personal tutorials. The training was mandatory, so those that tried hard to ignore her couldn't anymore.

I'm pretty sure the MCC hoped to appease us with Ginny's appointment, but it put more wind in our sails. At every turn, Ginny attempted to get her colleagues to understand how projects would stumble and perhaps fall because their design was fundamentally flawed. In those early compacts, it was a particular struggle. For example, in a compact with hundreds of millions devoted to agriculture, women's crops and roles were not recognized, even if they were readily visible once one simply looked at a farm. In the end, activities that were redesigned to accommodate women after the compact was signed were highly successful. The MCC leadership, now under Ambassador Danilovich, knew they couldn't risk failure under the congressional klieg lights.

A lot of the resistance to gender was coming from the countries themselves. The ministries of finance and other powerful people in those governments did not see why gender differences were important to economic growth. Their projects were about roads, irrigation, and electricity after all. There were few, if any, people with gender expertise—or even an interest in gender equality—around the table. So we needed more influence than Ginny's determined willpower and her intellectual force, though those were no small things. Women Thrive amped up the call to require a program to have a solid gender analysis, meaningful consultation with women's groups, and a design delineating women's exact roles in order for it to receive funding.

It was a thrill and a privilege to sit next to Ginny on the dais at the announcement of the Millennium Challenge Account's Gender Policy in January 2007 at the MCC headquarters in Washington. It was everything we wanted. I was most excited about certain words, like "countries will," "provide evidence," and, best of all, "disbursement of MCA funds may be conditioned." Not just because I am a policy geek, but also because these little words and phrases meant that integrating gender was not optional. Countries either did it or they put their money at serious risk. Here are some of my favorite parts:

- Countries will ensure that both women and men have opportunities for meaningful participation throughout the consultative processes.
- Based on an analysis of gender differences and inequalities, countries will identify those benefiting from the projects by sex and provide an explanation of how the programs are designed to take into account gender differences and correct gender inequalities that could impede economic growth and poverty reduction. When designing program, countries should ask:
  1. What are the policy, legal, and socio-cultural constraints to women and men becoming full beneficiaries of MCA investments, and what design elements are required to remove or compensate for these constraints?
  2. What are the different roles and responsibilities of women and men, and how do any differences affect the proposed project? How do these gender

differences vary by other demographic and social characteristics of the beneficiary population?

3. Are there gender inequalities in access and control of productive resources relevant to the proposed project, and how will they be corrected or mitigated in design?

- Countries will analyze the impact of investments on the people they aim to help and refine projects to ensure that gender differences and inequalities that limit economic growth and poverty reduction are addressed in project design.

- MCC will integrate gender into its oversight and assessment of a country's performance during implementation. MCC will assess the extent to which Compact programs reflect findings on gender differences and inequalities and meet intended gender outcomes, where relevant. **Additionally, some disbursements of MCA funds may be conditioned upon the satisfaction of targets and progress on indicators measuring project performance.** [Emphasis added.]

This gender policy was the most comprehensive and forward-looking of any government in the world. No donor had ever before linked the money to gender integration. I can't over-emphasize how huge that was. As we all well know, money talks. Loudly.

At the announcement event, I was last to speak, and I took the opportunity to thank the MCA leadership for creating a brilliant policy and also made sure they knew we'd be watching the MCA closely. "This gender policy will either spring to life or wither away based on how everyone at the MCA—starting with you, Ambassador Danilovich, and extending to every country team, negotiations officer, monitor, and clerk—chooses to stand by it or not," I said. "The gender policy will live or die in the thousand small moments when you must decide whether to hold on to it or let it go: when you either push a country to re-do its analysis or you just accept it; when you either make clear that a ministry must implement the gender aspects of its country's compact or subtly signal that they can ignore them; when you insist that there must be capable female program managers that the country can hire for their MCA project, or just accept the limp claim that no such women exist. Every woman and girl in every MCA country is depending on you to make the right decision in those moments. I hope you will."

# 19

# PULLING THE PLUG

The MCC never credited Irangani and Upali's work as the reason they made Sri Lanka do another consultation specifically with women's organizations, but I strongly suspect the 24-page women's proposal that Irangani and Upali sent to the MCC in Washington and to the Sri Lankan government had something to do with it. The government couldn't hide it, ignore it, or dismiss it, since the MCC's own country director, Darius Nassiry, was at the women's consultation.

According to Irangani, the MCC team was not only receptive to their proposals but also met with them often when they came to Colombo to conduct due diligence. "This was an unexpected quality from any government-to-government donor," she said. "We knew that they were interested in building the society as a loving family member who cares for betterment of the family. At times we wondered why we do not have such agency in our country."

When the government held that additional consultation in the fall of 2006, everyone was there—the minister of plan implementation who had been less than supportive during the first meeting, the deputy minister, the various ministers of this and that, their minions, and the US-based MCC team. The minister of plan implementation opened the session by saying, rather pointedly, that the government had already consulted with the people, to which Irangani sharply pointed out that that first consultation was "only with people in your government and your government-supported people." Irangani's steel backbone wasn't going to bend. The rest of the assembly went downhill from there.

A senior MCC official I talked with later reflected on that period: "We had hoped the peacemaker would be elected in 2005. But he wasn't, so the need for a good consultation process was even greater. In Sri Lanka, the MCA's core concepts were called into question. The democracy was doubtful and the legitimacy of the consultation process was suspect. On top of that, there was not a consensus in the White House or State Department about doing a Sri Lankan program with this new government. Senior decision makers were unfamiliar with Asia. There was less of an understanding of how to nuance and manage in that context. Asians are very different than Africans—they are not as desperate and they can tap into international bond markets; they have choices. So they'll act a little more defiantly with the MCC than others. We didn't have the same traction in country or in Washington."

On April 6, 2007, Freedom House, an independent watchdog organization dedicated to the expansion of freedom around the world, issued a press release that stated, "The serious human rights abuses and excessive restrictions on freedom of speech and association by the government of Sri Lanka merit the country's removal from a list of eligible recipients for Millennium Challenge Account (MCA) assistance." The problems with freedom of speech were only the beginning; the press release went on to say, "Human rights abuses linked to Sri Lankan government forces have increased over the past year. Human rights organizations have reported an increase in extrajudicial killings and disappearances by security forces and armed groups supported by the government. In an especially chilling example, seventeen local staff for an international humanitarian group were killed execution-style, allegedly by government forces. Despite assurances by top officials to investigate the actions of Sri Lankan security forces, no serious inquiry has taken place. While the independent National Human Rights Commission is empowered to investigate human rights abuses, it has suffered from insufficient authority and resources."[33]

Since the MCA program uses the data from Freedom House in rating countries on the criteria for ruling justly, it was particularly difficult to ignore their unambiguous call to nix Sri Lanka. A few months later, a small article appeared in Sri Lanka's *Daily Mirror* newspaper stating simply that "at a December 12 meeting, the board of directors of the MCC deselected Sri Lanka, based on the country's performance on seventeen indicators in three areas—ruling justly, investing in people, and encouraging economic freedom—sources said, adding that the government had been informed of the decision."[34]

I was very sad for the people of Sri Lanka. They needed this assistance. They were not to blame for their government's malfeasance, but they lost because of it. At the same time, I was very pleased that the MCC didn't fund the Sri Lankan government. It was the first time the MCC stopped working with a country because it backslid into bad governance. It was the right message to send to all countries that wanted to access the billions in MCA assistance. It basically said, "These are not dollars for dictators. We will stand by our criteria and our values."

I asked Irangani, Upali, and all the women who had worked so hard on the women's proposal and who were ready to start monitoring committees how they felt when the MCC stopped negotiations with Sri Lanka. One woman summed it up for the group when she said, "We were very sad that no money would be coming that might have been used to help women at the village level, but we were happy [the MCC didn't give the money to the government] because we felt that the government was going to get the funding and misuse it. We saved Americans more than $500 million." As a taxpayer, I am extremely grateful for that.

The MCA in Sri Lanka was closing up shop, but the women were only getting started. "By then we had decided we were going to work on women's projects. We had planned and we had raised awareness," Upali told me. Irangani added, "Our committees were in place, so we started to organize for local government elections, to propose projects for our villages."

The Tsunami Women's Network was one of the women's MCA committees that lived on long after the MCC exited Sri Lanka. In another district of Sri Lanka, the women went on to do some extraordinary things. The work they did on the MCA shadow proposal helped them prioritize projects for their communities. So during the elections in 2008, they met with all the party representatives at the local level.

"We were in the position to call a candidates forum," Somalatha, one of the key leaders of the Network, said. "We put our proposals forward and said to the candidates, 'No matter which party we belong to, we will vote for the party that will deliver the projects we want.' We listed and posted our local priorities on boards and put 35 of them in each village, each one with the title: 'Candidates Must Implement These Activities.' They could not be missed." She smiled. "The candidates were all scrambling to talk about these needs in their platforms and do little projects for the communities before the election. After the election we summoned all of the newly elected officials to a forum and posted our list of proposed initiatives. The community asked the winners, 'What's your plan?' Every Wednesday we women surrounded the office of the new village council-man and pressured him to implement our projects. He finally said, 'Stop coming and we will do it.' So we said, 'You do it and we'll stop coming.'" I was grinning unabashedly by this point in the story. "Now in 2012, they have implemented 30 percent of our priorities," she concluded.

Thirty percent seemed kind of anemic to me, so I asked her, "Are you happy with that?"

"Oh, we are happy!" Somalatha exclaimed. "If we had kept quiet we would not have gotten even that 30 percent! We are confident; we know we have done this. The village women were isolated before; now we work together and talk to the council about whatever we want."

Whether or not those women's incomes increased, they were no longer poor. They had power now, and power is the engine that propels people out of poverty. The story of these women's empowerment is an example of how the US government could make truly sustainable change and how considering gender dynamics is realistic, efficient, and fuels success.

# 20

# LIVING ON A DOLLAR A DAY IN SRI LANKA

In 2009, I lost four pounds in three days. Fad diet? Nope. I was simply living the way more than 1.3 billion people do: on a dollar or less a day.

My first attempt at living on less was in 2008, during a trip to Nicaragua. I wanted to see what it was *really* like to live on a dollar a day. It was not easy or fun, but it was very educational. After buying a cup of rice and a few ounces of beans, my dollar was pretty much gone. I could have blown it all on a small candy bar, and I seriously considered it, but most poor people are way smarter than that. So I opted for the more authentic (and bland) experience. I already had great respect for the tenacity and creativity of women living in poverty, but this endeavor took my reverence to a whole new level. Then a year later, I repeated the exercise in the mountains of Guatemala.

In 2010, I headed to Africa to spend 72 intense hours trying it again. This time, it was a 360-degree IMAX experience. No staying in a hotel at night, no cutting the day short by going to bed at 7 p.m. I had arranged to live with a family—one husband, two wives, and seven children—in their compound and perform daily chores such as fetching water and fuel wood, planting crops, weeding, and cooking.

This time I was anxious to try it in Sri Lanka. Irangani and Upali had arranged my stay with a small family of all women near Galle, end point of the infamous highway Irangani saved from riotous villagers.

My first impression of Malini's house was the smell. Earthy, pungent, strong. As if a sweat-drenched undershirt was rolled into incense and burned. The house itself was quite lovely. A proper cement and mortar house of four rooms—a living room, a kitchen, and two bedrooms—with a corrugated tin roof, a small garden, and a bathroom complete with flushing toilet and showerhead. They painted the house bright turquoise. I so love the riotous colors people in developing countries paint their houses. I feel like it's a rebellion against poverty: "We might not have much, but we have *colors!*" I'm not sure why, but all the pictures were hung several inches below the ceiling line so you have to look up to see them: a poster of roses with the caption "Have a Nice Day," another of a fuzzy little kitten right out of a Hallmark calendar. It all wasn't quite congruent with someone who lives on a dollar a day or less.

The house isn't actually Malini's house. It's her brother's, and she lives there with her three gorgeous nieces. It's because of those nieces that she recently fixed the wooden fence that runs around the yard. "I bought the wood and then had to carry it on my shoulders. The children would cry, 'Please, please don't get tired. Don't do things like this.' But I had to. Because when fences are broken, there is no security, for girls especially," she explained.

Dilki is the eldest at fourteen. I fell in love with her instantly. I first noticed a tough sweetness about her even though she is very shy. She is in eighth grade and would love to teach traditional Sri Lankan music and dance when she grows up. Sanduni is twelve years old and in seventh grade. She is adorably plump and all smiles. Malki is the youngest, eleven years old and in sixth grade. I first thought Sanduni and Malki were twins; they look almost exactly alike, except Malki's hair is cut short. They both reminded me so much of me at their age: chubby, shy, and curious.

When Dilki was about six and the littlest just three, their mother left them and "went with another man," to where they don't know. This was the second time I heard this story in Sri Lanka and it would not compute. A mother left her own three children just like that? No look back? No forwarding address? No "Darlings, I'll be back to get you as soon as I can"? At first I thought she was either pathologically callous or utterly desperate. But then I learned about their father, Malini's brother, who was a day labor fisherman who sold doormats when there were no fish. He was an alcoholic. Sometimes a raging alcoholic.

Now I was starting to get the picture.

After the girls' mother left, Malini would come and stay with the girls and would turn their father away from his house if he came home drunk. Given the situation, some of the family wanted to put the girls in an orphanage. With tears in her eyes, Malini told me she "could just not let that happen to these girls. They have family." So she moved into her brother's house, which at that time was made from mud, sticks, and a thatched roof. "I try my best to fulfill all their needs. I never want to send them to other households. Even though they do not have anything, I want to uphold their dignity." In the end, she told me, she wants the girls to study, build their skills, and find proper employment. "I want them to lead a good life, and I'd like to help them achieve it."

The girls' father is in prison now, charged with using dynamite to fish, an all too common practice in Sri Lanka. But it was the boat owner who was using the dynamite; that guy said it was his laborers and paid off the police, so the girls' father went off to jail. The poor work for nothing, and then when anything goes wrong they take the blame.

He is awaiting a trial; in reality the aunt doesn't really expect him to come back—either he will die in jail or not come back when he gets out. But they keep a room for him in the house, and no one sleeps in that bed because the girls think their "Tata" will come home at some point. They know their mother will never return.

Malini has her own family just down the road—a husband and a son who is married and who is also living there with his wife and small son. But that house is too small for the girls to join them there, and Malini's family can barely make ends meet as it is. So Malini spends the evenings, nights, and mornings with the girls and goes home to her house in the midday to help her daughter-in-law with the cooking, cleaning, and child care.

Someone has given them everything they have. The house was built by a Canadian charity after the tsunami washed away their little hut. All the kitchen pots, pans, plates, and utensils were found or handed down from a friend or relative. The furniture was a gift to Dilki from another aunt so that when Dilki marries she at least has this house and somewhere for her new husband to sit. Even all the clothes the girls wear—none of it is new, not even their underwear.

Before I arrived, I had talked with Irangani and Upali about what kind of gift would be appropriate to thank the family for hosting me. Irangani thought the experience of taking the girls and their aunt shopping to buy new things of their own choice would be deeply appreciated, more so than a gift of cash. And was she right!

Dilki, Sanduni, and Malki were giddy getting into the van to drive into Galle. How different from my sons, who have been dragged along on so many shopping trips they would pay me to let them stay home. Irangani and Malini decided that the highest priorities were school supplies and underclothes: backpacks, panties, undershirts, white school shoes, and fabric to make Sunday school dresses.

We landed in a busy strip of the city, with shops anarchically crowded together on both sides along 100 yards of asphalt and selling everything you could ever need (and an unlimited number of things you'll never need). Ironically, and apparently unnoticed by anyone but me, from one end of the street a beautiful, peaceful statue of Buddha looked down upon this capitalist chaos.

At the backpack shop, an old man pulled all kinds of packs off the shelf while Malki and Sanduni pointed to the pink one hanging in the storefront. My practical mama instincts kicked in and I tried to convince the girls that getting a black and red one with really good quality zippers would be a better choice; it won't fall apart and it'll last forever. Their faces fell. Through Irangani they said, "It's not pink." What is it about pink and girls? In every single country, across hugely different cultures and languages, girls *love* pink. It must be hardwired: The color of berries ignites our gathering instincts or something. So I agreed to go with the pink and the smiles came back. I'm a sucker for smiles.

A few doors down, Irangani took them to the back of a fabric store where the "unmentionables" were kept behind closed doors. And guess what? They had pink underwear! I was delighted, and I stayed out of the way this time. I let Irangani, the real professional, take it from there. We blew through the shoe shopping and then, finally, the highlight of the shopping trip: Each girl and Malini got to pick out fresh fabric from which a tailor would make a dress of their own design. In the United States, that would be insanely expensive, but in most developing countries, this is how it's done. How awesome is it to be able to pick out the fabric, design the style, and then have a seamstress sew it to your specific measurements? I made a mental note to build this into my plan next time I'm in Sri Lanka.

Our last stop of the afternoon was the supermarket. It was small but well stocked by developing country standards. And laid out just like an American supermarket—candy in the checkout lane ready to leap into your cart when your resolve is at its weakest, having said, "No, honey, you can't have that," 189 times throughout the store and then, "Oh, *fine, get the M&Ms! Just please stop bugging your brother!"

As Malini and Irangani worked on the staple goods—rice, beans, canned fish, and so on—I became frantic. It hit me that the girls don't get any protein. They eat rice—all carbs—three times a day. They are plump, but they are malnourished. Malini has diabetes, and I had no doubt it was from the starch-heavy diet. Where's the peanut butter? The milk powder? The high-protein cereals? I ran up and down the narrow isles finding things that could supplement their diet: canned sausages, fortified chocolate drink powder, chickpea flour, nuts. With no regard to the price, I grabbed armfuls and hurled them into Malini's already overflowing cart. The girls took the chocolate drink powder out of the cart and put it back on the shelf. I was totally confused. What kid doesn't like chocolate milk? Irangani's son noticed my blank look and asked Dilki why she took it out.

"We don't like chocolate mixed with water. It tastes horrible."

"Mixed with water?" I inquired.

"We can't afford milk," said Dilki matter-of-factly.

Feeling so totally stupid and terrible for making

her explain to me they are so poor they can't afford milk for chocolate, I hurried back to the powdered milk and picked up two big boxes, reclaimed the chocolate powder, and put it all in the basket.

It's frustrating to realize just how much little things can make a big difference in this family's—and others'—lives. Malini has space for a vegetable garden, but because it doesn't have proper drainage, storm water keeps washing the soil away. She doesn't have the money to hire someone to dig a drainage ditch, nor can she do it herself. Imagine how this simple act can impact the family's nutrition. And yet Malini can only fret about it. "I'm also concerned that over time, this water will ruin the foundation of the house," she told me.

We returned to Malini's bungalow tired and very happy from shopping. But something was nagging at me. The whole shopping trip left me feeling empty. All these objects, all this food, all of it will be gone in a few months or years at most. And really nothing will have changed for these girls. Is that the best I can do? It's like putting a Band-Aid on a child's broken arm and then expecting the kid to be grateful for it.

My thoughts were cut short by my aching hunger. I began the clock on my Dollar a Day at dawn that morning, skipped breakfast to save some money, and slept on the drive down to Galle from Colombo. When the van pulled into the village, I popped a handful of cashews (how expensive could those be since they're grown right here in Sri Lanka?) to stave off the hunger. Lunch was only a little rice and some snake gourd curry.

At long last Malini invited me to help in the kitchen. I could feel her internal struggle to overcome culturally sacred mores about guests (especially those from overseas):

*She's a guest!*

*But they told me she wanted to do everything I do.*

*But she's a guest, from the* United States!

*But I don't want to ignore her request to help.*

*Okay, maybe just a* little *help in the kitchen.*

She asked me to grind the milky pulp from the coconut into a bowl and pulled out a very odd contraption: a four-foot-long bench made of nailed-together wood scraps, about two feet high, with a pear-shaped set of serrated blades attached to a large crank handle that turns the blades on one end of the bench. A bowl was underneath the blades to catch the shavings as they fell. Imagine a gigantic pencil sharpener fastened to the end of an old plank of wood. Dilki took one half of a coconut, sat down, and deftly demonstrated, making it look as easy as a first grader sharpening a pencil.

*I got this,* I thought, taking Dilki's place at the end of the bench.

The bench tipped like a seesaw and if it weren't for Dilki catching it, I would have impaled myself in the head with the blades. Visions of explaining a Frankenstein forehead when I got home passed before me. "Yeah, well, I was in Sri Lanka and a coconut grinder came outta nowhere and whacked me in the forehead."

Thank goodness Malini wasn't in the room, or she would have gone right back to her culturally better judgment and banished me from the kitchen.

Among numerous giggles from the girls, I slowly and carefully spun the grinder and produced a fine dusting of particles in the bowl. Malini returned to the kitchen at that point and did not look particularly happy with my work. So I picked up the pace, only clipped the skin off a few of my fingers, and got through most of the coconut. Thinking I had done a decent job, I gave the tools back to Dilki, who then produced an equal amount of shavings in 30 seconds.

Coconut is one of the things I love best about Sri Lanka. It's crazy expensive in DC, but everyone in Sri Lanka, from the poorest villager to the business billionaire, eats lots of coconut. It's made into bread, put into porridge, rolled into rice, formed into at least 100 desserts, curried, fried, baked, and poached. I love it. And my love for it shows on my hips. While it's a delicacy for me, for millions of Sri Lankans it's a vitally nutritious staple that provides manganese, iron, phosphorus, and potassium, in addition to being one of the healthiest no-cholesterol oils you can eat. Best of all, they literally "grow on trees" that are abundant throughout the country.

Malini prepared some wonderful rice and coconut roti. Irangani had generously brought some additional food to feed everyone, and I took just a bit of beans from that communal offering. I blew through my dollar, even though once again I spent every penny of the dollar on food—something that is totally unrealistic for people who have to purchase everything their whole family needs with those 100 cents.

I could tell Dilki had some talent. Just the way she tilted her head with such sweet grace when she brushed and braided her long black hair; the tones in her soft voice that carried across the room so pure and true. My instincts were confirmed when we finally tricked her into giving us a little performance after dinner.

"No, I can't dance," Dilki lied.

"Well, you *can* dance and show us," Malini pleaded with her.

"No, I can't," Dilki persisted shyly, putting a hand over her mouth to shield her disobedient smile. "I need a drum."

"Ha! But you were singing and dancing right there in the living room before they came!" said Malini, outing Miss Dilki.

## RITU'S DOLLAR-A-DAY EXPENSES

| | Sri Lankan Rupees | US Dollars | Notes |
|---|---|---|---|
| **Nov. 24 (FULL DAY)** | | | |
| Breakfast (none) | 0 | $— | |
| Lunch (1.5 cups rice, 1/2 cup beans, 1/4 cup onions) | 25 | $0.19 | |
| Dinner (1 cup rice, 1/2 roti, 1/2 cup beans) | 20 | $0.15 | |
| 3 cups tea | 30 | $0.23 | |
| 2 "Hawaii" cookies (coconut) | 5 | $0.04 | |
| Handful of cashews | 50 | $0.38 | OUCH! |
| Snack (roasted rice ball) | 5 | $0.04 | |
| TOTAL | 135 | $1.03 | FAIL! |
| | | | |
| **Nov. 25 (HALF DAY)** | | | |
| Breakfast (leftover dinner, but less) | 17 | $0.13 | |
| Handful of cashews | 50 | $0.38 | BAD MOVE |
| 2 cups tea | 20 | $0.15 | |
| 1 cane sugar candy | 2 | $0.02 | |
| TOTAL | 89 | $0.68 | |

Upali took this as his invitation to demonstrate his prowess in Sri Lankan song and dance. "Naaaah, nah, nah, nah, naaaaa-aah, nah," he intoned in his crackly deep voice, way off key, and strutted around like a rooster. The girls were laughing, and I was thinking, *God, please make it stop.* This put Dilki over the edge, and forgetting about her shyness, she shouted out, "Not like *that!*"

"Okay, then," said Upali, laying down the gauntlet, "Show us how."

Then she sang a melodious, sweet tune. I don't know what it was about—perhaps about new love, new life, and new hope. Her flowing, wide steps and precise wrist flicks followed the beat of her song. I watched her little feet, shifting and shimmying on the bare cement floor, and imagined her high up on the stage she dreams about. How will she ever get there from here?

Well, once one sister showed off, another just couldn't resist. Sanduni brought out a small harmonium, with a tube to blow through, and a two-octave keyboard. She played us what seemed like a Sri Lankan nursery song; it must have been so familiar to everyone but me.

I looked at the littlest one, Malki, who was trying to hide herself behind the curtain that separates the living room from their father's room. Sanduni reminded me that Malki "only plays with dolls." Well, maybe next time.

Everyone had taken their turn in the shower, and it was my turn to wash away the sweat, smell, smoke, and dirt of this precious day. I was sad the day was ending but so grateful for the clear, cold water that splashed the heat from my skin for a few minutes. I dried off with a ratty towel and put my sweaty clothes back on again, saving my allowance of one clean shirt for tomorrow.

We had arranged for Upali to stay with us in the house; a man might deter any foul play since everyone in the village was well aware that an American with lots of electronic equipment was staying in the community. But everyone decided to stay. We had to fit Malini, Dilki, Malki, Sanduni, their second aunt, Irangani, Upali, their son, and me (that's nine of us) in one bed and two rooms. (No one wanted to sleep in their father's room.)

Malini of course insisted that I take the double bed all to myself. I obliged at first, but when the three girls and their two aunts squeezed in together on the cold cement floor next to me, I couldn't take it and invited Dilki to join me. She flew in before Malini could say a word.

I don't remember exactly how it happened—maybe it was because Dilki sang a song for me—but Sanduni asked if I would sing for them. I started with one of my sons' favorite lullabies, "Little Road to Bethlehem," and went through my whole song list: the "Shark Song," "Close Your Eyes," "Cradlesong," and "Blue Boat Home." Lying there with these motherless girls, thinking about how many times I've held my sweet boys to my heart and sang them to sleep, tears just started to flow down to the pillow. I ached for them. I imagined the empty tightness that must live in the heart of a child left behind by her mother. How they might wonder about what they did so wrong that she left them. How alone they must feel when their hunger peaks, and the one who should feel it in her belly, as if it were her pain, has abandoned them to the waves and the wind on the tip of a vast island in the Indian Ocean.

Then, breaking my silent sobbing, came a long *"phffffffffffft."* Someone liberated a huge fart. We couldn't stop giggling after that. I listened to the girls' laughter soften into long easy breaths. I tried to will myself to sleep.

I lay awake in the bed for hours. The mattress, sheet, and my black skirt were like layers of insulation holding and magnifying the heat against my back. Every window in the small house was shut and locked, not to be opened until morning. Malini could not afford to put bars on the windows to keep ill-doers away from the girls during the night. So at the end of each day, the windows were sealed tightly, and the cement walls that soaked the sun in all day would generously radiate their bounty, and the little house would become a sauna. Safety beats comfort every time.

My mind turned and twisted down the corridors of a hot, sleepless internal dialogue:

*I could help these three girls with their lives and make a ten-year commitment. I could figure out how to afford it. What to cut back on, so I can do it.*

*But what about the millions of other girls just like them? Who will help them?*

*It's the damn system that's broken. No safety nets to catch orphaned children or help their caretakers feed and clothe them. No help for a mother with an alcoholic husband. No jobs for women like Malini who would gladly work, earn an honest living, and raise other people's children.*

*That's why I'm working on these crazy systems, that's the whole point. Don't treat the symptom, treat the cause. Fix the hole in the bucket so all these kids don't leak out into the filthy, muddy alleyways of abject poverty.*

*And by the time that happens, Dilki, Malki, and Sanduni will be married off to old men, having babies, reliving their mother's dilemma—stay or go? Save myself or save them?*

*But I can't help every child I meet. I have stayed with families before and fallen in love with those little ones, and I will again and again. I just can't carry them all.*

At about 3 a.m., I gingerly peeled myself off the bed, scared that I would wake Dilki or Malini and offend their hospitality in giving me the bed. I found a small patch of real estate on the concrete floor—the *cool* concrete floor—close to the electric fan, borrowed for this occasion.

By dawn I had made up my mind.

Malini stirred at about 4 a.m. to go make her "rice cups" to sell in the little market kiosk down the road from the bus stop. A teacup worth of yellow rice, a little chili and onion sauce, inside a baggie and tied up in a neat little knot. Morning commuters would pass by, drop ten rupees into the basket, grab a portable breakfast, and hop onto the bus into Galle. Malini might earn about 100 to 120 rupees that day, just less than one dollar. Sometimes she sells them all and gets 130 rupees, if she's lucky. Often, only a few sell. This is *all* the income she earns.

I had no idea how she possibly makes it work. Upali and I sat with Malini and talked about her monthly expenses. She has arthritis and needs pain medication to beat it back enough to walk. The medication is free at the government hospital, but the bus fare to get there and back is not. School is also free, but again, it costs money to take the bus to and from school. It's too far and too dangerous for the girls to walk, so Malini feels this is a necessity. Water and electricity are cheap by our standards—totaling almost $7 a month. But this expense is almost 30 percent of her monthly bills. School clothing and supplies, while not a monthly expense, make up the lion's share of her fixed costs. Food is a variable cost in Malini's

## MALINI'S EXPENSES

| | Monthly Rs. | In USD | USD per day |
|---|---|---|---|
| Transport to hospital | 200 | $1.54 | $0.05 |
| Household items (soap, toothpaste, etc.) | 300 | $2.31 | $0.08 |
| Electricity | 500 | $3.85 | $0.13 |
| Water | 400 | $3.08 | $0.10 |
| Girls' bus fare to/from school | 800 | $6.15 | $0.21 |
| School clothing and supplies | 1,000 | $7.69 | $0.26 |
| TOTAL | 3,200 | $24.62 | $0.83 |

budget. Whatever cash is left goes to buy food. And when there is nothing left, there is no food.

I pulled Upali aside and said, "I think I want to help the girls. I mean with their education, and nutrition, and whatever they need to be success-ful. Do you think they would accept that help? I don't want to offend or—"

Upali cut me off with a huge grin. "Ah! This is delightful! Wonderful! Amazing! I must go tell Irangani!"

I took that to mean they probably wouldn't be offended.

Even with everything they've been through, these girls still have the light in their eyes, they still laugh, and they still like dressing up in pretty clothes. Sometime in the middle of the night, I decided I would cover all their current education costs plus all the things related to education that they've never had (extra underwear, sanitary pads, backpacks, tutoring help, writing paper, art supplies, good nutrition, and more), including all the way through college if they can get in. Yes, I signed up for twelve to fourteen years. It's a little nuts. I really don't have the money, but then what is money for if it's not for *this?*

We called an impromptu family meeting. Everyone gathered in the tiny living room, sitting on Dilki's wedding furniture, the floor, and a few plastic deck chairs. I told them in English, curtailing my enthusiasm so Upali could translate, that I was willing to make this commitment to them, if they would be willing to make a few commitments to me:

1. Malini must use some of the money to improve all of their nutrition, including *her own.* She protested, but I insisted or there was no deal. She can't die on these girls.
2. The girls cannot get involved with boys until they finish college. Malini signaled to me with a broad smile that she was on board with this and probably really liked having the extra leverage on this point. In this country, "getting involved with a boy" is a one-way street to marriage, which is the

exit ramp for education. There is no dating; there is no learning how to be in a relationship before picking the man you'll marry. Marriages are arranged, so "getting involved with a boy" is extremely unfitting for a young lady in more ways than one.

3. They must improve their marks little by little every semester. All of them are performing at about a C or D average, which makes sense given everything stacked against them. I hoped that with better nutrition, tutoring, and more support, they can improve their grades enough to get into college or at least a vocational school.

4. They all must study English and get passing marks in it. English is the entry code to the world, and I wanted to underscore its importance.

They all agreed to all the conditions. Irangani and Upali keep in touch with them and check in on them at least every six months. Actually, Irangani had already taken them under her wing after we'd been there for about fifteen minutes. Her only daughter got married and moved out five years ago, so she's tickled to have three more daughters to help raise.

Irangani and Malini worked out the budget for what expenses I will cover:

## EXPENSES FOR GIRLS

| | Monthly Rs. | In USD |
|---|---|---|
| Tutoring fees | 4,200 | $34.15 |
| Bus Fare | 800 | $6.15 |
| Nutritious food items (e.g., milk powder, fish, vegetables, etc.) | 5,000 | $40.65 |
| School supplies and clothing | 1,000 | $8.13 |
| Sunday school expenses | 600 | $4.88 |
| TOTAL | 11,600 | $93.96 |

I'm delighted to be able to do it. Still, I know that helping these three girls is not the best solution. The whole system they live in is broken. I'm hoping they will get educated, grow up, and change that system. Until then, I'll keep advocating for the big changes that Sri Lanka needs, because not every girl can find a sponsor. These were lucky.

# 21

# WHAT YOU CAN DO FOR SRI LANKA

But, you ask, how can we help families like Malini's from all the way across the globe?

## JUST ASK

Let's start with impact. Clothing retailers who want your business and the marketers who work for them are listening very carefully to what you say. Whisper campaigns have the ability to garner great attention from big business. Here's how we can start one.

The next time you're at your favorite clothing store in the mall, and the store associate asks if you need any help, this is your opportunity to respond.

You say, "Yes, actually. I want to know more about the clothes I buy. Can you tell me if your products are made ethically?"

He or she will probably become flustered. They might ask you to restate your question. "Made what?"

To which you respond, "Ethically, with good

conditions, good pay for the workers, things like that."

She or he might say, "Of course, they are made ethically."

You can then encourage them to let customers know more about their ethical procedures and process. "That's good to know. I'm sure many people would love to know that and would feel good about buying your clothes/products. Will you tell your manager I mentioned it?"

However, it's more likely they'll say, "I don't know." If this happens, you might respond with, "Okay. Would you please tell your manager that I asked?"

And just to make sure that your message gets through, you can print out a reminder note from our website at www.womenthrive.org/teacha womantofish/retail and leave it for the manager.

If a few more people ask the same store, the manager might pass it up the food chain. If a bunch of different stores pass it upward, they'll hear us loud and clear.

This even works at grocery stores. Just ask the person stacking the carrots up into neat orange fortresses if they carry fair trade produce or if they make sure that the farms in the other countries treat their workers fairly and don't pollute the environment. They'll probably say they don't know. That's okay. Just end with, "Thanks any-way. Would you tell your manager I asked?"

You can also write a letter directly to the CEO of your favorite brands. It's easy to identify the names of the CEOs on the Internet: just search [brand name] CEO. You can find their corporate headquarters information on the company's website. You don't need to write a really long letter; what's important is that you've taken the time to say you care. Below is a sample you can use or adapt:

Dear Mr./Ms. CEO,
First, I want you to know that I really love your products. I'm one of your loyal repeat customers. I also really care about how the things I buy for my family and myself are made; I want to feel good about what I wear and use. It's important to me that items I bring home are made ethically—in safe, environmentally sound conditions, with good pay, and where all employees are treated well. I hope that [brand] would share more about how you ensure that all your products are made ethically. Thanks so much and I look forward to hearing back from you.
[Your full name and address]

The goal is not to get retailers to do random spot checks of the factories that source to them, or to necessarily have their factories "certified." These inspections just capture a snapshot in time, and snapshots can be faked. Often workers are counseled about how to answer questions when an inspector shows up, even unannounced inspectors. The kinds of things we want to see in ethical manufacturing—the ability of workers to organize freely, good wages, safe conditions year-round, protection for the environment—require us to follow factories and their workers over time. Our goal is to create a shift in the overall ethics of manufacturing, which is only truly sustainable if the people who matter most to retailers and manufacturers—the customers—ask for it.

We also don't want retailers to just cut and run from a factory if something bad happens. That is the worst outcome for the women and men who work at these facilities since they won't have a job to support the people who are depending on them. They might end up in an even worse factory. And without any other options, women are sometimes forced to turn to prostitution. Those are just a few reasons why improving factories, not shuttering them, is so important.

Companies need to work with the country government, the unions, the workers, and the public interest organizations to improve the conditions for workers across the board. If you do your part to raise the stakes for stores, Women Thrive will do its part to raise the profile of issues that impact the women who work in these factories.

# TURN UP THE HEAT

You might have heard the old saying: Drop a frog into boiling water and he'll jump out. Put a frog in cool water, turn up the heat slowly, and the frog will never realize he's being boiled. The current United States approach to the corrupt Sri Lankan government is like boiling a frog, except what works for making frog legs doesn't work for obtaining results from corrupt dictators.

President Mahinda Rajapaksa was elected in 2005, with barely more than 50 percent of the vote, a few months after the tsunami. In 2009, he "won" the civil war in a spasm of unrelenting violence that killed the separatist leaders. He imprisoned his former opponent for the office, impeached the chief justice because she was actually trying to uphold the law, and changed the constitution to allow him to remain in office forever. He gloats in a superficial war victory and has resumed treating the Tamils with cruelty.

The violence of war is just underneath the country's surface, ready to explode. And yet, our country and many others are playing into the hands of this government by not pressing the issues of corruption and human rights violations with Rajapaksa.

In fact, all sides committed documentable human rights violations with impunity during the war. But Europe and the United States are so relieved the conflict is over that they do not want to stir emotions on either side by bringing the perpetrators of extreme violence, who now sit in comfortable government offices, to justice. The world doesn't want to see another war, and so we tiptoe around a tyrant; meanwhile, that very inaction and continued injustice will cause the two sides to snap once again.

Since Rajapaksa took office in 2005, the US government has raised the heat on him about one degree every year. So far, he's not jumping. At this rate, it'll take 204 more years to reach the boiling point. Sri Lanka doesn't have that kind of time before it slides back into full-blown civil war.

One action the United States has taken is to put forward two resolutions at the United Nations. The first calls on Rajapaksa to "ensure justice, equity, accountability, and reconciliation for all Sri Lankans" and "to present, as expeditiously as possible, a comprehensive action plan. . . ."[35] That is the diplomatic equivalent of saying, "Please, oh, please, will you?" The second resolution, approved by the UN Human Rights Council in March 2013, was only marginally stronger than the first from 2012, but still only "encourages" and "reiterates its call upon" the government of Sri Lanka to cease violating human rights and investigate previous allegations of abuse.[36] In the UN world, these resolutions are a necessary step, however futile, that must be taken before the

UN Security Council can approve international sanctions or other "kick in the butt" actions. The UN has to give countries every chance to make it right before they cause pain. But the United States can act without the UN, as we've done many times before and will do again in the future.

We've written sharp words and made stern faces at UN meetings, but we haven't taken real measures to make Rajapaksa change. Our aid to his government continues, while his violations of human rights become more flagrant and defiant. In August 2013, his military fired live ammunition indiscriminately at peaceful protesters, killing two teenage boys and one 29-year-old and wounding scores of others. What did the peaceful protesters want? They wanted a local factory to stop contaminating their drinking water with chemicals.

Rather than spending any time dealing with the legitimate concerns of Sri Lankan citizens and the international human rights community, Rajapaksa has instead hired a public relations firm in Washington, DC, for $800,000 to "educate the general public, business community, and political leadership in the United States on the processes of post conflict rebuilding and reconciliation undertaken by the Sri Lankan government, while suggesting that this complex effort needs reason-able time and space" and—get this—"arrange for positive letters on Sri Lanka to be sent by key

Senators and Congressmen to the president, secretaries of State, Defense, Trade, Commerce, et cetera of the United States. . . ."[37]

So what are we to do?

At Women Thrive, we do not advocate cutting aid that is helping people grow food, start small businesses, access the legal system, obtain an education, or immunize their kids. We strongly support US assistance that directly supports local organizations and bypasses corrupt governments. This kind of humanitarian and democracy-building help must actually increase to Sri Lanka. The trick is to turn up the temperature in ways that will actually cause pain to the people who need to change, not to the people we want to help.

There are several things the US government has the power to do but has not done. It could deny US visas for the topmost Sri Lankan government officials, most of whom are Rajapaksa's family members. Europe could do the same. The United States could also deny diplomatic credentials to any military officers who commanded units during the civil war and have allegations of war crimes against them. These steps don't harm the local people and don't stop Sri Lankan civil servants from carrying out their legitimate government duties. They do pressure the right people and make it clear that the United States, and the global community, are no longer willing to accept nods, smiles, and false assurances from Rajapaksa that "they're working on it."

Here's where you come in. None of this is going to happen unless we get uppity about it. We're going to write to the secretary of state.

Take out your nice stationery, because sometimes a handwritten letter on stationery will be seen by the official while a cold e-mail or form letter will never be put on his or her desk. Get your nice pen, the one you've hidden from your children so they won't make puddles of fountain pen ink to jump in, and think for a moment about what makes you feel mad about what Rajapaksa is doing to Sri Lanka. Maybe it's that he's squandering the resources Sri Lanka has been blessed with. Maybe it's because it's the twenty-first century and we shouldn't tolerate dictators anymore. What's important is that *you* say why *you* care. You don't need to be an expert in diplomacy or South Asian history. Your caring and taking the time to send a letter is enough. When you're ready, start your letter with "Dear Mr. Secretary," and just say who you are, why you are writing to him, and why you care. For example:

Dear Mr. Secretary,
My name is [your name], I'm from [your town, your state], and I'm writing to you today because I am deeply worried about the situation in Sri Lanka. It may be a

small country in the Indian Ocean, but what is happening there is despicable. I can't understand why our government has not done more to protect human rights and demand change.

Then you mention one of the ideas above, just noting that you feel the UN actions haven't done enough. You can say something like this:

I know that we have pushed Sri Lanka through the UN system, but that is not having any effect. It's time for us to cut off aid to the Sri Lankan military and prevent top government people from traveling to the United States. Thank you for your work.
Sincerely,
[Your name and address]

Be sure to include your home address after your name if you want a response, and make a copy of your letter if you can.

## JOIN THE MOVEMENT

If you've been inspired by Irangani and Upali and what they've been able to do with the tiny amount of resources Women Thrive was able to provide, imagine what they could do, and others like them, if they had real, sustained support. You can make a fully tax-deductible gift to provide resources to locally based organizations in Sri Lanka as well as more broadly in South Asia at the website address below. Your contribution will enhance capacity-building efforts and advocacy on women's economic empowerment, violence, education, and more. Just go to

www.teachawomantofish.org.

# PART TWO

---

# HONDURAS AND NICARAGUA

From left: Lena, Miriam, Ritu, Concepción, Doña Adina, Emilia, Suyapa, and Elena outside the COMUCAP a few days after the confrontation at the coffee plant. Source: Women Thrive.

Elena and I in a show of solidarity. Source: Women Thrive.

Carmen in front of the lush flower bushes in her small yard. Source: Women Thrive.

# 22

# SMELL THE COFFEE

I stood by the coffee plant's chain-link fence, just behind Elena Méndez, a woman of the Lenca people of the La Paz region of Honduras. Elena stood only about four feet tall, but her courage rose up to the bright blue Honduran sky. A few men and teenage boys on our side of the fence had come prepared with machetes and baseball bats to defend their mothers and sisters who were inside. I came prepared for anything or nothing; there was no way to know how the day would unfold. The early morning was still cool, but as the sun rose beyond the treetops, things were heating up.

Elena and about 30 other members of a local women's farmer association named the Coordinating Association of Rural Women of La Paz (COMUCAP) had just spent the night with their families on the cold cement floors of the coffee compound owned and operated by the association. It was not a slumber party. They were there to stop their former coordinator, who had recently been fired amid accusations of a range of corrupt activities, from forcibly taking over the plant as she had threatened to do a few days before. It

231

broke my heart to see this remarkable group of 257 peasant women have to fight back against someone who was supposed to fight *for* them, but who, according to them, never really did.

I had known the amazing women of COMUCAP since 2006, when Women Thrive partnered with them to influence the Millennium Challenge Account (MCA) program in Honduras, similar to what we did in Sri Lanka. Most of the women in the association are descendants of the indigenous Lencas of the region, and being indigenous meant they had little education or opportunity in a country still dominated by rich and powerful descendants of Spanish colonialists. Before the association, these peasant women lived in straw huts with banana-leaf roofs and worked small bits of land to coax out corn and beans for their families. Fifteen years after the association's birth, they have three thriving businesses: fair trade organic coffee for export, natural aloe products for the local market, and a mountaintop retreat center that caters to the growing business community in Honduras. Theirs is a story of taking nothing and turning it into something remarkable, a feat that is hard to pull off even for highly educated people.

In 2009, I sat in their little turquoise cement house on the side of a dirt road at the edge of town, which they call Casa de Mujeres (House of Women). I listened intently to Adina Lopez

Manueles, one of the founders of the group, tell me about its humble beginnings. "We grew up with the belief that we came to this life to stand beside a man, without developing ourselves, living in seclusion, and just having a family. We were not able to see beyond that, to see a happier life with more knowledge or personal growth for each one of us," she recounted.

In 1995, a local organization gave her an opportunity to receive personal development training. Doña Adina and two other women also received some guidance on how to train other women in personal development, but as she said with a smile, "It was learning by doing, as they say. One of us taught organizational skills, the other one taught positive thinking, and my theme was domestic violence. We were fully engaged, because violence has been very prevalent in women's lives. We did [the training] based on our own intelligence, on readings, and on practice, and constructing our own ideas on how to teach the other women." Whether they realized it or not, they were as much engaged with their own empowerment as they were in empowering other women.

When that training project came to an end two years later, the three women asked themselves what they wanted to do next, now that they were organized and on a roll. The answer was, without hesitation, "Push forward our own projects and become women organizers." The threesome visited different communities and gathered up women for their empowerment basket. When they had a critical mass of women in a given community, they were able to tap into funds from local foundations and international donors and help that community begin an income-generation project—and begin the deeper work of personal transformation and political enlightenment.

In 1998 the threesome launched their first project by obtaining loans so women could raise chickens. "It was the [project] with the chicken barns," Doña Adina said reaching back into her memory. "At the time, few women had the courage to take a loan of 2,000 lempiras (about $100) to build a barn, buy hens, and start up, even though as rural women, they have had chickens, a pig, whatever we were able to have before. It is the most common thing we do, chicken rearing! But many of the women who joined us did take the loans. We began to develop different projects in different communities. Little by little, we grew." They decided to become a formal association of women members and named themselves La Coordinadora de las Mujeres Campesinas de La Paz (The Coordinator of Farmer Women of La Paz). They go by COMUCAP for short. Gradually the association members pooled a little of their profits. "We were able to buy the land in El Mezcalito. Then we bought the El Caracol farm and the San Martin farm."

The women of COMUCAP planted their first coffee crop on the high-altitude, pine-covered slopes surrounding Marcala in 2000. The altitude, the air, the humidity, the sunlight, and the soil are all ideal for producing smooth, rich, gorgeous coffee without fertilizers or pesticides. By 2009, COMUCAP was exporting more than 10,000 pounds a year of organic fair trade coffee to caffeine-addicted, socially aware Europeans. The women had also built a rustic retreat center at El Mezcalito that hosts businessmen from the capital and foreigners from international agencies for their strategic planning meetings. And if that were not impressive enough, COMUCAP's members also started planting organic aloe vera; they turn it into soap, lotion, shampoo, and conditioner that leaves your hair just as smooth and silky as the professional stuff, which costs twenty times more and has all kinds of artificial ingredients in it.

Maria Molina was one of the early COMUCAP members who started the now thriving aloe business. She was born and raised in Chinacla, a rural village outside of Marcala, and has five children ages twenty, eighteen, sixteen, thirteen, and nine. I felt tired just listening to her rattle off their ages. She had her first child at sixteen. "A few women and I started as an informal community-based group that provided glasses of milk to children in the village," Maria said. "The Red Cross supported us at first. When we didn't have their support anymore . . . a member of COMUCAP arrived to help us. She told us that if we wanted to form a production sector, as a way to progress, we would have to start from zero. . . . [The women in my community] started to get together with COMUCAP's help. We shared information between ourselves and got trained in organic fertilizers, nurseries, and how to work on the farms in a collective way. After that, [COMUCAP] taught us how to produce aloe vera soap. Six of us got trained; we went to the top agriculture school of Honduras to get the training to produce the soap. And when we came back, we started to make the first test of soap. Zamorano [the agriculture school] gave us an engineer for an entire year to help us.

"COMUCAP also provided trainings in gender topics and nonviolence. The majority of women in our district, and in the soap company, were under the domain of their husbands. They had to suffer bad treatment and bad words. They beat us; they didn't allow us to be in that organized group [COMUCAP]. That was years ago. My children that are grown up today were small then. It was very difficult to attend the trainings, but I went. I always assumed my responsibilities as a house-wife and still made the time to be trained."

I had heard Maria's story many, many times

before on different continents. Her experience is the same as it is for hundreds of millions of women living in poverty. Really, the first part of her experience is *why* women are living in poverty, and the second part is the road map for how they get out.

Wherever I go, the story goes like this: a little girl has no access to education, or she leaves school when she marries as a child. That alone is challenging enough. With no way to get family planning, and definitely no way to say "no" to her much-older husband, she begins having children right away, one right after the other. Her sleep-deprived, weakened, and overburdened body is in no shape to till the soil, gather the harvest, and walk miles to the local market to sell the extra grain. But she does it anyway. Her husband beats her and berates her for over- or undercooking the dinner. And when she wants to go to a training workshop, her husband goes nuts and the abuse gets worse. But she goes anyway. She meets other women who live the same life as she does. She learns that it is her right not to be beaten and that there are ways she can stop having babies every year, without her husband having to know why. Better yet, she and her husband begin to make choices about childbearing together. Her sisters strengthen her. She stands a little taller. She learns how to earn some income working with her group. With that income she feeds her children better, takes them to the doctor when they're sick, and puts them in school. Her husband notices the positive changes and he treats her better, or she no longer puts up with his abuse and throws him out.

The biggest difference I have observed between women who succeed despite all the obstacles and women who fall back is the strength (or weakness) of their bonds with other women in the group. Certainly, there are singular women everywhere who bust through the hurdles by themselves and make it happen. But more often it's women who start a business with other women, who work collectively, and who share both success and the failure that rise out of poverty.

As Maria put it, "We did it as a group. When they [other women] saw our initiatives, more women joined the group and we became eighteen women. Now we are a community-based group and we have our own [private] company for soap and shampoo."

As you can imagine, Women Thrive was attracted to COMUCAP by a lot more than just their women-led income-generation projects and hair conditioner. These Honduran women understood completely that without raising women's awareness of their rights, assisting women to exercise those rights, and building political consciousness, they wouldn't be addressing the root causes of poverty—powerlessness and the inability to exercise basic human rights.

The vital importance of women building a supportive structure often gets lost on the road of good intentions. Take microcredit, for example, which people often glorify as *the* solution to poverty. Many microfinanced businesses remain microscopic and generate only micro-income as a result, even as the enterprises take up enormous amounts of women's time. Without access to any kind of banking infrastructure, women put their cash where they always have—tucked into their bosoms. Their money might be warm and cozy in there, but it's not safe. Women become targets for thieves or, sadly, experience *more* domestic violence as a result because their partners want some of that cash. What women need, in addition to a banking infrastructure to keep their money secure, is human rights education so they know that being battered is a violation of those rights. They need education for their partners and families so they can understand that a woman's new enterprise and access to income will strengthen the family, not weaken it. Very importantly, they need a space to support and coach one another through these difficulties. There are some microcredit firms that include these elements, but many do not. If you are an investor in microcredit, I encourage you to ask your chosen organization if it integrates gender and addresses the power dynamics within households. If they give you a blank stare, you might consider moving your money elsewhere.

For COMUCAP, women's economic empowerment is not an end in itself; it is the doorway to a whole new world of rights awareness and political action. All the women of the co-op have been trained in how to prevent and respond to domestic violence against themselves or their friends and relatives. They've analyzed the political history of their country and are savvy to the fact that one of the biggest reasons they are poor is because of politics tilted toward rich elites and racism against indigenous and rural peoples. COMUCAP is the kind of local organization with which Women Thrive loves to partner for our joint advocacy efforts. We want partners that are truly based in the community and led by the village women themselves. We look for women that are ready to go beyond their project work to take on govern-ments and get major resources so their entire community can move out of poverty.

As I stood in solidarity with COMUCAP's women and their families at the coffee plant that morning, I felt the tension of the impending conflict and prayed it would not turn violent. I was in awe at how these women were exercising their empowerment training in that moment. They were not leaders of countries or movements, but they were pursuing their rights with the same grace, dignity, and commitment to peace as other great leaders of our time.

# 23

# WHAT'S IN YOUR COFFEE?

For better or worse, most of us in America and Europe start our day with a cup of steamy coffee. Some of us dread to think what the day would be like if we didn't jump-start it with that little hit of caffeine. But one thing we don't often think about is where that coffee comes from, who grows it, and who benefits or is exploited by it.

The history of coffee is a bitter one, I'm afraid. It was one of the primary products that ignited the takeover of most of the world by European colonialists. Legend has it that coffee originated in the Ethiopian city of Kaffa and found its way to Arabia, where it became a popular social and medicinal drink.[1]

The Dutch managed to get a few fertile beans of coffee, despite an Arabian ban on their export, and planted them in the Dutch Indian and Indonesian colonies. The brown gold rapidly grew in popularity and profitability, no doubt boosted by its magical and addictive qualities. The Europeans wanted more land and more slaves to grow more coffee, as well as sugar, tea, and exotic fruits. The great explorers delivered.

Honduras and all of Central America were

"discovered" by Christopher Columbus, whose sails were financed by Spain. "Discovered" is in quotes because, of course, the region had become home for indigenous peoples thousands of years before. The land was not free for the taking. The Spanish conquistadors who followed Columbus were among the most brutal of colonizers. Between the slaughter of whole villages and the European diseases they spread, the number of native people in Central America plummeted from about 13 million to a small fraction of that in about 150 years.[2] Natives that survived hid themselves away or were pressed into slavery to build the Spanish empire. A generation of children from that era was born to mixed European and Indian parents; very likely, their mothers did not choose their fathers. The population of Central America is now 90 percent or more mestizo (mixed), but most of these mixed-heritage people are still considered somewhat lesser citizens.

Honduras declared "independence" from Spain in 1821, again in quotes because it was the Spanish-descended elites that led the government from that point forward, with a few exceptions here and there. When Americans went wild for coffee, sugar, and fruits like bananas in the early 1900s, many Central American countries, including Honduras, turned to American business moguls to finance massive plantations. Slavery morphed into low-wage labor in deplorable conditions. This is one of the primary reasons the United States supported cruel dictatorships throughout the twentieth century: to get their fix on coffee and exotic foods.

Indigenous and rural peoples, who had been murdered and enslaved for generations, tried to gain control over what used to be their land and livelihoods. The bloody and prolonged revolutionary wars in El Salvador and Nicaragua in the 1970s and 1980s were the result. Because those movements wanted to take back the land and distribute it to the people, they were called "communist" and the US government went to extremes, including illegal actions, to protect American plantations. Democracy, human rights, ethics, justice, and even our own humanity, I think, were casualties during those years. Every time I travel to Central America, I am shocked by the fact that the people there don't uniformly despise Americans. A Nicaraguan friend explained to me once that Central Americans, who have never viewed their governments as representing the people, make a big distinction between Americans and the US government. They don't blame the average American on Main Street for the past actions of the government in Washington. We should be thankful for that.

This history is why I strive to buy, whenever I can, fair trade coffee, mangos, sugar, bananas, tea, flowers, and other products. These goods are free of history's bitter taste because these farms depart from the past and treat workers and the land with the dignity they deserve. This new model for doing good and doing well emerged in the global marketplace in the 1980s, first by the Dutch, perhaps because of their role in starting centuries of coffee exploitation. They labeled the fair trade product "Max Havelaar," after a fictional Dutch character that fought for the rights of coffee pickers in the Dutch colonies. The label certified that coffee from Mexico sold in Holland was produced without exploitation.[3] In the 1980s and 1990s, the Max Havelaar label and others like it spread across Europe and into the United States, tapping into a latent consumer demand for delicious, exploitation-free coffee. In 1997, the various labels got together and created the Fair Labeling Organization (FLO) in Europe; shortly after that, Fair Trade USA opened its doors in the United States. Now, Fair Trade USA certifies almost 12,000 products, from sugar and spice (and everything nice) to spirits and sunflowers, which are sold in more than 100,000 stores in North America.[4]

So what does it take for coffee to be fair trade? Fair Trade USA has six principles with which products must align in order to use their distinctive green-and-black, boy-with-a-bowl sticker:

1. **Fair prices and farmer access to credit:** Farmers must receive a minimum floor price from buyers, or the market price if that's more, and an extra amount for organic products. Farmers must have access to credit so that they can afford to plant, and then pay it back after they harvest their crops.

2. **Good labor conditions:** Workers must be able to associate freely and form unions if they so choose, and have safe working conditions and sustainable wages. Obviously, forced child and slave labor are prohibited.

3. **No middlemen:** Importers buy products as directly from the farmers as is possible to get more of the profits to the community. The goal is also for farmers to develop the skills to succeed in a global marketplace.

4. **Community benefits:** A portion of the fair trade profits must be set aside for community development in areas like education, health care, business development, and organic certification.

5. **Democratic and open farmer organizations:** The farmers and workers decide democratically and transparently how to invest the fair trade profits for their community's benefit.

6. **Environmental protection:** Harmful chemicals and genetically modified organisms

are banned, and sustainable farming practices that promote health and eco-system renewal are encouraged.[5]

FLO has a slightly different set of standards, but they run along the same lines as those I just outlined. FLO certifies COMUCAP's products since most of its business is with Europe.

The organizational model COMUCAP uses is itself a rejection of their colonial past. While they still grow the crop responsible for the abuse of their ancestors, they have turned the tables by giving each and every member of the association a say in decisions and a piece of the profits. The profits (or losses) are to be shared among all the members, rather than concentrated in the hands of a few business kingpins. Producer associations and cooperatives are growing by leaps and bounds around the world because they unite some of the best aspects of a market economy—enterprise, efficiency, and creativity—with the values of equity, fairness, transparency, and shared prosperity. Associations and co-ops are part of America's economic fabric as well. There are more than 300 employee-owned cooperative businesses in the United States, including Ace Hardware, Blue Diamond nut growers, Land O'Lakes, and Sunkist, to name a few.[6]

# 24

# UPHILL CLIMB

I already had a few cups of coffee that morning in July 2013, but I was not ready to get on the plane to Honduras. I had been trying to get in touch with the general coordinator of COMUCAP for months. She had only written back scanty e-mails saying, "We welcome your visit and we will be at your service," with no acknowledgment about the women members I hoped to visit and stay with, or any other details that are nice to know before you land in a country. She did send a brief memo explaining that there was a conflict within the organization, but my Spanish wasn't good enough to read between the lines. I'd also moved into a new house with the boys only a week before, and everything was a mishmash of cardboard boxes, household items in the wrong rooms, and boy stuff strewn everywhere (taking full advantage of the temporary turmoil). I felt like I was going from chaos into the unknown. In retrospect, it's probably for the best that I didn't know what awaited me.

But my grumpiness floated away when I saw the houses on the terraced slopes of Tegucigalpa with their earthy terra-cotta roofs. It reminded me again that Central America is much like the Arizona southwest where I grew up, 60 miles north of the Mexican border. Everything here looked friendly, familiar, and close to home.

Tegucigalpa is a riotous, chaotic, crowded, and messy capital city tucked in the mountainous interior region of Honduras. Originally built on a flat valley, the town grew rapidly, and now both slums and modern megamansions splash up and down the steep mountainsides. COMUCAP is headquartered in the La Paz (Peace) region of Honduras; the town of Marcala is up many more mountains from Tegucigalpa at an elevation of about 4,000 feet.

I so love the drive up to Marcala. It is much like the rugged foothills of the Rocky Mountains, but with tropical vegetation mixed in with the towering pines. The winding road led us far above the frenzied city into cleaner air; my ears popped joyfully. Last time I passed this way the road was barely one lane each way; I'd gulped rounding every blind bend, ready for a head-on collision. The road we were on now was incredibly smooth, modern, and an unusual four-lane divided highway configuration. Our driver pointed out that this new stretch had been improved as part of the MCA's investment in Honduras. It clicked as soon as he said that; it looked just like any road in the United States.

I was still tense despite the scenery and smooth

ride. As we drove north, our translator, a lovely woman named Lena Zuñiga Rivera, asked me where our first stop was in Marcala. She translates for all the major nongovernmental organizations that work in Honduras, including Oxfam, Action Aid, and Plan International. Basically, she knows everything about everybody. I replied that we should go to the coordinator's house, and Lena's face fell. She brought me up to speed fast.

As Lena told it, an audit in 2011 caught the thread of an irregularity. When the COMUCAP board of directors pulled on that thread, a tangle of complicated financial transactions involving questionable real estate deals, coffee contracts, and bank accounts unraveled. The coordinator appeared to have been using various tactics to take more than her fair share of the profits from COMUCAP's businesses. The COMUCAP board fired her in spring of 2013, just a few months before my visit—but she neglected to mention that in her e-mail correspondence with me.

"So who's in charge of COMUCAP now?" I asked Lena, choking on shock and deep disappointment. She said that a new board had taken over, which included a mix of new directors and former directors with institutional memory from the previous board. She also suspected they had no idea I was back in the country. Lena picked up her smartphone and rang COMUCAP. Elena Méndez, the new president of the board, said she had no idea I was coming for a visit since I was, logically from my perspective, contacting the previous coordinator. Elena and the board don't speak with that coordinator much anymore. But by the time we arrived in Marcala an hour later, Elena had gathered all six of the democratically elected board members and was ready to meet us.

We sat in a small turquoise room that is the main office in COMUCAP's house; all of us squeezed in around a table and two desks. Elena started. She told us what happened in a distant, monotone voice, as if she were recounting the plot from a boring movie. It was clear, however, that the pain and frustration filled the veins right under her skin; any small prick might not stop bleeding. The audits they did showed numerous irregularities, according to Elena. When they asked the former coordinator to explain, she blew up and made it clear that she felt the financials should be no concern to the board. The board made the painful and difficult decision to fire their coordinator of twenty years. Shortly after that, someone stole all the financial records, as well as the organization's two computers and the keys to all the COMUCAP properties. Worst of all, the group was left with a debt of 8 million lempiras—more than $45,000. That is $175 for every COMUCAP member. At a rate of $1 a day in earnings, they each would have to turn over almost a half-year's worth of income to pay the debt. The businesses were inoperable at the moment because they had no management and no way to pay staff. The coffee buyers were unsure about who was running COMUCAP at the moment and were wary to send money. In sum, there was no way to cover the debt anytime soon.

How could this happen? Doña Adina's eyes brimmed up with tears as she said, "This is all my fault. I didn't know. If I had known, I would never have done it." Doña Adina was the chairwoman of the board during the time the ex-coordinator ran COMUCAP. She was serving on the new board because the association's members still trusted her and wanted to keep some of their institution's memory intact.

I waited patiently and quietly for her to continue.

She sighed heavily and said, "Years ago, when we were first starting, [the coordinator] told me that as the board president I should sign the power of attorney over to her. She said that it would make everything better for the board and the members of COMUCAP. I was still just a small, uneducated peasant woman, and I trusted her. I trusted her with all my heart and soul. I thought her life was dedicated to us. She had gotten an education, she had a degree, and she knew what she was doing with the business. So I signed it." She traced her signature with one finger on the palm of her other hand. She was trembling, and tears rolled down her deeply furrowed face. "I didn't know. I didn't know," she trailed off. My stomach tightened and I held back my own tears.

Juana Suyapa Garcia Sabillon, who goes by Suyapa, is a longtime COMUCAP member and now board vice president. She was furious and indignant. Not with Doña Adina, but with the whole situation. "Whenever we would ask about the money, to see the papers, or wanted some information about the businesses, the coordinator would get angry and tell us, 'You are just stupid peasant women, you wouldn't be able to understand any of that.' We stopped asking. We didn't know that it was our right, our duty as a board to see whatever information we wanted." It seemed crazy, but how would they know what a board of directors is supposed to do if no one ever told them? I don't fault women who barely got to second grade and were taught to be quiet and do what they're told for bowing to the pressure.

But, and this is a big *but,* the fundamental mission of COMUCAP is to empower women to challenge the status quo, to find out who wins when they lose, and to demand better. What was happening in Marcala was the worst kind of betrayal and the most pernicious kind of disempowerment. Nothing makes me madder than when the people who are supposed to protect and empower are the very ones abusing and repressing.

"We are humble farmer women that gave [the

ex-coordinator] power," Suyapa said with clear-eyed fury. "We put everything in her hands and made the international agencies believe in her. This is the moment we found out that she didn't love the women. She loved the money. She loved the traveling, and the opportunities for her family that our children didn't have."

"And she says we have 72 hours to give it all 'back' to her," added Elena.

My jaw dropped wide open. "She what?" I gasped.

# 25

# FOOLS NO MORE

The board members received the letter on July 18, 2013, the day before I arrived. I am pretty sure it was sent to coincide with my presence in Marcala. The ex-coordinator had convinced a few members of the association to side with her. She constituted another COMUCAP board and placed two former employees in the positions of president and vice president.

July 18, 2013
Dear Ladies,
The COMUCAP representatives signed below hereby inform you that you have

72 hours from now to revoke resolution number 173, regarding the administrative power granted by you to Maria Elena Méndez [the new board president] dated January 31, 2013, at the offices of Attorney [omitted]. We warn you that not making said revocation will result in legal action against you, and by your inaction you have committed a crime.

It was absurd. How in the world could a former employee think that they have the right to the organization and all its assets? And then it hit me. This is rural Honduras. There are no clear lines between employee and owner, or between what is legally yours and what someone else might just claim as theirs. This is a region whose body of history is heavily pockmarked by the powerful simply grabbing what they want from the poor. That is the model for how power has operated here since the Europeans began shipping Central America's resources back to the Old World centuries ago. Perhaps that was the mindset behind every move their ex-coordinator was making. Maybe she was simply trying to scare these peasant women into bowing down their heads and handing her back the keys to the castle.

"If she thinks we are going to back down, she is severely underestimating us. We are going to fight for what belongs to us," Suyapa said through gritted teeth. "We are waking up. We are waking up from the bad dream we were in where we gave her all our power and put all our hopes in her hands. We were fools, but we are not fools anymore."

I felt sick hearing her say that. My heart ached with grief and my head pounded with anger. I wanted to fix it all for them. But I couldn't, and shouldn't. As harshly unforgiving as the trail was going to be, they needed to walk it. They had climbed only halfway up the mountain of empowerment, became stuck in the clouds, and assumed they had reached the top. This is the wind they needed to clear things up. All I could do was offer them sustenance to keep on going.

My colleagues (my photographer, translator, and driver) and I left the board so they could go back to a training session on marketing that was in progress with some of their members. Of course, their real work was going on straight through the entire trauma. These women really won't stop for anything.

I knew I had to go see the ex-coordinator next and let her know that I could not travel around La Paz to see the COMUCAP members with her as planned; I had to work with the legal representatives of the organization. It really was as simple as that. I wasn't looking forward to that conversation.

The ex-coordinator's house was just down the

street from Casa de Mujeres, way too close to be comfortable. She was friendly, but distant, and I could see that the conflict was taking its toll on her too. Her eyes were sunken and surrounded by black shadows. Her lips were thin and her cheeks were sallow. She called out the two former employees-cum-board-members from some darkened back rooms of the house. I remembered them both from my previous visit and greeted them in my basic Spanish. I told them all I was very sad to learn about what had happened, and that seemed to lighten their spirits a bit, but they didn't know that I had already met with the real COMUCAP board. I let them tell me about what happened from their perspective, and while part of me hoped to hear something that would make this all just another episode in a "Massive Miscommunication" reality TV series, I didn't. It was as the COMUCAP board told me. They fired the coordinator. She felt she had built all the businesses herself and therefore, in essence, owned them. "Everything they have is because I did it for them," she said, emphasizing the *I*. I didn't think explaining to her that she was paid for her services would do any good at this point.

I kept it as brief as I could as I explained that I would be spending the rest of my time in La Paz with the new board and current members of COMUCAP. The ex-coordinator's face turned to ice; her eyes narrowed and pierced me. She realized she'd lost me. It was her look of surprise that made me wonder if she sent the 72-hour warning letter to coincide with my visit. Perhaps she thought I'd never go to Casa, never talk to the board or members, or never find out what had happened and that she could leverage my presence to further intimidate the peasant women. I wanted to say, "My dear, if I was that stupid I would not have made it all these years in Washington. If you want to see power games . . ." Instead, I just said, "Lo siento." And I was truly sorry for everyone.

The next day we were up early to meet the board at Casa de Mujeres and to see some of their members who had received assistance from the MCA. A few of the board's women were still sleeping on floor mattresses at Casa when we got there. Elena's hair was still wet, sleek, and silvery black from the shower. Suyapa's face and eyes were red from a night with a lot of anxiety and a little sleep.

We piled into two trucks and spent the day bouncing up and down rocky mountain roads talking with women farmers who had created beautiful, bountiful farms after they accessed irrigation through the MCA. Their stories lifted our spirits; the thousand shades of green and dark wet earth grounded and calmed me.

Elena's two cell phones rang constantly

throughout the trip. Our reverie came to an abrupt end when she got a tip that the ex-coordinator had recruited people to take over the coffee, aloe, and retreat facilities by force, before the 72-hour deadline. The board needed to mobilize the members to sit in and watch over the facilities *pronto*. I decided it would be best to retreat to the hotel and stay out of the way.

My dreams that night were bizarre. In one of them I heard gunshots, only to awaken at about four in the morning and realize that part wasn't a dream. I stared at the ceiling until it seemed safe to get up. The hotel management didn't seem flustered at all. Apparently everyone here has a gun since the police system is dysfunctional, so late night and early morning joy fire is pretty routine.

We went back to Casa in the afternoon to check on everyone. Elena, Suyapa, and Doña Adina looked bone-crushingly tired, but they were also somewhat elated. "What happened last night?" I asked . . . after we had coffee first, of course.

The board mobilized and talked to almost all the members of COMUCAP, one by one, explaining what the ex-coordinator was doing. Up until that point, the board had been trying to resolve things amicably and without confrontation. But the time for that had past. Elena and Suyapa were surprised and heartened by how the members stood up, rallied their families, walked miles to the coffee

## Some Basic Good Governance Practices for Associations and Cooperatives

Every cooperative, association, or membership organization needs to have some basic practices for good governance and financial management. If these are not present, something might be fishy.

- Organizations should **have a constitution** or bylaws, which explain how the group is governed and run. This document sets the rules for which actions the board may take on behalf of the membership. For example, it is customary for the membership to give the board the authority to hire and fire a coordinator for the group. Every member (not just staff and board) should fully understand the constitution.
- It should be known to all that **only the individual membership base can vote to change the constitution**. Under no circumstances should employees be able to alter the organization's constitution or bylaws.
- The organization's **vision, mission, and objectives should be very clear** to every member. Ideally, they should have indicators for success, even if that is just comparing the past to the present on an annual basis.

- **Budgeting should be done collectively and transparently**, including budgets to donors. For very large projects, it is a good practice for all members to know what is in the budget.
- **All expenses should be supported by documentation**, and spending reports should be regularly submitted to the board and any member that requests it.
- **Checks and balances must be present.** For example, the director should not be able to complete financial transactions without the signature of another officer; the board should approve all major financial transactions.
- **All members should receive the financials and a yearly report** of activities at an annual meeting. The financials should be audited by at least a local cooperative inspector, which is inexpensive. Any member should be able to ask for clarifications and receive an understandable response.

Questions to ask individual members of an organization to check if all is in order:

1. Are you aware that there is a constitution or bylaws that govern your cooperative/ organization? Do you feel that you understand it?

> 2. Do you know what the expenditures, income, and profits are for your organization? Do you participate in any budgeting or financial reporting processes?
> 3. Are you aware of projects that have been done recently and what the benefits of those projects are? Does your group have any way of monitoring progress?

plant or retreat center, and spent the night guarding their communal property.

"I didn't know what to expect," said Elena. "I didn't know if they would stay with the board or leave us. I didn't know if they would be scared away. But they were so brave, coming out from their homes and going to where they might face conflict. They are ready to stand and fight for what is theirs."

"How long will they have to stay and guard the facilities?" I asked.

"As long as it takes," Suyapa replied. "It could be days, weeks, months; we don't know. But we will stay there until we feel safe again that no one will take it from us."

A sad look came over Elena's face. "But we don't have anything to give them to eat. They have been there since last night and it's now evening."

I looked at my colleagues and they immediately

understood what I was thinking without my having to say it. We had a decent meal budget for the trip. I asked our driver to take some of the board members and buy enough food to feed everyone for at least a week. They returned about an hour later with boxes of eggs, masses of corn flour for fresh tortillas, blocks of pure white farmer cheese, sacks of shiny red beans, gallons of oil, and a couple pounds of butter, sugar, and salt. The cost to feed 100 people for a week: $400. Being able to support these women in their final push toward true empowerment: priceless.

About an hour later, dinner was ready for the members at the coffee plant and El Mezcalito retreat center. I asked if they would prefer me to come or head back to the hotel. They had been waiting to ask me to come but didn't want to push for too much. I assured them there was no place I would rather be.

It was a pitch-black night, so dark that the star-filled sky made me dizzy to look at as we wound our way up the mountainside to El Mezcalito. As we pulled into the retreat center it looked deserted. But then our headlights hit the front porch and temporarily blinded the families who had been sitting quietly in the night. I had expected to find mostly men, husbands and grown sons, of the COMUCAP members. But whole families were there standing guard with their sweet newborn babies, teetering toddlers, bored teenagers, and sleeping grandparents. Everybody had come out in solidarity.

The board asked me to say something to encourage the women to continue their fight. I looked around at their faces. "You humble me. You amaze me. You built this place with your own hands. This beautiful place is your work. You own it," I said. "And you should defend it. We will stand with you as long as it takes." The women straightened their backs and stood a little taller as I said those last words. They realized they weren't alone in this.

# 26

# TASTE OF VICTORY

Early the next morning, which was the end of the 72-hour handover deadline, the board wanted us to go with them to the coffee plant to be there as outside observers. I knew that a confrontation could easily become violent, but the COMUCAP women felt that our being there would make them safer, so I agreed.

When we arrived at the plant, the women said that the man next door, who was likely friends with the ex-coordinator, spent the night running his machete along the fence to intimidate all those inside. The women's sons and husbands got their machetes and baseball bats, and slept outside in case the man's clanging was an overture to serious violence. By morning, everyone was exhausted and stressed. These COMUCAP members had slept on cold cement floors for several nights, gone without food, left their fields baking in the sun, and held strong in the face of threats and harassment. There was so much at stake: twenty years of literal blood, sweat, and tears to build these successful businesses, which were also the means of lifting their families out of poverty for the twenty years ahead.

All was calm initially, so we went into the aloe processing building to see how they peel, squeeze, puree, and cook the aloe for the first steps of making soap and shampoo. Just as we were finishing up, one of the ex-coordinator's board members, the young woman who used to manage the coffee plant, showed up at the fence. The woman said that the COMUCAP members all needed to leave. Elena just looked at her, with no expression on her face, and responded with a flat, "No." Elena explained to the young woman that she was getting in over her head, that what she was doing was illegal, and as the president of the fake board, she was going to be held responsible. I could see wheels turning in the young woman's head. Elena went on to say that the COMUCAP board would be willing to provide the young woman with the severance pay she had been demanding, but not until the harassment and illegal seizure of COMUCAP's property stopped. After about twenty minutes of Elena's reasoning with her, the young woman finally handed over the keys. Then she left. It didn't look like much, that moment of her hand reaching through the bars of the gate and putting the keys in Elena's hands, but it was a huge victory for the women of COMUCAP. It could have gone much worse, but the day's trials were far from over.

An hour later, three men came by, saying that they wanted to have some coffee ground and asking if they could come in. Elena knew them and knew the chubby one with greasy hair was a lawyer and relative of the ex-coordinator's who was helping her. Elena looked at the men and said, "We know who you are." There was no more conversation after that.

Then the young lady came back with the former director of the coffee operation, who happens to be the ex-coordinator's son-in-law. They brought a document showing what shipments of coffee had gone out to what buyers in Europe and the United States. They wanted Elena to sign it to acknowledge that all the coffee was accounted for, which would let them off the hook for stealing any coffee. Unfortunately for them, there was a small issue. Apparently, they had opened a fraudulent bank account under COMUCAP's name and sent an e-mail to the main buyer in Germany telling her to deposit funds in that new account. To her credit, the German buyer wanted to make sure the account was legitimate because she had been wiring money to a different account for years. She called the COMUCAP office to check. The board knew nothing about a new bank account. The son-in-law director denied it all, saying he was just a neutral party and wanted to remain friends with everyone. One of the board members said she knew he had opened the account because the buyer had sent COMUCAP a copy of the e-mail, which came from *his* e-mail account. He turned red and said his account must have been hacked.

During this whole conversation, a loose piece of sheet metal kept banging loudly against the roof, sometimes so noisily that it was hard to hear anything else. It was as if the coffee plant itself was revolting against a hostile takeover.

The young woman who had managed the plant wanted severance pay for herself and her husband, the plant's security guard who was also fired. Elena said that if it were owed to them, she would honor the debt, but now wasn't the time to work it out. Besides, COMUCAP was 8 million lempiras in debt and had no money. The young lady could argue until she was blue in the face, but nothing was going to happen right then.

Elena finally said to them both, "We received your letter very quietly. I talked with my colleagues and asked them what we should do. Everyone was so angry and wanted to defend themselves. I said, 'No, not with aggression.' I want to do things face-to-face. I don't send messages. The people who only send messages are not interested in fixing the problem. I am not afraid of anybody because I know when you are saying the truth God protects you.

"If you want to start another association you can do it, but don't use the name, the official stamps, and the partners that belong to the members of COMUCAP. And now you have also beaten us with letters that have been sent to donors and buyers. I ask myself, 'Why are they doing this to us humble women?'

"We are still here. We are living through this and it hurts a lot. But I know that here we are strong. Even without money, we are going to continue taking care of these businesses, because these are the assets of the 257 women. I made a promise to the women that the day we can say, 'This is ours,' we are going put up our flag and take care of our fort. And now, we women have the ownership and the power. The sons, daughters, and husbands of the members have been our companions on this great journey we are on. I thank God and the international donors that are with us in this moment."

The two former employees got their personal items and Elena went through an inventory of everything at the plant to make sure all was in order. I checked the computer to make sure the association's document files were intact, which they were, and then changed the password.

I stepped outside into the afternoon sun. Suyapa was pacing across the compound on her cell phone while her voice was booming from the radio of a beat-up old pickup truck. She was on the local station being interviewed about the day's events. The reporter asked her tough questions about how the board let this happen and what they were going to do now. Suyapa didn't pull any punches. She named names and accepted responsibility on behalf of the board while asserting the members' rights to the profits of their labor. The COMUCAP crowd listened intently and when she finished applause erupted. After months of fighting, the women wrested back their organization. As we drove away from the compound, I rolled down the window, saluted them, and shouted out the Spanish equivalent of "You go, girls!" The women of COMUCAP laughed and cheered where they stood on the loading dock of the coffee warehouse, now in their control.

I won't remember that day just because the women of COMUCAP stood strong against intimidation and threats of violence. I will remember it because this small group of rural Honduran women, who took a wrong turn along the path to empowerment and gave their power to someone else, finally took real ownership of their future.

# 27
# THE FARMER AND HER HUSBAND

In much of the world, a farmer is not a guy in overalls with a pitchfork, but a woman with a baby on her back.

More than two and a half billion people (40 percent of the world's population) work less than five acres of land to feed themselves and their families.[7] Women are the majority of these small-scale subsistence farmers. They cultivate half of the food the world consumes and about 80 percent of the food that sustains Africa.[8] So it is painfully ironic that of the almost 870 million hungry people worldwide, eight out of ten are farmers, and six of every ten are women.[9] This is because, as Doña Adina said during one of our conversations, "We women are the first getting up, the last going to bed, and the last to eat if there is anything left." Subsistence farmers work the land in order to simply feed themselves and their families. They cannot afford to buy food, and they are not making a living by selling their produce. In other words, if they don't grow it, they don't eat it.

Every single year, hunger kills more people than AIDS, tuberculosis, and malaria combined—and those three diseases claim millions.[10] It's a vicious cycle: Malnourishment makes people much more likely to contract, and die from, these diseases, and farmers exhausted by sickness cannot be as productive in their fields, which creates more hunger and malnourishment.

So why can't farmers grow enough food to prevent themselves from starving? There are so many reasons, and at the core of every one of them lies powerlessness. I want to explore two of the principal causes here: history and discrimination against women. My choice of these as principal causes might surprise you. Usually, we hear that droughts or floods caused by climate change, or rapid population growth, are reasons why people die of hunger. Those are certainly major contributing factors. But if we peel back these phenomena, we find the same root cause again and again: the inability of certain people to access what they need because other people are preventing it.

During the nineteenth and twentieth centuries, the best land was taken from indigenous peoples by colonial powers to create massive plantations for export crops such as coffee, tea, sugar, and fruit—and also to dig into the earth to feed a new industrial world with an insatiable appetite for minerals. After independence, some countries redistributed a portion of land back to their citizens. Most didn't. Private companies replaced the colonial powers, and even now, a lot of territory still produces export commodities and is off limits to poor farmers.

The land that remains is in high demand. Women, the least powerful among the powerless, are given land that is practically uncultivable. Women's land frequently comes in tiny, disconnected parcels. Their plots are farthest from the well or water source and are depleted of nutrients by past farming and poor management. After all, if it were good land it wouldn't belong to a woman. I shouldn't say *belong,* because land rarely is owned or controlled by women. Normally, their husband or another male family member lends them a plot to grow food for the family. In some regions of the world, the man's land is used to grow cash crops for market; he keeps much of the proceeds for himself (though women must spend hours working their husband's land before they toil on their own land).

Women have little incentive to invest in their own plots. If a woman improves her land by putting in fertilizers, growing crops that regenerate the soil, or planting trees to enhance water retention and create shade for tender seedlings, it's a good bet that a man will take the newly productive land away from her. So why bother? This is why it's so vitally important for women to own the land they farm. Ownership justifies investment, investment improves yields, and yields feed children.

Rather than addressing these and other root causes of hunger, our global community has long opted for an arrangement that gets food to the starving but helps the donor country much more in the process. The major fault of our modern food aid system lies within its underlying assumption: There is not enough food where people are starving, so we have to move food across the world to the hungry. In many cases that assumption is simply wrong, but decision makers in the United States keep ignoring that fact.

Food is often present or not that far away, but subsistence farmers are too poor to buy it. Within the same country or region, variables such as climate change, weather patterns, and soil quality mean that one area may struggle with famine while another experiences an excellent harvest. The United States doesn't connect the hungry with the food produced in their region by helping them purchase it or by bringing that local food to them. Instead, the US government buys food from American farmers and ships it tens of thousands of miles away, at great cost to taxpayers and with significant environmental impacts.

The saddest part is that we end up hurting poor farmers with this kind of food aid. When thousands of tons of free food enter a country, the glut pushes the price of basic foodstuffs in the local market down through the floor. People who could buy food from local farmers don't, because local grains actually cost more than the cheaper foreign commodities. Sometimes hands reach in the basket as the food travels from the dock to the hungry farmer's table. Occasionally, you hear about corrupt government officials stocking up their pantries with freebies. Tons of food are stolen from warehouses and then find their way into the market at low prices. In addition, donor countries use a technique called "monetization" in which they sell (at a low price) or give grain to national governments or international aid nonprofits. These actors then process, package, and sell the food, using the proceeds for a variety of projects—some related to hunger and some not. Whether through corruption, theft, or cheap sales on the open market, the result is that local farmers who might have excess harvest can no longer sell it, thus pushing small-scale farmers deeper into poverty and making them more likely to depend on food aid than they were before.

European countries have moved away from sending food commodities from afar and toward purchasing food from local farmers (helping them earn an income) and distributing that food (which is fresher and locally appropriate) to hungry people in the same region. This alternative system of purchasing foodstuffs from neighboring countries or local farmers is called "local and regional purchase" and is welcomed by the hungry people we want to help.

Why does an ill-advised system continue to operate? Power and money, of course. The United States is the largest contributor of food aid in the world (supplying about half), and the law governing this aid says that 75 percent of the food must be sourced, processed, and packaged by US agribusinesses. Not many agribusinesses get contracts with the government through this arrangement, as only a few can maneuver the complex system well enough. A small pool of players means that taxpayers are shelling out an average of 11 percent above normal market prices for these commodities, which is another layer of absurdity.[11] Then the law says that up to 75 percent of food must be carried by US-flagged ships at taxpayer expense, which pushes up the cost of food aid even more. Almost 40 percent of the food aid budget is used to cover shipping.[12] USAID estimates that it could reach four million more people with food aid for the same cost to taxpayers if it were allowed to buy food locally on the open market and transport it more quickly and cheaply.[13]

Both George W. Bush and Barack Obama asked

Congress to let them spend more of the food aid budget on local purchase. Now, if these two men can agree about it, everyone ought to be able to agree about it. But on this topic, US farmers and shipping companies have a lot more political leverage with Congress than even the president. The powerful farm and shipping lobbies keep yanking the choke collars of congressional members from agriculture states when they dare to think about supporting local purchase. So we taxpayers are paying with one hand to push farmers into poverty in the name of feeding the hungry, while the other hand is paying to pull them back out of poverty. It is truly obscene. It doesn't have to be this way. In the What You Can Do section that concludes Part 2, I'll walk you through how we can change this nonsense.

The second major problem with the global food system is that one-third of the food grown in the world for human consumption goes to waste. One researcher estimated that all the hungry people in the world could be well fed just by the food that British and American consumers, retailers, and restaurants waste.[14] While that is in itself a wise idea, we don't even have to do that to solve the problem. In developing countries, billions of pounds of grains and vegetables rot before they can be consumed or even make it from farm to market. Small-scale subsistence farmers around the world don't have the proper facilities to keep food fresh so that they can use it during a future bad season or to sell the excess in the market. Eliminate the waste, improve the distribution system, and world hunger is solved. Of course, it's not that easy, but as a global community, we are not focusing enough resources on this part of the equation.

The ultimate solution is to help people everywhere—especially women who are responsible for feeding their families—to grow nutritious, fresh, and plentiful food. However, over the last three decades, global donors from the United States and European Union to the World Bank moved away from funding agriculture. The Green Revolution of the 1970s, which spread the use of hybrid seeds to stop diseases that were decimating crops across Asia, seemed to have solved the problem of feeding the world. During the 1980s and 1990s, the International Monetary Fund (IMF) and the World Bank were also driving developing countries to "modernize" by moving away from agriculture-based economies toward industrial export-driven economies (hey, what worked for us should work for everybody, right?). Lots of countries were not in a position to argue, as they desperately needed loans from the IMF and World Bank. These nations swallowed the whole prescription and cut back their support programs for farming, as well as for vital social programs. They focused on attracting foreign investment to build industries for exports and on paying the interest on their debts. None of this was helpful for preventing hunger.

Thankfully, sanity is making a comeback in international agriculture. Both the IMF and World Bank have changed their strategies to promote and protect investments in social programs and farming. The G8—the group of industrialized countries that includes the United States, Canada, Germany, France, Britain, Italy, Japan, and Russia—has focused several of its heads-of-state summits on growing investments in farmers. Soon after President Obama took office in 2008, he began working on a new signature initiative to end world hunger. At the 2009 G8 Summit in Italy, Obama announced the US government's Feed the Future (FTF) initiative, pledging $3.5 billion for agricultural development and food security.

The original FTF strategy correctly put the focus on small-scale farmers, but it did not recognize the centrality of women as the farmers who are feeding the world. The first FTF strategy relegated women to a being a "vulnerable group" that would need a little extra attention. Women Thrive mobilized its coalition members and sent a strong message to the State Department, USAID, and the White House that women needed to be at the center of this new initiative. We were much happier with the next version of the strategy, which made small-scale women farmers a major focus for all interventions. It's still too early to say whether FTF has been effective in actually working with women farmers or successful in reducing hunger overall, but at least they are heading in the right direction.

# 28

# PURCHASE FOR PROGRESS

The Rome-based World Food Programme (WFP), the world's largest humanitarian agency helping hungry people, decided to try an experiment in 2009 with the support of the Howard G. Buffett Foundation, the Bill & Melinda Gates Foundation, and a number of countries including the United States. Purchase for Progress (P4P) is a five-year pilot in twenty countries—including both Honduras and Nicaragua—that seeks to increase the amount of food that WFP buys directly from small-scale farmers; in other words, local purchase. P4P connects the World Food Programme with farmers' organizations to offer them opportunities to learn the requirements for crop quality and quantity necessary to access commercial agricultural markets and become competitive players in those markets. WFP helps the farmers' organizations get training and technical assistance from local NGOs, and then it purchases the crops that meet WFP's standards. Farmers also use what they learn from the P4P program to sell to others outside of the World Food Programme. While P4P integrated a gender perspective from the start in order to ensure women's participation, the Honduran and Nicaraguan programs have recently put more serious focus on recruiting women farmers.

After saying an emotional good-bye to the women of COMUCAP, I went on to spend a day with women farmers participating in the Honduran P4P program. The following week, I was able to sit down with women farmers in Nicaragua. Each of the groups had been working with WFP for about a year. What amazed me was how far they had come in those twelve months. I have spent time with women's farming cooperatives all over the world, most of which operate without any outside assistance whatsoever (which is what we are trying to change). The training, facilities, technical support, and financial assistance provided by P4P put these women's groups on a fast track to becoming successful, self-sustaining, and profitable farmer organizations. They were so far beyond other women farmers in their own countries, and they didn't even know it.

The 21 women in Honduras who call themselves Mujeres Unidas en Acción (Women United in Action) are focusing their energy first on red and black beans, the staple protein of Latin America. In 2013, P4P provided $9,000 to build a small warehouse and equip it with some basic tools to handle and process beans and grains. The women of Mujeres Unidas en Acción contributed the land to build the warehouse, some of the building materials, basic construction labor, and about 300 pounds of beans to be processed and sold in the market. The women proudly showed me their six shiny, new, stainless steel silos, each about the size of a minivan if you stood it on one end, full of their initial bean capital. Their enterprise is sorting the beans by quality, packaging them in smaller units, and then reselling the beans in the market to local families. The profits they make will go right back into their facilities and farming. At the same time, they are beginning to farm some land, growing corn and beans with the goal of feeding their families and selling the extra to the WFP.

One of my first questions in these situations is always about the kind of training women have received. I'm curious about several things. First, does the program address the sticky issue of gender relations, particularly violence and repro-ductive health, to ensure that at a minimum, women are not put at risk by participating in a program? Second, are the farmers offered all of the options from traditional and natural methods to high-tech, high-input cultivation? Most importantly, are they *really* educated about all the risks and benefits of these techniques, for example, how to use chemicals properly so as not to destroy their health and their precious land in the process? Are they channeled toward expensive techniques by receiving free seeds and chemicals for a few years, becoming dependent on these inputs, and then having to pay for these things to keep their farms alive? And do they truly have the power to decide for themselves?

There is a lot of discussion and disagreement around the world among hunger advocates, donors, recipient countries, consumers, and researchers about these very questions. There is no consensus about how small-scale farmers should go about increasing their productivity. Many people feel farmers should only learn how to grow more food naturally, sustainably, and solely with locally available inputs. Others feel that climate, soil, and other conditions necessitate the use of chemicals and genetically modified (GM) plant varieties. These interests will never agree. But do they have to? Perhaps we are being excessively narcissistic by thinking *we* get to decide what's best for subsistence farmers. We can decide whether or not to feed our own families certified organic or GM foods, but we should not get to decide what's best for a small farmer whose family might starve if whatever technique we are pushing doesn't work out well.

The most important thing is that farmers know the options, fully understand the choices and their short- as well as long-term impacts, and have the power to decide for themselves.

Gladys Montoña, president of Mujeres Unidas en Acción, remembered that one of the first P4P trainings, conducted in partnership with the organization UN Women, was on the rights of women in rural areas, the different roles of men and women, and how women's work in rural areas is more complicated because they have to tend the household at the same time. "We realized that everything we, as women, did on the farm and at home was not valued," said Gladys. "We had to value ourselves." They also held workshops on domestic violence and the different kinds of violence—physical, sexual, and psychological. "We have learned about the reproductive health and rights of women," Gladys continued. "That the life conditions we experience should not be imposed on us. P4P and UN Women have strengthened us a lot in our family lives as well as in our group life." Another participant in that training added, "Before we got together we were housewives in the kitchen making tortillas, taking care of the children, sweeping, and mopping. Now we have gotten out of the kitchen. Before we were hoping to receive something from the men. We don't want to be that way again."

The women sitting around me ranged in age

from 20 to 60. One of the younger members held a one-month-old baby boy who looked exactly like my older son did when he was born. She let me hold him after we finished our meeting, and I was transported back fourteen years in an instant. More than half of the women in the group were single mothers.

The conversation turned to the field schools P4P sets up in tandem with the training. These field schools are critical for farmers to experiment and see for themselves what techniques work best in their particular soil and climate. P4P recognized that experimenting with new methods on the land people depend on for food is too high risk. Karin, one of the leaders in the group, said, "In the field schools we learn during the whole process from sowing to harvest. We learn about the chemicals that protect the foliage from pests, when and how to apply them properly. For example, in the flowering season we don't apply anything to the plant. We learn about the right doses and what substances have the greatest toxicity. We know how we should use the pesticides and the dangers we are facing when we don't use them correctly. We have acquired a special suit to protect ourselves." I was glad to hear that the chemicals came with appropriate protection and training, but I still wanted to know if their curriculum included natural and agro-ecological practices as well.

After our group discussion we walked about a

half mile to a plot of land where the group is growing maize for home consumption and for WFP. The Honduran countryside in this region is so intensely gorgeous that I could sit and look at the vistas for days. The deep green fields of corn fill the valley. The wind moves their leaves in long, undulating waves and fills the air with a peaceful hush. Volcanoes rise above the valley in every direction. Most of them went dormant long ago, and their sides are carpeted with thick tropical foliage. A few are still active, and whispers of smoke twirl into the blue sky above them.

Mujeres Unidas en Acción is renting one manzana of land from another farmer for 2,000 lempiras ($100) per season. *Manzana* literally means apple; in Latin America it refers to a unit of land of varying size depending on the country. In Central America one manzana equals about 1.7 acres, which you can picture as one and one-third football fields. The organization planted corn to harvest in the late fall and will sow beans to reap before winter comes. As we walked through the rows of corn, I asked the women if they were taught or were using any natural techniques. Gladys said they were trained for it and that the goal is to grow naturally and sustainably, but since they are renting the land they don't want to invest in it. Growing with chemical-free methods can take several years of adding natural fertilizers and putting nitrogen back into the soil by cultivating certain crops. The women do have a plan to save profits each year to be able to buy their own land as soon as possible, but one manzana costs 30,000 lempiras ($1,500). They haven't completed a full season yet, so they do not know what profit to expect from their hard work.

The P4P women's program in Nicaragua is a little further along than in Honduras. Edwin Sevilla, P4P country director in Nicaragua, gave me the rundown on the overall progress there. So far, P4P Nicaragua has purchased 2,300 metric tons of food from local farmers, mostly maize, some beans, and a little rice. The food purchased in Nicaragua has been for local distribution in the country; it supports school feeding programs and assists families in extreme poverty. As we jostled along the road to see the women's cooperatives, I asked Edwin how the work with women and the related gender issues like violence and household power were going. "I think mainstreaming of gender has to be a priority," he said. "It actually takes a lot of effort, concentration, and resources. There are times when resources should be directed at women and times they should be directed toward men, so that mixed male-female cooperatives will be open to women's participation. It's important to carry out activities exclusively for women, but we cannot overlook the importance of coed activities for raising awareness. In recognition of this, our country office has hired an expert with background in gender issues to be a focal point to work with both men and women."

I was impressed with that answer. I can tell when someone doesn't have a clue about what gender integration really is when they say things like, "Fifty percent of our beneficiaries are women." Or when I ask what their budget is for gender work and they say, "We don't need any resources for that, we just fold it into everything we do." Those are big red flags flapping in the wind.

The P4P facility in Nuevo Segovia, Nicaragua, was massive. It had a warehouse the size of a football field with numerous silos around the perimeter. In back was a large covered area with machines for husking, sorting, milling, and packaging, as well as a few tractors. Inside the warehouse were about 60 women representing six or seven different cooperatives. They had each drawn a picture at a recent workshop to represent the current development stage of their cooperative. The joy they exuded while they presented each one to me was infectious and wonderful. It was clear to me that the women felt like full owners of their male-female cooperatives. Johanna, the gender focal person for her cooperative, pointed to a picture of an umbrella and said, "I see the cooperative as an umbrella that covers and protects those of us who belong to it. On the top right corner there's a cloud and on the other side a sun. The cloud represents the difficulties and storms that the co-op undergoes to support its members. And the sunny side reflects the small strengths and support we receive from abroad, in this case from the World Food Programme." There was a small boat off to the side of the drawing not under the umbrella. Johanna added at the end, "That little boat represents people in my community who are not part of our cooperative and this program. They are exposed and without help."

As the women each described their land and techniques, whether they had validation plots (small areas of their land used to experiment), and what they were learning at the field schools, the issue of natural and high-tech methods came up again. It was fascinating. This Nicaraguan group also described in detail the precautions for using chemical fertilizers, herbicides, and pesticides. Some of the women were hoping to be able to plant a hybrid variety of corn. They wanted to increase their yields dramatically—along with their profits. Another woman named Cruz, wearing a maroon business suit with matching tennis shoes, wanted to take the no-tech approach. "For me, I prefer sustainable and natural. The yield could be a little bit lower, but the truth is that we want to protect our health and our family and have better quality for sale. Sometimes when we buy the chemicals, the products are so damaging to our health, our children, the soil, and even the health of people who eat that food. There are other products used to force or delay ripening, but the quality is lower. We have received training on how to make our own natural inputs, like fertilizer. WFP has helped us to learn these things."

Cruz and other women farmers were indeed lucky to learn these things. Other women's cooperatives that I've visited in Central America, which have received little or no outside assistance, have been working for ten to fifteen years and don't even have a building to their name, let alone storage facilities or milling machines. They occasionally snag some training if they can convince someone from the agriculture ministry to visit them after the "real" training is done for male farmers. My P4P visits drove home for me, more than anything else, that having access to money, training, and outside support makes a huge difference. There is more than one way to teach a woman to fish. You can give her a stick and a hook, point her toward the lake, and then hope for the best. Or you can really support her, with high-quality training, good nets, bait, and a boat, and watch her bring in the catch.

# 29

# HELPING WOMEN, ONE MILLION AT A TIME

Some days at work are particularly good. The day in 2006 that one million African women got the right to have property in their own name and be treated as full adult citizens was one of those days.

The Kingdom of Lesotho, a small country tucked inside of South Africa, was in negotiations with the Millennium Challenge Account for a $363 million program. But they hit a little snag. This was around the time MCA had started to pay real attention to gender. It came to light that married women in Lesotho had the same legal status as children. They could not own property, sign a contract, get a loan, take legal action, start a business, or complete a host of other basic tasks without the written consent of their husbands. During the time of Lesotho's conversations with the MCA in Washington, I had the opportunity to meet with its ambassador to the United States, who happened to be a woman. (She must have gotten written consent from her husband to take the job.) She told me how ludicrous it was that even she, an ambassador, had to put real estate in her son's name to "facilitate" the transaction. For rural women living in poverty, the lack of property rights made their lives impossible. If their husbands died, they and their children were automatically evicted from their homes and farms. They had no other assets because it was illegal for them to possess any. The law essentially condemned widows to extreme poverty, forced marriage to a husband's relative, or death.

Women's rights advocates in Lesotho had been pushing a piece of legislation called the Legal Capacity of Married Persons Act for more than a decade. The male leaders of Lesotho had waved it off like it was a pesky fly. But the MCA didn't see it like that. They saw the legal discrimination against half of Lesotho's population as a "significant constraint" to the country's economic growth. The MCA money just wouldn't be as effective if women had to get their husbands' permission to become economic actors. So "the passing of the Legal Capacity of Married Persons Act was a precondition set by the Millennium Challenge Corporation (MCC) before moving forward with the Lesotho Compact."[15]

The day the act became law, we celebrated not only for the women of Lesotho but also because it was an unmistakable signal that any other country that wanted to get MCA funding had to start paying close attention to women's legal status. We at Women Thrive didn't have our hands directly in the dough in Lesotho, but as I discussed earlier, we were up to our elbows in making the MCA care about gender overall. That is what I love about the advocacy we do. If we can get a whole big institution to take women's rights and gender seriously, then we don't have to be involved in every single fight in each country around the world. The way I see it, Women Thrive's work is about creating a framework that women's organizations everywhere can use as leverage to change what they want to change in their own countries. After all, local women's advocates know best what they need and how to get it done. We just tip the balance more favorably in their direction through our advocacy in Washington, DC.

In 2013, the MCA looked back to document how the passage of the married persons act made a difference. A mediator with the High Court of Lesotho said, "The gender laws that have been introduced now let married women file a case in their own name without their husbands' consent. This has improved accessibility of justice for women and has been instrumental in empowering women by giving them access to legal services. They are now able to make their own decisions and fight their own legal battles."[16]

This was the MCA at its best. But promoting gender issues didn't always work in every country. Take Honduras, for example. It was one of the first MCA programs, before they had a gender specialist and the Gender Policy. The Honduran consultations did not invite participation from NGOs in general, and women's groups were barely even informed about the MCA coming to their country. Women Thrive did a case study with Columbia University on the Honduran consultation process. As a result of that work, we sent three pages of strongly worded recommendations to the MCA on how they needed to help country governments conduct real conversations with their citizen organizations. To their credit, the MCA took a lot of what we said and put it into practice.

Ginny Seitz, the senior gender adviser, and others at the MCA Washington office tried to retrofit gender into the Honduran proposal and managed to get a requirement that 20 percent of the beneficiaries of the agriculture program should be women. But getting any real consideration for women was a constant fight. One of the contractors implementing the MCA project on agriculture agreed to hire female trainers to work with female farmers, but they required all trainers to have a degree in agronomy. Virtually no women in Honduras had degrees in agronomy. It took a lot of cajoling to get the contractor to agree to pair women trainers with more seasoned agronomists as a work-around. Of course, they did not consider the issue of gender-based violence up front, which is always there, and the female trainers started getting attacked during their excursions to communities. In the end the contractor said there was no way that they could hit the 20 percent female beneficiary quota; they said they could do 3 percent.

By this point, more than halfway into the MCA's five-year program in the country, Women Thrive had helped COMUCAP build its capacity to pressure the MCA Honduras on gender equity in the projects. While we pushed in Washington, COMUCAP pushed in Tegucigalpa, and we were able to raise the bar to 8 percent. When I was in Marcala during COMUCAP's crisis, I met with a few women who were part of that extra 5 percent of beneficiaries. The help they received with their irrigation and crops has been transformative for them and their communities.

"This is the reason we are now so insistent that the core team that develops the Compact has someone looking at gender, so that it's built in from the beginning," Ginny said to me. It became painfully clear that gender had to be there from the very beginning of the MCA's work in a country—starting with the consultations, ending with the postproject evaluation metrics, and covering every single step in between. Eight percent was better than 3, but it was still too little.

Nicaragua's MCA program came not long after Honduras'. The contrast between the two was stark. The MCA Washington team working with Nicaragua pushed gender from the start, but more significantly, Nicaraguan women's organizations were well organized and ready to meet the MCA toe-to-toe when it arrived.

# 30

## SYLVIA

Nicaragua is the poorest country in Central America, and Central America has many poor countries. It shares much in terms of its history, geography, and people with Honduras. But one big difference it has from Honduras is that the people of Nicaragua fought a long, bloody revolution against their dictatorship. Honduras has had its own dictators, still does in fact, but Hondurans were spared all-out civil war only because their country had a massive military bankrolled by the United States government, which quashed any whisper of revolt before it could grow into a shout.

Perhaps as a result of people organizing themselves for a civil war, Nicaragua has many vibrant grassroots organizations working to solve their particular poverty puzzle. Women's groups in Nicaragua are some of the strongest of any I've seen in the world. Many of the women in these groups fought, lived, and slept in the jungles of Nicaragua for years during the war, right alongside their male counterparts. These women are tough. They do not take no for an answer. They can organize a serious demonstration in a few minutes. They know how to look power in the face and say, "Wrong answer. Try again."

Sylvia Torres is one of these women. I first met Sylvia at the event to announce the MCA's gender policy in January 2007; she sat right next to me on the panel. Sylvia worked for the Nicaraguan government on their MCA program, but she didn't strike me as the usual developing-country government type. She was way too outspoken. Turns out Sylvia didn't actually want that job. But the women's movement talked her into it, and it's a good thing they did.

Sylvia was born into a very poor family from the inner city of León. Many of the families there didn't value education, but hers did for a very unusual reason. Sylvia's uncles, grandfather, and mother worked as janitors at the university. While they would stand in the back of the classrooms waiting to clean the blackboards, they'd soak up the knowledge being shared with the students. They came to value education as a rare and precious gift and put an emphasis on educating their little ones.

"Even though we were poor we went to school and studied hard," Sylvia said. "That was different than other kids in my neighborhood. When girls finished middle school they flew away with their boyfriends. They started having a baby every year and then the violence and poverty would come. I swore I would get out of that neighborhood. I vowed not to marry. Being the oldest, I had to take care of the seven children my mother had."

Sylvia's leadership skills blossomed as she grew up. At age thirteen, she was volunteering at a literacy school, had won a prize for writing, and was a community organizer for clean water. The approach she learned in those early years formed the foundation for her later work in the women's movement and with the MCA. "I would listen to the people closely," Sylvia told me, "and would try to respond to their needs *with* them, not *for* them." She was taking the participatory approach to development, though being just a teenager she didn't realize it. "I learned those years to how to keep up a fight, and later in life I learned to fight with more maturity and grace."

She won a full scholarship to the same university where her family members had worked, coming full circle. After that it was a natural progression into the guerrilla movement. "I never was a fighter," she clarified. "I was an educator and organizer of the rural people. I heard what they said and I understood their lives. I started writing about it in the local papers. That's how I ended up being a journalist. The local newspaper, part of the official Sandinista media, decided to send me to their national paper. I studied how to be a real reporter and ended up with first-page stories!"

It was during this time that Sylvia became part of Nicaragua's vibrant women's movement. "I was part of a group of feminist journalists led by Sophia Montenegro. We started covering issues of regular people, not just politicians and the mainstream agenda. We talked about things that were not fashionable, like ethnicity, women's empowerment, violence, abortion, and rape. Now everybody talks about these things, but not back then."

Knowing that knowledge was power, Sylvia decided she needed to learn English. She found her way to the United States through another scholarship and attended Duke University and the University of Pittsburgh to study anthropology. Sylvia definitely got out, way out, of the neighborhood in which she spent her childhood. Back in Nicaragua, Sylvia returned to the women's movement and was perfectly placed to take on the MCA.

When the MCA landed in Nicaragua, women and their organizations were already a strong part of local development councils, something for which they had fought hard. "At that time, we had already begun to develop women's leadership at the departmental level because the local development councils already existed," Sylvia recounted. "The local mayors wanted us women to participate in smaller committees, not decision-making bodies. We said, 'No, we won't participate under those conditions.'" I could just see Sylvia looking those guys right in the eyes and saying, *"Wrong answer. Try again."* "They said women could chair the health section or women's and children's section, stuff like that," she continued, almost laughing out loud about it. "Women said, 'We are about everything, not just the home.' That's how the women's movement got a seat on each local development council. If we had not done this, we would not have been in a position to negotiate with the MCA when they came."

The MCA was aware Nicaragua already had a structure in place to get local participation in development programs and asked the Nicaraguan government to use this system to develop their proposal. "The MCA was the first megaproject to work with local institutions," Sylvia said. "It broke the pattern of international institutions working from the center of power in the capital city. In a way, I think this was the MCA's greatest contribution—respecting the local institutions that existed at the time, and ensuring that there was accountability and inclusion in the process. That's its legacy." I was happy to hear that the consultation element of the MCA had improved considerably since they were in Sri Lanka and Honduras.

However, it was Nicaraguans, steeped in a culture of machismo, that were the problem. The MCA proposal from Nicaragua had a strong element of rural business development in it, primarily focused on dairy producers. But the proposal was utterly gender blind. Literally. Women were invisible to them. If a dairy farmer was a man, they counted him in their estimate of project beneficiaries. If the farmer was a woman, she didn't exist. The surveyors said they couldn't find *any* female dairy producers. Rural women are all over the Nicaraguan dairy business. They buy raw milk from the (male) ranchers and turn it into an assortment of the most delicious cheeses. Other women buy the cheese products and then walk through town selling them to people on the street. This "industry" provides an income to thousands of women.

Sylvia continued her explanation. "The MCA people from Washington and our government talked about inclusion all the time, but was it going to be real or not? Even though they paid lip service to inclusion, the truth was that it was a gender blind approach. They did not acknowledge women as vital actors in the economy. Everything was directed at men. When they said farmers, they meant male farmers. We knew we had to make them recognize women's role in the economy. The women's movement told the Nicaraguan MCA developers that they could not go forward with the proposal as drafted. Their response was that 'women are housewives.'" Once again, that was the wrong answer.

The women's advocates didn't back down. They got some money and prepared a study about what economic activities women were doing in the area. They sent it to Washington and to the Nicaraguan MCA team. Based on that, the MCA Washington said the Nicaraguans had to redo their proposal design. "It was the women's movement that guaranteed inclusion," Sylvia proclaimed. "Not those who talked about inclusion. Women are more than 50 percent of the population in these areas and vital to the economy. How could they not be included?"

The Nicaraguans made some minor changes in a gesture of compliance to get the money. When the United States and Nicaragua were about to sign the agreement, Congresswoman Nita Lowey of New York arrived to visit with the government and Nicaraguan women's organizations. Women Thrive had fully briefed her on how poorly the Nicaraguan proposal incorporated gender. Representative Lowey did not waste much time on the ground before she said to the American and Nicaraguan MCA officials meeting with her, "I really don't see gender, and the women have told me that they have not had their voices heard."

Representative Lowey said that the Nicaraguan government had fifteen days to present a plan on gender to her or she would not sign off on the project. Representative Lowey, you may recall, is not just any congressperson. She sits on the powerful Appropriations Committee, which holds the purse strings for the MCA. The Nicaraguans, of course, agreed to develop a gender strategy.

"We women worked during long, eight-hour sessions, sometimes more than 300 of us," Sylvia recollected. "We did a complete gender analysis of the current proposal and wrote all of our recommendations." The government included more gender considerations than before but still did not embrace the women's priorities. The MCA Washington requested that Nicaragua include women on their delegation for the important trip to Washington to present the changes to the US decision makers, including Representative Lowey. But at the last minute they did not. "We women were ready to go," Sylvia said. "It was almost as if they pulled us out of our seats on the plane."

That was not going to stop the Nicaraguan women's movement. They sent their recommendations directly to the US embassy and asked that they be forwarded on to the Congress. "All the politicians in León laughed at us saying we were such arrogant women," Sylvia said with a chuckle. "The US embassy was very impressed with the professionalism of the proposal. What they liked the most was that we weren't complaining about being poor, but we were saying to them, 'This is how you can solve the challenge.' This was a huge success for us. It proved that we weren't crazy women! It gave us legitimacy and the inspiration to keep working."

Representative Lowey and the other members of Congress who had visited Nicaragua were not completely satisfied with the proposal the government had submitted, but there was at least a framework to include women, so they did not stand in the way of Nicaragua and the United States signing the project agreement. The Nicaraguans had to create a gender strategy to outline exactly how women were going to be included in the MCA-funded programs.

As you read earlier, Women Thrive had fought hard to get a senior gender adviser hired on at the MCA headquarters in Washington because we knew that if no one were in charge of gender integration, it simply would not happen. We had seen again and again that even if the right words were on paper, if it wasn't anybody's job to make those words reality, it wasn't going to happen. So we also pushed strongly for the MCA's gender policy to require every country to have a gender specialist at a senior leadership level. Nicaragua had to hire someone to create the gender strategy for their overall work and ensure that women were being included all the way along.

Whenever you tell someone in government they should do something, you always run the risk that they'll turn around and hire you to do it. The US government has snatched up quite a few of Women Thrive's people for this very reason, which I consider a mark of success. So be careful what you advocate for. Sylvia was shocked when she got the call asking her to be the senior gender adviser for Nicaragua's MCA program. She was reluctant and kept putting them off for three months straight, but they didn't stop asking her. Her sisters in the movement encouraged her to get on the inside. "I was so reluctant, but I finally decided that I had been fighting for this, and I could do it as the movement dreamt it. I had to keep that commitment to women," she said with a sigh. "The MCA Nicaragua thought I would keep my mouth shut if I was on the payroll. But they were never able to co-opt me."

Sylvia reached back to her teenage leadership years in which she listened carefully to what people wanted. She did not take the top-down approach to gender integration that many organizations do. Her method was to talk to local women and figure out what concretely needed to change to get them access to the projects. Sylvia also drew on her older, wiser self, which knew she had to choose her battles carefully. "I couldn't go asking everybody to become a feminist," she said. "I had to set a clear and realistic goal. So I told my colleagues that we just want women to be part of this program. They could keep their *machista* attitudes, but women must have access."

She's not sure why, but the MCA Nicaragua put Sylvia on the committee that approved all project contracts before they went forward. "They thought it was some menial job just pushing papers around, but it was one of the most powerful positions in the program," Sylvia explained. "Every time I saw a contract that had no gender in it, I wouldn't sign it. They would complain and harass me, but I would say, 'I don't care. I'm not signing.' I would go to the contractor and tell them, 'If you want your contract, I have to sign it. So let me help you. Come and sit with me and I will design with you how to put gender into your work.' "

It didn't take long for the first big confrontation to occur. The American contractor hired by the Nicaraguan government to implement the dairy project only identified twelve male cattle owners. They proposed that 5 percent of the beneficiaries be women. The local women's organization in Western Nicaragua identified 400 women cheese producers. Each of the male cattle owners would hire two additional people through the project, resulting in an employment increase of 24 people. On average, the women cheese producers already each had four employees working for them. If employment was the goal, it made a lot of sense to include women in the project. But the contractor wasn't thinking like that. In its mind, development meant that raw milk should only go to a modern processing facility, be sterilized, put into aseptic little boxes, and sold in supermarkets. Even worse, the contractor's plan could have hurt women. To participate in the MCA project, it was proposed that the cattle owners sign a contract saying they would sell all their milk to the processing plant. They would no longer provide raw milk to the women artisanal cheese makers. "We presented all of this to the contractor, but they had no vision," Sylvia said flatly.

A few months later, the senior agriculture director from the MCC went down to Nicaragua to see how things were going. The head honchos at the MCA Nicaragua did not allow Sylvia to get on his calendar for the trip. "So I waited for him at the entrance of our building and when he came out, I introduced myself," Sylvia told me. "He said, 'You're not on my agenda.' And I said, 'I know, that's why I'm here. Give me five minutes, just five minutes while you eat your lunch. You eat and I'll talk.' He agreed. We spoke for two hours and he became one of my best allies.

"I said to him: 'This project has two indicators—employment and income. You're going to get income, but not employment. And that income is not going to be distributed among the poor. In fact, you are making poverty worse. All the women processors see the MCA as an enemy that's going to ruin their livelihood and the livelihoods of many, many people.'

"So the agriculture director made a huge thing out of it. He called everybody and said that they had to address this issue, that I was going to be in charge, and that I was the boss. It was like God's word. Now they were open to listening. So I presented the study again. And the contractor said they wanted to redo it themselves, because they didn't 'trust the study' we put together! They decided to pay somebody that they trusted. The irony was that their researcher went even further with the conclusion than we did. He even calculated the 'internal rate of return.' He proved that with better practices for making cheese, they could raise the income of women producers by $500 annually, and with more investment they could increase it by $2,000 annually. Ha! They spent all that money because they didn't believe our analysis was correct. And then it came back even better."

Sylvia got her way, of course, and the MCA Nicaragua helped women cheese artisans to modernize their production, improve the quality of their delicacies, and grow their businesses exponentially. "We were able to help almost 40 cheese producers," she said, "and each of those grew their businesses to hire four or five more employees. For each of these women, their workers, and all of their families, it was life changing."

# 31
# BEAUTIFUL CHEESE

On a hot day in July 2013, I sat at Doña Erlinda's street-side *quesillo* stand gratefully enjoying a special treat. It was halfway through the first day of my fifth dollar-a-day experience, this time back in Nicaragua where I first tried to do it on a whim. Doña Erlinda gave me the quesillo for free, and I was very thankful to have some expensive protein, which would be hard to afford on my one-dollar allotment. A quesillo is a thick corn tortilla layered with a disc of boiled farmer's cheese that is soft, chewy, and tart, and then topped off with pickled onions and cream. The cheese has a wonderful consistency that is a little firmer than fresh mozzarella, but still stretchy and moist. Lots of people stop at the stand, hop off their mopeds, and grab a few bags of the delicious and nutritious snack. Doña Erlinda's are particularly sought after.

If a kid could design a grandmother from

scratch, I think she or he would make one like Doña Erlinda. Her deep-set eyes are wise and kind, and the way she looked at me made me feel like she'd understand my thorniest dilemmas and have just the right words of counsel. She's just plump enough for a kid to melt into her lap and fall fast asleep, but not so plump that she couldn't get you in a game of tag. She was wearing a pink T-shirt, bright green cotton skirt, frilly apron, and black grandma shoes with the thick rubber soles and laces just at the top.

Before she started working with MCA, she was one of the ladies who sold the cheese other women would make in their homes. "I would walk all around Managua selling cheese out of a big pan I carried on my head," Doña Erlinda told me as we sat outside her cheese-making room. "I have seven children and that was the only way I could feed them. What I earned on a daily basis was entirely invested in food: rice, beans, and occasionally beef or chicken." Once again, another rock of a woman who did whatever it took to prevent her children from going hungry.

Doña Erlinda never saw herself as a business-woman back then, but she sure does now. "One day a woman came who was with the MCA. She told me that she could help us because the MCA was looking for small entrepreneurs. When she saw me there she thought I had a whole business behind me, but I was just buying the cheese from others and selling it there on the street. When she asked me if I had a source for milk to make the cheese, I immediately said yes. She said, 'Good, I'll be back tomorrow.' I ran home to my neighbor, who knew a dairy farmer, and asked her to get me five gallons of milk so I could show the MCA woman the next day." Doña Erlinda knew she had to do whatever it took to get this opportunity for her family.

The MCA project trained Doña Erlinda and other women on proper food handling, how to make the soft cheese for quesillos, and basic business practices. Doña Erlinda started processing five gallons a day and soon reached the point where she and her family were turning fifteen gallons a day into cheese. "This was the first time in my life I felt I could breathe easily," Doña Erlinda said. "I knew we would have enough money at the end of every day to feed the whole family and send the children to school." The MCA saw that she was taking full advantage of all they were offering and chose her to receive a de-creaming machine, materials to build a separate room for cheese processing, and university classes on business development. It was like water for seeds tucked in fertile soil. Her business has grown so much that five of her family members work with her full time. One brings in the milk; another does the coagulation and creaming process; her daughter-in-law makes the pulled cheese; her daughter tends the street-side shop; her other daughter works the vendor cart at the central park. When her husband is not driving trucks, which he does for a living, he helps bring the milk in and cream it. She decided to name her shop, aptly, Quesillos Mi Familia.

"I feel extremely proud to have been part of the MCA program," Doña Erlinda said with a smile. "I say thanks be to God and to the MCA for bringing us up from where we were. What we've learned has been very useful, and with what we've been able to do, we eat, have a roof over our heads, and the clothing on our bodies. But I don't want to stop there, I want to keep developing." She is hoping to get the mayor's office to help her construct a mini processing plant so she can not only produce more but also pay it forward and teach other women how to make cheese people will love to eat. She learned to fish and fed everyone, and now she's going to teach many other women how to do it too. That's just how women are.

Before we ended our visit, she wanted to add one last thing. "I would just like to make a call for women to continue to struggle," she said. "I know we get tired. I know we get weary. But we can triumph! We are entrepreneurs and we can get ahead. There's a saying that God helps those who get up early. We have to keep that in mind, but we shouldn't wait until dawn to get up."

It made me feel so happy and proud to have

played a part in getting the MCA to support women like Doña Erlinda. Meeting her, and women like her, is the best reward I could ever have. The paramount reward is that the MCA's work in Nicaragua didn't just touch a few women. Out of the almost 6,000 people the MCA assisted in starting or growing new businesses in Nicaragua, 2,641 were women (30 percent).[17] As opposed to Honduras, these are the kind of results I like to see.

Women Thrive's advocacy to get the senior gender adviser position and the gender policy in Washington, combined with Nicaraguan women's persistent activism and smart leveraging of that policy, yielded big dividends for rural women and their families. Nicaragua was a lovely harbinger of a good trend for women and the MCA in other countries, including Burkina Faso, which you'll learn about in Part 3.

# 32

# CARMEN

Juan had been eyeing Carmen for a year before he asked her out. She ran a little fruit smoothie stand next to the school where he studied to be a physical education teacher. He passed her every day, taking in her creamy skin, silky brown hair, and effervescent spirit.

She never noticed him. Carmen didn't pay much attention to the guys around the neighborhood. Overhearing their conversations every day, she considered them ill-bred, vulgar, and only into sports and chasing tail.

But when Juan introduced himself, he seemed different to Carmen. He was well educated, intelligent, dedicated to his courses, and gorgeous. They had been dating for three weeks when he asked her to marry him. She refused and said that she had bigger plans in mind for herself.

I met Carmen on the aloe-covered hillside of COMUCAP's El Mezcalito retreat center in 2009. I was interested in interviewing handicraft producers to understand if and how they got their products into the United States. Carmen ran a project helping local women crafters market their wares to tourists coming through La Paz. She had worked with COMUCAP before, so they connected us. My Spanish was basic and her English was spotty, but somehow we hit it off and within a few minutes knew everything important there was to know about one another: She had a son, I had two, and we were both going through a divorce. We chatted on the bumpy truck rides between handicraft sites like a couple of hens. As she shared more with me it became clear that, while she wasn't living in poverty like the women she was serving, she was going through her own version of hell. Later that evening, we sat down at my hotel with a translator and she told me her whole story.

Carmen Elena Marquez Bautista was born on a coffee farm near Marcala. Her family was neither poor nor rich. During the school year they lived in the city, and during vacations they would go up to the mountain to harvest coffee. "My early childhood was one of the nicest periods of my life," she recalled. "At five in the morning we would be deep into the coffee plantation along with the workers. We would gather coffee for a while, and then all of us, siblings and cousins, would lose interest and play. The plantations are on slopes, so we would slide down the steep hills, or climb trees to eat the oranges and other fruits. My father would catch us and say, 'Aha! And I thought you were picking coffee!'

"For me, it was a marvelous experience. Even though we played a lot, it taught me the meaning of work and gave me a sense of responsibility. My parents instilled moral, Christian values in us, as well as an understanding of how to work together as a family. Even now when I have free time, I go back to the plantation to pick coffee. Harvest is a very happy season.

"Believe it or not, I used to play with boys more than girls. My brother had toy tractors; I would build roads with them, and then put my dolls on the back of the trucks. I loved playing soccer with my cousins and even with my father's workers. It

313

was a constant struggle for my parents. They used to tell me, 'Child, you must play with girls, not with boys!'"

Carmen was not a girl that just did what she was told. She was a free spirit with an iron will, and as she grew up she only became more solid in herself. If I had seen her as a child, I would not have predicted she would fall into the trap she did. But then again, that trap snares many women you would not expect—rich women and poor, educated women and illiterate.

Carmen's two older sisters were already in college when she finished grade school. When she was sixteen, her parents broke the news that they could not pay for her to attend college too. Carmen shrugged her shoulders and said, "I am sorry, but I was not born to stay here and be a housewife. I want to succeed in life and I will do whatever I need to do to have a real job." Carmen packed herself up and went to work in Tegucigalpa as a maid, despite her parent's protests. When she began to feel uncomfortable around the men in her employer's house, she quit and tried to get a job at Hotel La Ronda, where a cousin of hers was working. Her father caught wind of this and went to Tegucigalpa to bring her home. He told her she would be able to study starting the next school year; he would find the money for her. She had won.

The following autumn, Carmen started at a

technical school in business administration in Tegucigalpa. Her family couldn't afford the university, so she chose a practical path to get to her dreams. In her third year, the program required her to start a small enterprise to learn about running a business in the real world. Carmen created the smoothie stand, which was so successful that she and a friend decided to keep it going after they graduated from business school. Still, she had bigger plans.

Carmen had refused Juan's hand in marriage, but unfortunately she did not refuse him in any other way. "I ended up pregnant with my son," she recounted. "I did not know what to do. I felt the sky had fallen down to the earth because I didn't know how I was going to face my parents. That's what I was worried about, facing my parents, nothing else. Not how I was going to take care of my son or how I was going to live. I felt I had betrayed the confidence my parents had in me.

"When I told Juan I was pregnant, he just said, 'What are you worried about? Let's get married.' I knew I wanted to have a home and a family, but not like that, not in such a hurry. He took me home and told my parents we were getting married in a few months. They were surprised, but they accepted it." Others did not take the news as well. Carmen's friends begged her not to marry Juan. "There's something wrong about him," one of her closest friends warned. "He's jealous all the time and he's too possessive." But they didn't know Carmen was pregnant.

"In the end I was married and went to live in Colón to do what I did not want to do, that is, to be completely dedicated to being a housewife. I gave up everything I wanted and tried to be happy with the relationship. I did everything to be, as macho husbands say here, 'the perfect wife.' I was the one who obeys orders, is completely dedicated to her home, is fully devoted to her children, and has no other aspirations than attending to her house and her husband. Deep inside me, I knew that was not who I was."

Carmen's only light was her baby son, and she focused herself completely on that source of joy. "I had incredible dedication to him," she told me, smiling. "I would get up at four in the morning to wash his clothes because I enjoyed doing that by myself. He would only fall asleep in my arms because I never put him down. He made me so happy that I forgot about everything else. But after that first year, I started to realize how I was living. I would think while I was doing laundry, oh my God! What am I doing here? I should be working in an office, sitting at a desk. I should be somewhere else, doing something productive."

That's when she began noticing the changes in Juan. He would come home late, with no explanation. He would go away for days with his friends. He would yell curses at her, insult her, and berate her. "But then I met the wife of one of his friends," Carmen said. "She told me her story and she had it worse. Her husband hit her. Everyone knew that he was unfaithful and a drunk. When she went to work, he would go out with other women openly on the streets. So I would say to myself, 'Well, mine is not so bad, I can bear it.'" Or so she thought.

Years went by and Carmen became pregnant again. That's when she found out about Juan's affair with a girl in their small town. He denied it, of course. But now when Juan yelled at Carmen, she yelled back. "I was no longer the humble woman who spoke in hushed tones," she said. It was just gasoline on Juan's fire. "Things got much worse. He wanted to hit me and I would say to him, 'If you are going to hit me, you'd better kill me, because if you leave me alive, I will kill you or put you in jail.'" Carmen's voice was hard and angry as she told me this. "That was the only way, because he is six feet tall and strong. I could only defend myself from that man with the words coming out of my mouth.

"After that, the strong abuse began. I had a cruel pregnancy. I started having problems and almost lost my baby. I would spend every day at the doctor's office being medicated to prevent my baby from coming out, lying down with my feet up. When I was about seven months pregnant, a woman came to my house and told me, 'Right now Juan is with his girlfriend at the bar downtown.' We had a gun at the house; I put it in my robe pocket and ran out. I was running, running crazy uphill for some twelve blocks. Someone told him I was coming and so she was gone when I got there. If I had found him there with her, I was going to shoot that woman. I was crazy. I had lost all judgment. I was resentful and hurt. I was so in love with him, I believe, at that moment. It was so strange, because when I married him I was not very in love, but somehow while being with him I fell in love."

How sad and common that is. Even strong-willed women can be caught in the undertow of the abuse-then-adore cycle. A man hits and then in deep remorse buys roses, chocolates, and says sweet things. Women forgive and soak up the temporary affection.

The gun in Carmen's pocket didn't deter Juan from going out with his girlfriend. When someone told Carmen that Juan was, once again, out around town with his lover, she snapped. She went home from the doctor's office, threw her clothes in the car, grabbed her son, and started driving home to Marcala. Someone called Juan and he caught up with her after about 70 miles. Carmen told Juan she didn't need him to take care of herself and her children; that she would do just fine on her own. But somehow, the day ended with her back at home with him.

"My daughter died inside me," Carmen said with tears coursing down her face. My heart sank when she said those words. "That is truly what I cannot recover from." Her voice quivered. "I always wanted to have a daughter. When I saw her and she was dead, the pain was profound. She would be seven years old now, eight this August."

Carmen continued her story after we sat in silence for a while, letting the pain of her loss dissipate. "I made the decision to go back to studying and begin a new career in teaching. I thought, well, this man is no longer my priority; my priorities are my son and my studies. But just the same, the problems continued. He was at his worst behavior. If he ended a relationship with one woman, he would start another with a different woman. I became hard and indifferent."

Carmen was getting ahead in her career as a teacher and working at the same school as Juan, but in September 2006, the problems intensified. Juan not only had a student as a lover, but he was also seeing a coworker. What's more, Carmen discovered that he had a years-old relationship with a married woman, with whom he had a daughter! "She was a little girl the exact same age as my daughter would have been," Carmen sighed, and I winced. Just as Carmen's baby died inside her, another daughter was being born to Juan.

One day, Carman was with a friend working on some school projects. Juan had left the house three days before. "He called me and asked, 'Where are you?' I said, 'I am with my friend Adilia doing some work.'" Juan thought Carmen was lying and was with another man. "That made him crazy," Carmen continued. "He told me, 'Carmen, if you have any shame, go home, take your things, and leave.' So I went home and started putting things together, but he followed me all over the house, so I couldn't pack anything. And then he lost it. He hit me hard. I grabbed my son and ran out of the house."

The following day, Carmen went to the police station to file a lawsuit and have them arrest Juan. "Within five minutes the whole world was there—all his friends, the mayor, the deputy mayor, everyone. 'What happened?' they asked me. So I told them, 'Your friend is in jail because of domestic violence, that's what happened. With all of you gathered here, the only things missing are your poker cards and beer so you can have a party.'

"I told the police, 'If this man kills me it will be your fault. You have let him stay free. I am a victim of domestic violence and you don't know how violent he can be.' They said, 'Well, at least you filed the claim.' And I said, 'Aha, so you're saying a record will be there stating that Carmen Elena filed a claim, and even so, the man was let go and then he killed his wife.' It is incredible! In this country there is no justice for us women. That is why they kill us!

"I was furious. From that point on, I started letting out the real Carmen Elena I am, the one who does not stand to be humiliated, to have her rights violated, to be manipulated, or to let people succeed in their misdeeds just because they have connections and because we live in a country riddled with corruption."

Juan fought back in the worst way possible—he would not let Carmen take her son with her when she left him. "I was staying with my friend, and he would come to her house with my son and beg me to come back. I said to myself, 'No. No more, Carmen Elena. No more humiliations.' So I called him one day and asked him to come over. I had all my son's things and told him, 'OK, you won the war. You wanted my son. So here it is: these are his clothes, these are his toys, and these are his documents. Here you have them, because even if you take my son, I will not stay.'"

Carmen tried to figure out how she could get her son back through legal means. But the only way was to go take the boy out of the house with the police and the Human Rights commissioner. "I did not want to traumatize my son," Carmen said. "I did not want to expose him to that ordeal. It was too much. That day I cried like a crazy woman. I thought I would die from crying. But I did not die.

The next day, I woke up and took the first bus to Marcala. I left with a broken soul because my son stayed with his father. I went into a deep depression. I knew I had to continue living, but I didn't want to."

# 33

# FACING THE FACTS

Right now, as you read this, a girl of maybe ten or even eight is pinned down to a cold concrete floor by a hairy, sweaty man-beast, being raped for the first time as her initiation into forced prostitution. A refugee mother is performing fellatio on some man and vomiting up his semen to get the daily ration for her kids. At this very moment, a teenage girl with just-budding breasts is screaming as a soldier rips off her tattered dress and pushes her toward a broken bed with his bayonet.

While the statistics don't give you these images, they show that this is the mathematical truth. It is mind-blowing. The scale of violence is so massive and its reach so pervasive that it is a rough and ugly thread in the fabric of women and girls' daily lives. The most recent research from around the world finds that 35 percent or more of women will experience violence at some point in her lifetime.[18] An earlier survey conducted by the

World Health Organization (WHO), PATH (a global health research organization), and the London School of Hygiene and Tropical Medicine in fifteen locations across ten countries found that up to half of girls ages fifteen to nineteen have experienced physical or sexual violence from an intimate partner.[19]

Let me rephrase that in case it didn't hit you in the stomach: Up to half of teenage girls had been or were currently being abused by boyfriends or husbands. Not all those girls between fifteen and nineteen even had intimate partners, so among those that were in a relationship, the rate was even higher. What if boys at your child's high school were roughing up half of the girls? Can you imagine parents and teachers *not* going nuts about it? But for girls in the ten countries studied, basically no one gives a damn.

Here's more: WHO did a comprehensive and carefully developed global survey on violence against women in 2005. They found that in sub-Saharan Africa, between 36 and 71 percent of women have experienced physical or sexual violence at the hands of a husband or intimate partner.[20] Again, let me rephrase. The *lowest* rate they found was that more than one-third of women have been abused at some point. That's incredible.

What is even more disturbing is that in many countries women themselves felt that the violence against them was justified. More than 60 percent of women in rural Ethiopia thought that a husband's beating was justified if she didn't complete her housework. More than 40 percent of women in rural Peru believed the same thing. If a woman disobeyed her husband, almost 80 percent of rural Ethiopian women felt that wife-beating was appropriate; about 50 percent of women in Tanzania and rural Peru agreed. Our challenge is not only convincing men that violence against women and girls is wrong; we have to educate *women and girls* that it's wrong too.

A 2010 survey by UN Women found that 87 percent of Afghan women were beaten on a regular basis.[21] The *American Journal of Public Health* reported that 1,152 women—that's 48 per hour—were raped daily in Congo in 2011.[22]

Shall I go on? I think you get the picture.

Gathering accurate data on violence is tricky. You can't just walk door to door with a clipboard and ask women if they've been raped or beaten lately. The statistics I cite come from highly reliable sources that carry out their surveys in adherence with strict ethical guidelines and rigorous protocols. These are real numbers, not flimsy estimates based on hearsay. The WHO study defined physical and sexual violence very specifically so there would be no room for interpretation about what is or isn't really violence. Their definitions are in the box on page 325.

# World Health Organization Descriptions of Physical and Sexual Violence

Prevalence estimates of physical and sexual violence were obtained by asking direct, clearly worded questions about the respondent's experience of specific acts. For physical violence, women were asked whether a current or former partner had ever:

- Slapped her, or thrown something at her that could hurt her
- Pushed or shoved her
- Hit her with a fist or something else that could hurt
- Kicked, dragged, or beaten her up
- Choked or burned her on purpose
- Threatened her with or actually used a gun, knife, or other weapon against her

Sexual violence was defined by the following three behaviors:

- Being physically forced to have sexual intercourse against her will
- Having sexual intercourse because she was afraid of what her partner might do
- Being forced to do something sexual she found degrading or humiliating[27]

If you think that violence only hurts the woman or girl taking the beating, think again. The costs to businesses, health care systems, and educational achievement are staggering. A survey in India found that women who experienced even a single episode of violence lost seven working days on average.[23] A World Bank study estimated that Colombian women who suffer physical abuse have 14 percent lower earnings than women who do not experience violence. This added up to a 4 percent loss in gross domestic product for Colombia in 2003.[24] That's serious money.

Boys and girls pay a price too when their mothers are abused, beyond the trauma of it all. An academic study found that children of women victims of violence in Nicaragua left school an average of four years earlier than children whose mothers were not abused.[25] When their moms are violated, children have lower rates of immunization, higher rates of diarrheal disease, and are more likely to die before age five than other kids.[26] When boys witness their father or a male authority figure abusing women, it can become their template for male-female relationships. Violence is an injustice that multiplies injustice.

I believe it's the unquantifiable impacts of violence that are most profound. Like the nightmares that make you relive the rape or the flashbacks that intrude persistently during the day.

The way it's impossible to think about anything else for months, making it difficult to complete any productive task. Lots of women fall into a pit of debilitating depression, especially if they must keep the violence a secret. Others who have been tortured or brutally abused might leave their bodies emotionally and spiritually and become like walking dead.

Sexual violence to me is the very essence of evil. It reaches into the most precious part of a woman—the place where she creates new life and experiences the pleasures that come with being human—and rips it out of her, sometimes literally. Recovery is a long, hard, and painful road, even with access to counseling. Most women never even have the chance to walk that road. For too many women survivors, reclaiming self-esteem, feeling alive, and enjoying their God-given sexuality are impossible.

And that right there is the goal of sexual violence: to break a woman's association of sex with pleasure, and even more so, to isolate her from the power within her. From an individual point of view, violence serves to keep a woman or girl under the thumb of a man. From a global point of view, violence against one-third of all women and girls, with the other two-thirds living in fear, keeps *all* women down. This is the ultimate cost of violence. It robs the world of inconceivable amounts of creative, brilliant, and probably earth-changing contributions from half of the human race.

This distorted balance of power between men and women on a massive scale is killing the human race and our planet. The innate male drives to build and demolish and to hunt and survive are not necessarily horrible. But when they are not balanced by female energy to restore, cooperate, and live in harmony, things go haywire. The way forward is to bring the power between men and women into balance on a global scale. To do that, we must end violence against women and girls.

People often ask me if that's even possible. They say that we can't realistically protect every woman and girl out there. And we can't change all men either. My response? Ask women survivors of violence what they think is possible. When we at Women Thrive decided to address violence on a large scale, that's what we did. We started with women working at the grassroots level directly on the problem. Over a period of six months in 2005, we interviewed more than 40 organizations worldwide, as well as survivors and violence program experts. We had two big questions: What works, and what should the United States do to help? Here's what we heard loud and clear:

- **This is a big problem that needs big solutions.** That means governments have to be involved, from passing and enforcing laws against violence, to running massive public education programs, to setting up health care systems that identify and treat survivors. Charities cannot address this pandemic alone.

- **The US government absolutely should get involved.** In fact, women thought that US leadership on violence against women and girls would boost their efforts by simply bringing more attention to the issue, even if the United States didn't put any new money on the table. Violence is a gross violation of human rights, and if the United States wants to be a global leader on human rights, this issue cannot be ignored.

- **Trust women at the local level to know how to get things done.** Women who live and breathe their culture and religion every day know the best ways to navigate the sensitive and dangerous topic of violence. Muslim women know how to tap the Quran to show that Islam does not condone violence against women and girls. African women know how to talk to their village chief about how violence against girls in their community reflects poorly on the chief's leadership. Trusting local women is also the way to inoculate America from intentionally or unintentionally engaging in cultural imperialism. The United States should support the women on the ground who are already doing great work and avoid the mistake we make so many times—setting up a well-meaning but tone-deaf new infrastructure to deliver programs.

- **Focus on preventing violence, not just dealing with the consequences of it.** The American approach to violence against women and girls in our own country has largely focused on services for survivors (which are good) and on law enforcement capturing and prosecuting perpetrators (which is also good). However, in most developing countries, women won't take advantage of services because of the stigma or danger involved. In addition, their legal systems are corrupt, dysfunctional, or both. The best way to approach it is to stop the violence from happening in the first place. In the long run, it's also much cheaper.
- **Work with men and boys too.** Both men and women in many developing countries think violence is an acceptable means of communicating within human relationships, not because they are inherently flawed as people, but because this is what they have learned. They can unlearn it as well. There are programs all over the world to change how people think about family planning, from soap operas and billboards to political

speeches and street theater. We can employ the same kinds of techniques to alter the way people think about violence. Reaching men and boys with new ways of thinking is especially effective. They are thirsty for it. In fact, the number of male allies from all quarters grows each day. Organizations like Promundo and Men Engage are leading this new movement. Men can be some of the most persuasive and effective messengers.

- **Weave antiviolence interventions into health, education, and economic projects.** If you hang out a shingle saying, "Come on in for your violence prevention and recovery services," women are not going to rush in and partake. In many societies, including our own, being a survivor is a low-status position. However, when women and men are participating in a project to improve their health, and antiviolence discussions are just part of the health care curriculum, they accept it and behavior does change.

- **Boost women's economic independence, especially their ownership of property.** The data are now irrefutable. If women own real assets like land, livestock, a house, or money in a bank account (rather than in a bra), it prevents violence against them. A number of studies have correlated women's ownership of land or property to decreased rates of domestic violence. A woman's status within her relationship is elevated if she has her own money or property. And if she is abused, she is able to leave that situation without completely risking her own well-being and that of her children. A rigorous study in Uganda by world-class researchers at the International Center for Research on Women found that "cash holding is associated with a seventeen percentage point lower likelihood of experiencing such violence."[28]

- **Talk to the men with the guns.** Women from around the world were crystal clear about this one: Military and police forces must stop being the instigators of violence against women and girls, especially rape, and start fulfilling their obligation to protect. Sadly, it is not uncommon for international peacekeepers to take advantage of their status and guns, temporary residence in a foreign land, and the chaotic situations they find themselves in to sexually exploit or violate women and girls. The United States funds peacekeeping missions to numerous volatile areas and, like it or not, also gives huge amounts of training support to militaries and police forces around the world. The US military can play a very positive role by including in their training for foreign forces information on why abuse of women is unacceptable, how to prevent it, and what to do to stop it when it happens. And our government can also push for this training of peacekeepers when we are footing some of the bill. At a bare minimum, the US military must have zero tolerance for violence against women and girls within its own ranks, including partaking in prostitution, sex trafficking, or sexual assault.

Our marching orders were clear. The next question we had to answer was, What was the US government already doing on this issue? We knew we couldn't get that information ourselves as a bunch of nonprofit folks, so we went to Representative Nita Lowey, our most reliable ally, and asked if she would get the Congressional Research Service (CRS) to do a quick report on the current US response to gender-based violence globally. It is CRS's job to nose around the government and find things out for members of Congress, and when CRS calls, people answer the phone. Of course Representative Lowey said yes. The answer came back many months later: US government agencies had small, uncoordinated projects here and there. No one was tracking how much money was being spent on violence prevention and treatment. And it was far from being a priority for anyone.[29]

While we waited for the CRS report findings, we decided that a way to have immediate impact was to get the US government to put some money into the United Nations Trust Fund to Eliminate Violence Against Women. The Trust Fund is the biggest source of funds for local women's organizations around the world that do anti-violence programs. The application process is rigorous but navigable for small women's groups, and the Trust Fund evaluates its grantees' work extremely well. Since the US government wasn't contributing anything, there was nowhere to go but up. Working shoulder-to-shoulder with Amnesty International USA, Futures Without Violence (formerly the Family Violence Prevention Fund), International Center for Research on Women, and the National Spiritual Assembly of Bahá'ís, we began campaigning for the Trust Fund.

In 2004, the Trust Fund had only $987,000, most of which came from Spain. Our triumvirate coalition (Amnesty/Women Thrive/Futures) went up to Capitol Hill and got $1.5 million for the Trust Fund, effectively expanding its budget by 150 percent. We continued to push every year for a more respectable US donation, and in 2011, we got it up to a high of $3 million. Since 2005, we've leveraged almost $14 million from the US government for the Trust Fund's work. I'm really proud of that.

But the Trust Fund could use a lot more money. In 2012, they got requests from groups around the world totaling $1.06 billion, but they could only support $8.4 million worth across nineteen countries.[30] Even if half of those programs are worth supporting, the Trust Fund needs $494.6 million more.

It was a good but small start. We had to do something much bigger and better. Women and girls deserved nothing less.

# 34

# BIGGER AND BETTER— THE INTERNATIONAL VIOLENCE AGAINST WOMEN ACT

Our coalition of organizations was fired up by our success in getting more money for the Trust Fund. We decided to take on the ambitious task of developing a piece of major legislation. There were a lot of reasons to do this.

First, the only way to make the US government do something permanently is to pass a law. Otherwise, it is just at the initiative of a president, and presidents change. I have witnessed grand programs for women and girls at the highest levels of the White House and State Department shrivel into dormancy in the basement of the same White House and State Department under the very next president. If programs for women and girls are written into the law, that can't happen.

Second, it was abundantly clear that President George W. Bush was not going to pick up the issue of violence against women and girls as his cause célèbre. He had chosen instead to put his international affairs political capital behind the creation of the President's Emergency Plan for AIDS Relief (PEPFAR) and the MCA, both great new programs. But this meant the leadership would have to come from Congress.

Finally, and not insignificantly, we wanted to design the architecture for a US response to violence against women and girls globally to stay true to what we heard from women and girls around the world. That meant that we, with our allies on Capitol Hill, needed to craft the legislation ourselves.

You may be a bit surprised to hear me say, "We craft legislation." You might be thinking, "Doesn't Congress do that?" Well, sometimes they do. However, the vast majority of legislation is actually developed first by public interest nonprofits, trade associations, or the private lobbyists everyone loves to hate. The truth is that most congressional staff people each cover four or five gigantic issue areas at once. Lots of the aides we work with don't only lead on foreign affairs or women's issues, they are also responsible for things like Social Security, Veterans Affairs, environment, and small business administration, all at the same time. Very few congressional aides are lucky enough to specialize in any one area. They are ridiculously busy and not able to be expert on every single issue. They really have to focus on working Capitol Hill and keeping their bosses on the right track.

It is actually a very good thing that thousands of organizations with deep expertise take time to research, consult with others, identify the best solutions, and share those with Congress. It does mean that different groups will propose different solutions—often diametrically opposed solutions based on their particular point of view or constituency. But to me, that is the beauty of democracy. People should get together with others, generate ideas, and then debate them in the public space. It's messy and overwhelming, but the alternatives are worse. Thousands of people are fighting (and dying) right now to have the right to engage with their government in that same way.

Let me be clear, however. As outside groups, we can draft legislation, propose legislation, and comment on legislation, but we cannot actually *write* legislation. At the end of the day, members of Congress, their staffs, and their lawyers do the writing. They hear our proposals, read our drafts, understand our arguments, and then make it their own. The members that lead the introduction of legislation, called sponsors, decide what goes into it. We don't always get everything we want. There's a natural push and pull. Our job as advocates for women and girls is to push for as much as we think we can get, and then push for some more, but without breaking the relationship with sponsors. The sponsor's job is to pull out the best of what they hear, add their own knowledge and experience to the mix, and decide what is politically possible without losing the support of us advocates.

Nonprofit organizations are allowed to work on legislation and lobby without losing their tax-exempt status as long as it's just a portion of their work. Those that wholly devote themselves to lobbying are not charities; they are political advocacy organizations that cannot receive tax-deductible contributions.

In 2006, our coalition approached Senator Richard Lugar, a Republican from Indiana and the chairman of the Senate Foreign Relations Committee, to inquire if he might be interested in sponsoring the first International Violence Against Women Act (IVAWA). We needed to start at the top of the committee; there's an unspoken rule that the chairman has first right of refusal for any legislation emanating from his committee. We didn't think he'd be that keen on it because he's not known for his feminist perspectives, but his office was enthusiastically interested. In their view, violence against women and girls was a human issue, not a partisan one. We were beyond thrilled. To have a male Republican head-of-the-key-committee lead IVAWA would send just the right messages to every member of Congress: This is a big deal and this transcends politics.

Senator Lugar's team was outstanding. We worked as hard and fast as we could, but they couldn't complete the legislation and introduce it before the November 2006 elections. It was no fault of theirs. Creating a new piece of legislation as important as IVAWA takes many months, sometimes years. The Democrats took control of the Senate in that midterm election by a margin of one seat. Starting January 2007, Senator Lugar would no longer be chairman of the Foreign Relations Committee. We had to go ask the new guy if he wanted to sponsor IVAWA: senator, now vice president, Joe Biden from Delaware.

Senator Biden was the original lead sponsor of the US Violence Against Women Act (VAWA)—the domestic "older sister" legislation of IVAWA. The US VAWA was first passed in 1995 and has helped significantly reduce violence against women in the United States over the last eighteen years. Senator Biden was very excited to be in the lead. His office didn't ostracize Senator Lugar's, however. They operated in a truly cooperative, bipartisan manner, the best I've ever seen in my 23 years working with Congress.

New heavy-hitter organizations joined our coalition and brought their expertise—and thousands of supporters—to the table. The International Center for Research on Women provided the top-notch research that grounded the ideas in the bill. The International Rescue Committee led the way on how to reduce violence against women in humanitarian emergencies. CARE jumped in with their 75 years of experience in children and women's protection. American Jewish World Service brought to bear their knowledge from funding grassroots women's organizations around the world for decades.

Together, we constructed the most cutting-edge legislation to internationally address violence against women of its time. The bill was a kind of 360-degree strategy to prevent, and eventually eliminate, gender-based violence. The following were some of the most important provisions of the act:

1. **IVAWA put one person in charge of the task for the US government.** If no one is really in charge, things tend not to happen in the world of government. So IVAWA proposed a new office inside the State Department—the Office of Global Women's Initiatives—to "design, oversee, and

coordinate activities and programs of the United States Government relating to international women's issues," including efforts to "prevent and respond to violence against women and girls throughout the world." An ambassador at large, who would report directly to no one else but the secretary of state, would lead this office.

2. **IVAWA called for a coherent whole-of-government strategy to reduce gender-based violence.** Putting the strategy together required a review of what everyone was already doing across the government, a very useful undertaking. It also required conversations between government folks and the women's community to ensure that what women wanted remained front and center. The strategy had to have the following basic tenets:

- Don't try to save the whole world; just pick ten countries with severe levels of violence against women and girls.
- Analyze what the country governments and local organizations were already doing and decide if there were opportunities for good work to happen. If not, the country should not be included in the strategy because taxpayer resources would likely be wasted there.
- Identify who, both within the US

government and among international partners, was going to do what. Don't duplicate what another actor might be doing in the country; look for where the US government could add unique value.

3. **IVAWA encouraged a comprehensive approach to reducing violence rather than a silver bullet.** Just as women asked for, IVAWA supported legal system reform, a variety of health care initiatives, public awareness programs to change social norms and attitudes, improvements in women's economic opportunities, and better educational attainment for women and girls.

4. **IVAWA talked to the men with the guns**. It mandated that US training for foreign military and police forces include instruction on preventing and responding to violence against women and girls.

5. **IVAWA demanded attention for mass outbreaks of violence against women and girls.** The bill required the secretary of state, director of national intelligence, and the secretary of defense to take action when women and girls were being raped or otherwise brutalized as a weapon of war.

It was a very special moment when I held that baby in my hands, all 59 pages of her, for the first time.

# 35

# LEGISLATIVE LABYRINTH

The next three years of pushing IVAWA through Congress were like being in the Minotaur's labyrinth. Just when we'd cleared one hurdle, another one jumped out at us and took a swipe.

Getting a bill introduced into Congress is just one step on a long journey through that labyrinth. A bill sponsor won't generally move a bill until there is enough support to ensure that it will pass through a committee vote and a vote on the floor of the full House or Senate. Our coalition had some heavy lifting to do to familiarize members of Congress with IVAWA, gather up support from the committee members, and recruit a critical mass of Republicans to cosponsor the bill. Just getting the bill placed on the agenda of the Foreign Relations Committee takes a number of committee members asking the chairman to do it. Senator Biden and his committee had their hands full with the wars in Iraq and Afghanistan, the Nuclear Nonproliferation Treaty, and numerous other foreign policy crises. And then he got even busier in early 2008 running on the White House ticket with fellow senator Barack Obama. We also had to get IVAWA introduced into the House of Representatives. Representative Howard Berman, a Democrat from the Los Angeles area, was the chairman of the House's parallel Committee on Foreign Affairs, and he agreed to take up the mantle. But with Senator Biden out of pocket, we knew all we could do was try to set the stage to push IVAWA through in the next Congress.

We pulled out all the stops for the next two years. Senator John Kerry from Massachusetts, who is now secretary of state, took over the committee and the bill from newly elected Vice President Biden. Congressman Bill Delahunt, a Democrat from Massachusetts, offered to sponsor the House version of IVAWA. We also acquired a very unlikely but incredibly dedicated ally from Texas: pro-life Republican Ted Poe. He was a former state prosecutor who had won convictions against men that committed heinous acts of violence against women and girls. Working together, the coalition got one-third of the *entire* Congress to cosponsor the bill. Several organizations around the IVAWA table pitched in and we bought $50,000 worth of ads in *Politico Magazine*, which Hill staffers read every morning. Working with UN Women, we even managed to get Nicole Kidman, their goodwill ambassador, to come to Capitol Hill and testify on IVAWA at a House hearing. She didn't mince words at the hearing when she said, "Violence against women is not prosecuted because it is not a top government and urgent social priority. We can change this by exerting leadership, making wise investments and building local partnerships. . . . IVAWA represents an effective cross-cutting approach that elevates the issue so it will count and be counted."[31] We recruited religious leaders from the Christian, Muslim, and Jewish faiths to throw their weight behind the bill. Amnesty, CARE, International Rescue Committee, and many other coalition members asked their thousands of supporters to write and call Capitol Hill and urge them to pass IVAWA.

The sun really came out on women's issues at the State Department the day Hillary Clinton became secretary of state. One of the first things she did was create the Office of Global Women's Issues, a move right out of the IVAWA playbook (we called it the Office of Global Women's Initiatives, but who cares?). She appointed her longtime friend and adviser, Melanne Verveer, as the ambassador at large. Ambassador Verveer was one of the very few people who could call Secretary Clinton in the middle of the night and get through to her. It meant that when Verveer spoke, you could assume the words could have come from the lips of the secretary. It made the ambassador one of the most powerful people at the State Department. Our IVAWA coalition was ecstatic. We pushed the Senate hard to vote in favor of Verveer's confirmation. Women Thrive made behind-the-scenes calls to assuage fears among conservative members that Verveer and her office would promote abortion overseas.

Abortion politics had become another big, ugly monster in the labyrinth with us. It was getting to the point in Congress that if any bill had the word "woman" in it, it became a battleground for abortion politics. We had worked incredibly hard to keep the issue of abortion out of IVAWA. There was unwritten agreement with both pro-choice and pro-life cosponsors of IVAWA that this bill would not become another place for either side to wage a war on abortion.

However, as soon as passage of the bill looked likely, the US Conference of Catholic Bishops (USCCB) started to focus on it. If the bishops say no to something, it can be very difficult for pro-life members of Congress to support it and still keep the bishops' support. We went around in circles with the pro-choice community and the USCCB. We tried various different combinations of words—even altering the definition of violence—to come up with a solution acceptable to everyone. If one side said they could swallow it painfully, the other side said they would oppose IVAWA if those particular words were in it.

By August 2010, we knew our window was closing. It was looking like the Republicans were going to take the House, Senate, or both in the upcoming midterm election. With abortion now in the mix, we were left with only one very unsavory option: pass the bill with only Democrats voting for it. Our coalition had bent over backward to keep IVAWA above the bloody partisan fights. Allowing it to go there was a high-risk strategy.

Senator Kerry agreed to put IVAWA on the committee calendar for late August, right before Congress went into recess. We didn't know exactly when that meeting was going to take place. At that point in the congressional year, nothing is scheduled very far in advance. Committee meetings spring up with a few hours' notice; we were lucky and got about a day's notice. We called every single Democratic senator on the committee to make sure they were going to show up for that particular vote. They all said they'd be there—but they weren't. Senator Kerry had to pull IVAWA off the agenda. When I got the news that IVAWA had been withdrawn because not enough Democrats turned up for the vote, I was so angry I could barely breathe. Of all the bills I'd worked on over twenty years, I'd never seen one go down because members just didn't show up for a committee meeting. Sometimes members intentionally miss a vote, but the senators that didn't show were solid yesses. Congress would be back in session for a few weeks that September, and maybe again in December for a lame-duck session postelection, so we had another chance. Even so, if IVAWA passed the Senate Foreign Relations Committee, it would still have to pass the House Foreign Affairs Committee, the full Senate and House floors, have the differences between the House and Senate versions worked out, and then passed again by the full House and Senate. That's six different votes, and each of them would require huge effort.

# 36

# TURNING TABLES

W hen I lost my son, I was so depressed that I had no interest in anything." Carmen continued her narrative where we spoke at my hotel in Marcala about her struggles. "I had to be forced to pee, to change clothes, to get up and eat something; it was a horrible depression. I felt that without my son I would die. But I knew I had to continue living because one day my son would come back."

One of the leaders of COMUCAP, who knew Carmen from her childhood, told her about a wonderful job opportunity in Marcala (the job she was in when I met her). Although she had to scrape herself off the floor and pat her swollen eyes with makeup, Carmen went to the interview. She noticed that her potential employers were listening to her very carefully, and she left feeling surprised but happy. They offered her the job. Maybe her luck was changing.

But Juan would not leave her be. He'd call every day begging for her to take him back. He'd come to Marcala every weekend with her son, using him as lure. "Every time he left with my son, my heart would break. What a terrible situation! I knew that Juan did not mean anything to me, but my son was everything. It got to the point that I could not get Juan out of my house. One day he showed up at my house with all his things, saying he was willing to do whatever it took to save the relationship. I believed absolutely nothing he said, but I wanted to get my son back. So I told him, 'Okay, you can stay here, but you are in a trial period.'"

Juan didn't like the life Carmen had built for herself. "When he saw the work I was doing, all the meetings and travel, going for days to Tegucigalpa, and being invited to conferences, he could not stand it. When I came back home, he would take my cell phone and start going through it to see how many calls I made and how many male names were in my phone. I would think to myself, *The moment will come when this bomb will explode, sooner or later, because we will not stand each other.*

"One day I got a call for a special assignment over the weekend. Juan was not at home; he was still involved with his coworker at the old school and he would disappear with her for days. So I took my son and left. When I came back, he was very angry. I told him, 'I'm sorry, but I will never again leave my job to please you. Those times are over.' He said to me, 'You are not even the shadow of the woman I knew. Who have you become? You are such an arrogant, haughty woman.' I replied, 'It is not that I am arrogant and haughty, but now I defend myself and I don't let you humiliate me.' I no longer allowed him that. I was in my own home and I was not going to give him that. If he wanted to, he could humiliate himself, but not me. Not anymore.

"That night he attacked me. He was close to strangling me. I said to myself, 'This really is the end because if I don't separate from this man, he will kill me.'" The next day she found a divorce lawyer and sued Juan for domestic violence. She went to the forensics office, which issued a report that showed the marks his hands left on her neck and documented that he was close to asphyxiating her. She won a restraining order. He could not get closer than three blocks from her house, her office, or her.

"The judge also gave me custody of my son, ordered Juan to pay me child support, and said that I could let my son be with Juan whenever I wanted, or not at all. I thought, Look at how the roles have changed. Now I have my son and I am the one setting the rules. Juan had to go back to Colón."

Carmen had also bought her family's coffee farm. "When I leave my house now I can breathe. I feel alive. I am a happy woman. I go wherever I want to go and I do whatever I want to do. If I want to let Juan be with my son, I do, but if I don't want to, I don't.

"Ritu, good always triumphs over evil. I have suffered a lot and there are things I have not recovered from, that I have not overcome, and that hurts. But I am very well without Juan. I feel that life smiles on me now. I am happy to have met you and I hope that this story might be useful as an example for so many women who are victims of domestic violence and who cannot lift up their heads. In this country, there are thousands of deaths due to domestic violence. Right here in this town, a husband cut off the hands of his wife. He left her crippled and with five children. And do you know why? Because she put him in jail and they let him out. I can't stand it. When I find out about women who are victims of domestic violence, I go and talk to them. I tell them how they can start freeing themselves. I tell them that they have to come out, raise their heads, and nurture their self-esteem. The problem is that when one is buried there, deep under violence, one loses even oneself."

# 37

# GOOD ALWAYS TRIUMPHS

Senator Kerry didn't put IVAWA back on the committee agenda again until December 14, 2010, during the lame-duck session after the election. The Republicans were going to own the House of Representatives in the next Congress beginning January 2011. They had no incentive to work out a solution on abortion for IVAWA. They could just wait until the new year and then call the shots. The partisan speechifying during the 2010 election was downright disgusting. The vituperative and nasty attacks both sides made during the election destroyed the historically polite decorum on the House and Senate floors. Facts no longer made any difference. Getting things done was not the objective; in fact, many members of Congress made obstruction their sole purpose. The rhetoric on international issues emanating from some of those mouths made former senator Jesse Helms, a superconservative from North Carolina, look like a hippie.

That was the backdrop against which the IVAWA vote in Senator Kerry's committee took place. When he placed the bill on the table for debate, the Republicans made statements pledging their allegiance to the world's women and girls. And then, each and every one of them voted against IVAWA, even Senator Richard Lugar, the man who helped create IVAWA in the first place. The bill was still approved since there were more Democrats than Republicans, both on the committee and in the room that day.

Technically it was a win for IVAWA, but I felt sick about it. Women and girls, who were fighting for their lives every day, got caught in the dual political buzz saws of abortion and partisan politics.

One big reason we couldn't pass IVAWA that year was because we didn't have *you.* Our coalition got hundreds of Americans to call and write Congress, but it wasn't enough. We needed tens of thousands to call, write, meet with, and demand that Congress pass IVAWA. In early 2013, when Congress needed to re-up the programs contained in the domestic Violence Against Women Act, they started playing political football with it. The roar that arose from American women scared them so badly they put away their usual partisan playbook and passed VAWA in a few days' time. It was like Congress got a collective purse-whack upside the head from women. That is what it's going to take to pass IVAWA. At the end of this section, I'm going to show you how to join the movement and help us get this done for women and girls *everywhere.*

But for the IVAWA in 2011, Congress was a lost cause for the moment. We would have to go to the White House to get something done. Before the end of the year, Women Thrive organized a coalition leadership meeting with Tina Tchen, head of the White House Council on Women and Girls, to push the administration to create a comprehensive strategy to address gender-based violence globally in lieu of IVAWA. As a result of that meeting, the National Security Staff convened the executive branch agencies from the State Department and USAID to the Centers for Disease Control and Prevention to scan current international antiviolence programming across the government and analyze how the United States could adopt a more comprehensive approach.

At the start of the next Congress in January 2011, the outlook for IVAWA was grim. The House turned over to the Republicans. Given what happened in Senator Kerry's committee, he wanted the House to go first, but the new politics of the House made it impossible to get a bipartisan bill introduced. We decided to focus our energies on the Obama administration. With only two years left in his first term (we didn't know if there would be second term or not), we didn't want to leave anything to chance. We worked with our friends on the Appropriations Committees in both the House and Senate to include a sentence in a major spending bill requiring Obama to create a comprehensive strategy to prevent and respond to gender-based violence globally. That bill was signed into law by the president in the fall of 2011. Among the many items the bill contained was our sentence requiring the president to essentially implement IVAWA through executive action. In December 2011, the administration created a new position on the National Security Staff to coordinate action on violence. A bright young lawyer from the Justice Department named Mala Adiga moved over to the White House and began crafting a strategy to engage the entirety of the US government—from the State Department and Centers for Disease Control to the Department of Labor—in stopping violence against women and girls. But by that time, we only had one year left to get the provisions of the IVAWA put into practice.

By June 2012, we were getting really worried that the strategy wasn't going to get done. The White House was focused on getting the boss reelected. When they missed the deadline to submit the strategy to Congress, as required by the bill, and our colleagues on the Hill hadn't heard word one from the administration about it, I decided we would have to get a little uppity. I called a few friends at the White House to let them know that if they delayed longer we would have to start publicly criticizing their slow pace. We were coming to the end of a very long road. As an advocate for women and girls, I was obligated to speak up when something that was supposed to happen wasn't happening. I can never really know if that call made a difference, but the strategy started to move again after that.

I sat in the ornate Indian Treaty Room at the White House Eisenhower Executive Office Building on August 10, 2012, and listened to Valerie Jarrett, senior adviser to the president, announce the United States Strategy to Prevent and Respond to Gender-Based Violence Globally. I was deeply honored to speak after her on behalf of our coalition and to present her with a giant thank you card signed by more than 600 women and men from around the world.

A strategy is only as good as its implementation. If nothing happens with it, it's not even worth the paper on which it's printed. As I write this, it's been just over a year and a lot has happened. Now, every USAID country office has to report how much they would like to spend on antiviolence programs. In 2013, they asked for a total of $150 million. Even though CRS couldn't figure out how much money was being spent back in 2006, there's no doubt it was a big change. USAID proposed spending the base $150 million plus an additional $31 million in 2014. When Women Thrive meets with country-level USAID staff, it is clear to us that they have heard loud and clear from their leadership that gender-based violence is a priority issue that must be integrated into their work. We know that USAID staff are getting training on how to concretely blend violence prevention into their areas of work, from infrastructure to education. USAID Bangladesh is launching a pilot to test holistic approaches to preventing child marriage. The US government is adding another $10 million to its efforts in the Democratic Republic of Congo to assist rape survivors and give them new access to medical and psychosocial care, legal assistance, and income-generating activities.

But we still need IVAWA. If a future president of the United States is not that committed to women and girls, all this forward movement could so easily slide backward to the days when no one thought twice about violence. We need these policies to be law, not just presidential projects. Senators Barbara Boxer, a Democrat from California, and Susan Collins, a Republican from Maine, will reintroduce IVAWA into the Senate in 2014. Representative Jan Schakowsky, a Democrat from the Chicago area, led IVAWA's reintroduction in the House in late 2013.

Now all we need is you.

# 38

# NEW LIFE

After Carmen and I met in 2009 we lost track of one another. There was a lot happening in both our lives. But when I returned to Honduras in July 2013, I knew I had to find her. I got a number for Carmen from COMUCAP's ex-coordinator (before I told her I couldn't work with her anymore). I was thrilled when my translator, Lena, talked with Carmen and set up a time for us to meet a few days later. I was practically jumping out of my skin as we pulled into her driveway. A lovely woman in her mid-forties greeted us at the door. The house was part restaurant and part living room; I thought Carmen must have started a side business to stay afloat. We sat down and I waited for Carmen to come in. Lena began chatting with the woman and then nudged me to say something. I whispered to her, "Where is Carmen?" Lena looked at me sternly and replied, "Ritu, this *is* Carmen."

We had the wrong Carmen. The kind lady was about the same age, with brown hair, and had survived an ordeal with domestic violence, but she wasn't my Carmen. We apologized profusely for her trouble and excused ourselves with tails tucked under our legs.

How in the world were we going to find the real Carmen? We went back to COMUCAP's office and they had a good laugh when they heard what happened. One of the board members said she thought she remembered my Carmen; she knew Carmen's mother. She didn't have a phone number, but she remembered where Carmen's family lived in Marcala. We hopped back in the truck and headed over there.

There aren't really street names in Honduras, nor house numbers, so we had to ask people on the street if they knew where Carmen Elena Marquez Bautista lived. Someone said she lived in the last house on the road across from the soccer field. How many soccer fields could there be in one small neighborhood? A lot. We stopped at every house that was the last one across from a soccer field and knocked on the door. The final one was painted a lovely mauve with white trim, with rose bushes in the front garden. That's unusual for Honduras. Nobody has a garden in front of the house facing the street. The gardens are always safely behind the front wall where no one can vandalize them. I thought to myself that if Carmen had a house, this is exactly what it would be like. She would have roses in front for all the world to smell. A young housekeeper answered the door when we knocked, and said yes, Carmen lived there, but she was still at school and would be home in about two hours. She called Carmen on her cell phone. When I heard the voice on the other end, I knew I found the real Carmen.

We waited nearby until she came home. I gave her a big hug when she came out the front door, or I should say, I tried to give her a big hug. She was eight months pregnant! I said to myself, "Please God, don't let this be Juan's baby."

It wasn't. After Carmen left the handicraft women and got her degree in teaching, she soon met David at her new school. They were just good friends during that first year after they met; Carmen was in no hurry to have a man in her life again. "He told me all about his life and I told him everything I had been through," she said. "He was so supportive of me. We started to get involved in March 2010, about a year after I met you. It's been a wonderful relationship, based in a lot of love and respect. And now I'm having another baby! I'm so happy. I always wanted to have another child."

I was thrilled for her. "Do you know if it's a boy or girl?" I asked.

"It's a little boy," Carmen replied. "His name is Keneth Gadiel. It means divine fortune."

The rest of that day, I couldn't keep from smiling. Even after everything that Carmen had been through, the glowing light within her did not go out. Now it was shining brightly. She was living her big dream at last. Not only was she a successful teacher, but she also got to love again—and after much pain, hold a new baby in her arms once more.

# 39
# LIVING ON A DOLLAR A DAY IN NICARAGUA

I was supposed to spend a day living on a dollar or less with one of COMUCAP's farmer members in Honduras. But as you can imagine given the situation I walked into, it wasn't safe for me to stay outside the hotel in Marcala. I asked Sylvia Torres if she might know someone in Nicaragua who would be willing to let a strange *gringa* shadow her for a day. Of course Sylvia did.

Lorena was incredibly gracious to welcome me into her home in Ponoloya, on Nicaragua's Pacific coast. There was a lot going on the day I showed up. Her eldest daughter, named Miss Lady, had just returned from business school in the United States a few days before I arrived. Miss Lady grew up not knowing what her name meant until she arrived in the United States, at which point she changed the spelling to Misleydi to avoid being teased relentlessly by her classmates. Misleydi's younger sister, who was in her late teens, had just delivered a beautiful baby boy the day before I arrived. The father of the child didn't want to marry the young mother but was willing to be in the child's life. I couldn't help but note the divergent trajectories these two daughters' lives were taking. They both were raised in the same situation, with the same parents and the same opportunities, but they were taking different pathways into adulthood. While I was happy to see a perfect baby boy arrive in the house, knowing all of the joy and cuteness he will bring, I still felt sad for his mom. The statistics are not on her side. She will likely not complete her education, and she will earn far less than her sister with a college degree.[32]

Early motherhood almost always ends a girl's educational career, thereby seriously stunting her potential for future economic self-sufficiency. Misleydi's achievement of winning a full scholarship to Florida State University is extraordinarily uncommon in Nicaragua. In fact, only two women were sent from her country that year to participate in the program.

Teenage single motherhood is not uncommon in Central America. Twelve out of every 100 girls in Nicaragua have a child before the age of twenty. In developing countries overall, an astounding one-quarter to one-half of girls will become mothers before they reach twenty years old, most of them because they are child brides.[33] By comparison, the US rate is just less than six out of 100.[34]

I wondered what Lorena thought about her two girls' contrasting lives, choices, and futures. On the outside, she did not seem fazed by it at all. She was efficiently accomplishing numerous household tasks simultaneously. But I remember well how overwhelming it was with that first baby, when I did not have a clue how to get him to breastfeed well, what caused a small squeak or openmouthed wail, or how to hold his little body without breaking him. My mom helped me so much, and I'm sure Lorena's daughter needed help as well. Lorena had to be a little stressed. I didn't feel comfortable asking her about it—especially not her deepest feelings about her new grandson and his mom.

Lorena's house was the same as many I have seen all over the world—a two-room cement bungalow with a corrugated tin roof. It was basic, but her family had a few amenities that included an old color TV and running water. The kitchen was out back under a makeshift veranda of sticks, with a grass roof, a tin wall on one side, and the wood-burning hearth in a far corner—very typical for low-income families. The location of her home is what was remarkable. The little house sat only 100 yards from a beautiful tidal estuary, where a stream joins the Pacific Ocean. The marsh teemed with small fish, snails, and grass shrimp. It would be primo real estate in the United States.

Just like my other Dollar-a-Day experiences, my host didn't really want me to help in the kitchen. It is understandably awkward to meet someone for the first time and then say, "Hey, can you wash all my dirty dishes?" So I just jumped in and figured I couldn't mess up washing dishes too badly. Once Lorena realized I actually wanted to help her make dinner, she had me chopping pork and vegetables, frying rice, and preparing the broth for the stew. She deftly maneuvered a shallow steel bowl over the fire, covered on the outside with a thick black crust from years of open flame. I am not used to cooking over a wood fire and kept burning my forearms on the edge of the bowl while stirring the rice in spattering hot oil. After the third time I charred my arm, I figured out I could just use a longer spoon than Lorena did.

As I attempted to cook a half decent pot of rice, I noticed that Lorena's sons—a twelve-year-old named Marlon and a twenty-something named Cairo—were busy with all kinds of household chores, from washing more dishes and sweeping up the dirt compound to doing laundry at the side of the family's well. It stuck in my mind. That was very unusual to see in Central America, where boys learn machismo before they learn to talk.

Dense smoke filled the kitchen veranda. Someone brought the newborn baby out there while he was peacefully sleeping in his car seat carrier. I wanted to scoop him up and take him back inside, away from all that smoke, but that wasn't my place. The fumes give children asthma, upper respiratory infections, and more serious lung problems later in life. But I realized this was normal for them. Families all over the world need efficient, safe, and smoke-free stoves. They would save so much time, sickness, money, and trees.

Dinner was a lot more than I had left in my daily budget. My Dollar-a-Day started out in Managua with a half cup of beans and rice and two small slices of watermelon valued at about 22 cents in US currency. I had no coffee; it would have been too expensive, especially with sugar, without which it is undrinkable for me. The spectacular *quesillo* from Doña Erlinda's shop turned out not to be a free lunch for my Dollar-a-Day experience. My traveling companion from the Women Thrive staff and I decided that even though she did not charge me, it would be cheating not to count it toward my tally, so I paid up the 15 córdobas (60 cents) and only had 8 cents left for the day. I could not be rude and refuse the pork stew and rice Lorena and I had prepared, so I ate only a little of it, but I'm certain it was more than 8 cents worth. My body had passed through the I'm-feeling-a-little-hollow stage hours before; I was now in the I'm-gonna-faint-if-I-don't-eat stage. It was really hard not to ask for seconds, but that would have meant I would be fasting the next day.

The hazy Central American sun went down soon after dinner, and I settled into my fabric hammock. I had to sleep under the next-door neighbor's banana-leaf roof cabana because there wasn't any room in the house with the new baby and Misleydi back from school. The whole family had to fit into one bedroom divided into smaller sections with fabric curtains. There were no walls around the cabana, so forget about locking doors. I asked our driver to sleep under there too so I could feel a little safer. I could see he wasn't thrilled about it, but he did it anyway and I was grateful. Then Marlon and Misleydi decided to also keep us company. Marlon hung up two more hammocks from the rafters; I heard the deep, rhythmic breathing of sweet sleep from his direction a few minutes later. I listened to Misleydi and our driver, an old family friend of theirs, talk for a long time about her experience in the United States and his time in Cuba. I understood a few sentences here and there about the difficulties of reentering an old life after seeing the possibilities of a new one outside Nicaragua. I could imagine the reverse culture shock that Misleydi must have been going through. She had shared a two-bedroom apartment with a friend of hers while at Florida State, which must have been enormously spacious compared to this childhood home. She had seen the huge houses, well-equipped schools, megasuperstores, and manicured roadways of America. I know she was so happy to see everyone again, but it had to be painful to be back in this impoverished setting after experiencing a far more comfortable existence.

I pulled up the fabric of the hammock as far as I could on both sides of me so I was tucked into the deep fold of a giant peapod, sprayed a good dose of DEET on any exposed skin, and dozed in and out of sleep. It's often late in the night when I miss my boys the most. I knew they would have loved sleeping out there with me in a tropical cabana, despite the bats, heat, and mosquitoes.

We all got up well after dawn; I'm not sure how I managed to sleep that long. Marlon realized he was late for school and literally sprung from his hammock directly into the shower. I helped prepare the strong dark coffee and simple sweet rolls from the bakery for breakfast, which only cost me about 5 córdobas (20 cents), thank goodness.

At seven in the morning we walked a half mile to El Rancho de Juan, an ocean-side bar/restaurant where Lorena works as the morning cook, waitress, and cleaner. My translator explained to Lorena, again, that I wanted to do all the things she does at the restaurant. Lorena shrugged her shoulders, said "Bueno," and assigned me to wash the last evening's dishes without running water.

Soaping them up was easy enough. But rinsing them off involved scooping bits of water up from a plastic basin with one hand and splashing the dish while holding it in the other. I tried to balance the need to wash all the soap off with the need to use as little water from the bucket as possible. I didn't want to make Lorena fetch more water for me. I can't say they were sparkling afterward, but I rationalized that the soap residue would act as a protectant from bacteria that might land on the dishes after I washed them. I then wiped down all twenty or so tables, which were covered with a coat of dust from the dirt floor and a salty film from the ocean air. Then I fried up more rice and chopped peppers.

Lorena invited me to roll out a tortilla. I thought it couldn't be that different than making Indian roti, which I did for my mom growing up. It was completely different. The masa (corn dough) used to make tortillas is soft and moist. As I tried to pat it out with my fingertips as Lorena had done, I just put holes in the fragile discs. Indian roti dough is much tougher, more elastic, and very forgiving. Lorena took over the tortilla making.

While she flipped the masa between her hands, I talked to her a little bit about her life. Lorena was raised right there on the Ponoloya beach. She had two brothers and an adopted sister; her grandmother raised them all after her parents separated. Countless women in developing countries take in their children's children and go through the rearing process all over again, even if they are desperately poor. Their own children must leave their hometown, and often even their country, to find work. Or they may have died because of HIV/AIDS, malaria, war, or domestic violence. Lorena's grandmother was one of these women who raised children twice. She did all kinds of things to support her second brood. "She would collect mussels and sell those," Lorena said. "She would collect fire wood from the mangroves, and sell that. She had a little farm with fruit trees, so she would sell oranges and lemons. She had a few cows and she could make raw cheese. She did a little of everything. When I got older, she opened a restaurant and bar." Through her grandmother's efforts, Lorena was able to go to school through fifth grade. After that she helped her grandmother in the restaurant. "She taught me how to make fried fish," Lorena shared. "And also mussel cocktail, cheese, and tortillas, and lots of other things. Her specialty was fried fish. People would come from all around to have her fish."

When she was nineteen, Lorena met the man with whom she had Misleydi and Cairo. She later met and married her current husband, who welcomed in Lorena's two children, four and two at the time. The couple had three children together. "He's a good man," Lorena said. "When people ask him how many children he has, he says five, even though my first two are not his." When Lorena wasn't working as a cook at a restaurant, she would go out with her husband to fish and collect shrimp, a job she enjoyed for the freedom it afforded.

Lorena had been working at El Rancho de Juan for four years. When I asked her about her hopes for the future, she replied, "It would be great if we could have our own business in the future, and if my children can make something of themselves." I mentioned that Misleydi told me she might open a restaurant now that she has a business degree. Lorena smiled and said, "Yes, she's got lots of plans, that one." She continued, "I want my children to be able to work in fields that they want, I want them to do what they choose. That is what I wasn't able to do. Even from our position of poverty I will help them in every way I can as long as I'm alive."

If there were an anthem for mothers around the world who are raising children in poverty, it would go something like this: I want them to have a better life than I have had, and I will do everything I can to make sure they have a chance to live well. The greatest hope for so many women is that their children will be free from the illiteracy, deprivation, and suffering they have endured. Every mother wants the inheritance of poverty to stop with her.

I asked Lorena how she got Marlon and Cairo to help so much around the house. "I told them that they have to learn how to cook, to wash clothes, and clean the house. They shouldn't think that's women's work. They have to learn it all as well. I said I'm not always going to be around and when I'm not, they need to know how to take care of themselves. They shouldn't have to pay someone to do it for them." She is definitely setting up those boys for success, at least with their future wives.

I was beginning to slump and decided to have a small piece of cheese with one tortilla—twenty more cents spent. I asked Lorena what I could do next. I think she took pity on me at that point and asked if I wanted to sort red beans before she boiled them. I gave her an enthusiastic "Yes!" I always volunteered for bean sorting when my mom would make *dahl* (Indian beans). It's a simple task of pulling out the small rocks and bad beans that snuck their way into the bag. I find sorting beans very meditative. It keeps my mind busy enough to not think about my everyday dilemmas and worries, but it's simple enough not to demand many brain cells.

Eleven a.m. came very quickly while the beans mesmerized me. I still had a very long day ahead—driving two hours to meet with another women's cooperative that had partnered with the MCA Nicaragua, and then a three-hour drive to our next pit stop for the night. I was exhausted not just by the short, but punishing, Dollar-a-Day, but also by the previous COMUCAP "adventure" in Honduras. I could tell that Lorena was

# RITU'S DOLLAR-A-DAY EXPENSES—NICARAGUA

| | *Nicaraguan córdobas* | *US Dollars* | *Notes* |
|---|---|---|---|
| July 29 (FULL DAY) | | | |
| Breakfast (1/2 cup beans and rice, 2 slices watermelon) | 5 | $0.20 | |
| Lunch (1 quesillo) | 15 | $0.60 | Expensive, but worth it |
| Dinner (1/2 cup rice, 1/2 cup pork stew) | 20 | $0.88 | |
| TOTAL | 40 | $1.63 | Tomorrow is going to be hard |
| | | | |
| July 30 (HALF DAY) | | | |
| Breakfast (coffee and roll) | 5 | $0.20 | |
| Lunch (piece of cheese and 1 tortilla) | 5 | $0.20 | |
| TOTAL | 10 | $0.40 | |

exhausted too. I had no doubt she'd be happy to take care of one less person. We had to say good-bye quickly because her employers were minding the restaurant at that point, and our car was waiting to go. I gave her a big hug, congratulated her on her gorgeous new grandson, and wished her all the best for her growing family. I wished I could have stayed another day. It's usually the second day when the formality wears off and I really get to understand these amazing women, with their fears, dreams, and triumphs.

I collapsed into the backseat and let the cool air-conditioning blow into my dirty, sweaty face and hair. I got to leave, but Lorena had to stay and work until afternoon and then go home and begin her second shift. The last day proved to me, again, that I could never survive that kind of life. Since I had to speak in complete sentences and stand up straight for the rest of the day, my colleagues took pity on me and we decided to call Dollar-a-Day done for Nicaragua. It was just a day and a half for me, but a lifetime for Lorena.

# 40

# WHAT YOU CAN DO FOR HONDURAS AND NICARAGUA

At the end of Part 1, I showed you how you might influence corporate America and the Department of State. Now, I want to help you take on the US Congress.

## GET THE INTERNATIONAL VIOLENCE AGAINST WOMEN ACT (IVAWA) PASSED

Lots of people think writing or calling their member of Congress doesn't make any difference.

I am here to tell you that it makes a *huge* difference. As I said before, Hill offices tell us every single day, "We're not hearing anything about this from back home." That sentence is usually followed by a polite smile from the aide and a wave bye-bye. Your collective voice is more powerful than that of any advocate, and even more powerful than the voices of women from developing countries who we take to Capitol Hill to tell their stories. Those women are amazing and eloquent . . . but they're not voters. You are.

The truth is that Congress hardly hears anything about global poverty and international women's matters. This issue is not like health care reform or raising taxes. For those things, congressional offices metaphorically stack up the letters by pro and con and weigh them in bulk to see which side is winning. But on our issue, if an office on the Hill gets 50 letters from their district saying, "Pass IVAWA now!" that sounds like a roar. So, the good news on IVAWA is that we don't have to generate millions of letters or calls to win this one. So please do not think that your action won't do anything.

Some actions are incredibly effective. Other actions are helpful if there are thousands of people doing it. There's actually a loose hierarchy of voter input to a congressional office. The following methods are ranked from useful to incredibly impactful: clicking "like" for something on a

Congress member's Facebook page; signing a petition to Congress; posting a comment on a member's Facebook page; sending a form e-mail where all you have to do is hit a button; sending an e-mail where you enter a personal message; mailing a preprinted postcard that you sign; calling a congressional office; writing a personal letter; coming to Washington, DC, to join a citizen advocacy day; attending a town hall meeting and speaking up; and at the very top of the impact curve, meeting your senators and/or representative in their local office near your home.

In terms of impact per hour of your time, a meeting is the very best. This action is worth more than a hundred letters. You can gather up some friends and take them with you to meet with your senators and/or representative in their district office. You can start with just one meeting if you like, or go for all three (your two senators and your single representative). If you're inspired to attend a town hall, you can find those dates and places on the website of your member of Congress.

If you're not sure who your senators and representatives are, don't feel bad. It's really confusing to keep track of who's who when you're trying to remember to call the doctor, change the laundry, pack the kids' different lunches, and put together that PowerPoint for your board meeting in your head. All you need to do is come to our website (www.womenthrive.org) and click on "Get Involved." You'll find a place where you can enter your name, street address, zip code, and hit enter, and a list of your congressional senators and representatives with their local offices will pop up. Whatever you are ready to do, we can help you do it. We have lots of information as well as how-to instructions under our Get Involved tab.

If you're not quite ready for a meeting or town hall forum, then get out your nicest stationery—the stuff you bought at Papyrus last year and haven't had the occasion to use—grab your favorite pen, and write a letter. What's really critical is that your note comes from your heart. You don't need to know any statistics or have the technical solutions; that's our job. What you do need to say is why you care. Perhaps you think what's happening to women and girls is wrong and unjust. Perhaps you think that our country should be part of the solution. Whatever your thoughts, whatever your reasons, they are important and valid. **Be sure to ask your member to cosponsor the International Violence Against Women Act**. Here's a sample to give you the idea:

Dear Senator/Representative [Insert Name],
My name is [your full name] and I live in [city, state]. I know that every day horrible

acts of violence are taking place against women and girls worldwide. I think that our country should be part of the solution by supporting for programs that work. I would like you to do everything you can to end violence against women and girls, especially for you to cosponsor the International Violence Against Women Act. Thank you.

[Your name, full address, and e-mail]

The fact that you put in the time and effort to write a personal, handwritten note may get your letter on the member's desk rather than in the in-box of a "Legislative Correspondent," whose sole job is to open and reply to the mail without the member ever seeing it.

One challenge we face is that we can't just write once and forget about it. Members of Congress need to hear from people, even the same people, every step of the way: from before a bill is introduced, as it gathers cosponsors, gets voted on in the committee, and then voted on the full floor of the House and Senate. We have to create a growing and persistent drumbeat to get Congress to move.

One fun thing to do to keep it interesting is to add wine, friends, and stir. Gather your favorite posse of friends for an evening of wine-ing and writing. Ask everyone to bring their choice stationery and favorite pen, put on some world music, pour some wine (or your favorite beverage), and ask everyone to finish these two sentences: "When I think about women and girls being raped and abused, I feel . . . ," and "I want you to support the International Violence Against Women Act because . . ."

## EAT, DRINK, AND DRESS FAIR TRADE

This is an easy action we all can enjoy. You can find fair trade products in every grocery store these days whether you're in the United States or Europe. All you need to do is look for the fair trade label. In the United States, it's a logo of a man holding a bowl with "Fair Trade Certified." In Europe, it's a man with one arm raised against a blue, green, and black background with "FAIRTRADE." These products may cost you a bit more than their non-fair-trade equivalents because there is no exploitation involved. But your fair trade coffee with exploitation-free sugar will taste that much smoother and sweeter.

You can find a greater variety of fair trade products online by going to Fair Trade USA's webpage, www.fairtradeusa.org/products-partners, which lists the products they certify and their partner companies. In Europe, Fair Trade International has a list of items they certify at www.fairtrade.net/products.

If you want to spread the joy of buying fair trade, you might try inviting your friends to an all-fair-trade dinner or potluck. You will be amazed at what you can create from the bounty of fair trade foods, wines, and spices.

# PART THREE

## BURKINA FASO

Paul, Madame Sirima, and I wait to talk with women's association members until the men disperse. Source: Julie Dixon.

Mariam fits me with a traditional wrap. Source: Paul Kinda.

Members of Mariam's women's association demonstrate how to make soap. Source: Women Thrive.

Mariam's family standing outside the newly constructed hut. Source: Paul Kinda.

Mariam's daughter prepares to cook in the kitchen area. Source: Women Thrive.

# 41

# SCHOOL GIRLS

I smiled as I watched hundreds of kids enjoying their recess outside the blue-and-tan-walled primary school in Pissila, Burkina Faso. I was baking under a harsh, hot, and unforgiving sun, but the heat didn't seem to slow the kids down a bit. I could feel the soft skin of my neck drying, tightening, and then blistering after only a few minutes. It was my warm welcome back to Burkina. I had traveled 4,997 miles to see for myself the laughing, running, and jumping products of a successful piece of advocacy Women Thrive had done about eight years before: girls, lots of girls, going to school.

Far too many girls—about one-quarter of those who live in developing countries (36.6 million)—never get to go to school.[1] Girls who live in rural poverty are at greatest risk of not receiving an education. They are some of the most marginalized and forgotten people on the planet. Their families are too poor to pay for a uniform, books, and pencils, even if the schooling is free. Their parents often prioritize education for their brothers, since daughters will only be married off as soon as possible, educated or not. Or, as is often the case, parents keep girls home from school to protect them from the potential violence they will experience on their way to and from school, or in school at the hands of their teachers. Girls' days are often filled with endless work helping their mothers care for their younger siblings, assisting with farming, or working to bring in a little income. I could go on for pages about all the reasons girls are shut out of learning. It always comes down to the same thing: Women and girls go without because society values them the least.

We all understand the benefits of education from our own experience. Imagine what your life would be like if you could not read this book, fill out a basic form, get a driver's license, or even read simple instructions. Where would you work? How would you get by? When I consider the prospect of a life devoid of education, everything feels cold, black, and heavy. If you're a parent, you might feel, as I do, that the two most important things you can give your children are love and a good education.

Beyond just knowing in our bones that education is essential, the power of educating girls has been proven by many years of research. If a girl in a developing country gets seven years of education, she will, on average, marry four years later than she would otherwise and have about two fewer children.[2] Several studies found strong links between education and future wages—a link that is stronger for girls than for boys. Going to primary school alone boosts girls' lifetime future wages by 5 to 15 percent. For boys, primary school increases their wages between 4 and 8 percent.[3] In Thailand, Ghana, and Ivory Coast, the different rate of return between boys' and girls' education was even greater: Girls' secondary school completion boosted their future earnings 15 to 25 percent more than it did for boys.[4] Now, this is not to say that educating boys is unimportant. Educating all children is important. The point is that holding girls back not only violates their basic human right to an education but also keeps families in poverty and robs the world of economic growth.

The great news is a higher percentage of children, and of girls, are enrolled in school than ever before in human history. Progress really accelerated in 2000 when world leaders gathered at the United Nations to agree on a set of global goals for poverty reduction, education, health, hunger, and other areas, all to be achieved by 2015. These targets are known as the Millennium Development Goals (MDGs). Two MDGs prioritize education. The first is that all children, no matter where they live, should have access to free primary schooling by 2015. The second goal is to close the gap between girls' and boys' enrollment in primary school by 2015. Back in

2000, in most poor countries, boys far outnumbered girls in school.

Just setting common goals for the world galvanized billions of dollars from donor countries and international institutions such as the World Bank and United Nations. Developing country governments became focused on trying to reach the specific MDG targets. Together, the world has made incredible progress. Even the poorest countries have improved their primary school enrollment rates, from less than 60 percent of children in 1990 to more than 80 percent in 2008.[5]

These happy numbers, however, mask some difficult underlying problems. They measure enrollment, which simply means a child's name appears on a school registration list. It does not mean the child goes to school regularly or even at all. When we look at primary school *completion* rates, we get a more accurate picture of progress. These numbers have also improved, from 44 percent of children in developing countries completing primary school in 1990 to 63 percent in 2008.[6] Things are getting better, but only 63 percent of children finishing primary school means 37 percent have virtually no chance of succeeding in a globalizing economy.

The really tragic setback we uncover when we look under the hood is that even though children may be going to school, the majority of them are not learning even the very basics of reading, writing, and math, let alone critical thinking and problem solving, which are more essential than ever. An estimated 200 million children in primary school are learning so little that they cannot even read basic words like "you" or "me" in their native language.[7] In Uganda, more than one-quarter of kids in seventh grade could not read and understand a simple story written at the second-grade level. Nine out of ten second-grade students in Mali studying in French could not read a single word in a short sentence.[8] In Africa, girls' learning outcomes are worse than boys, whereas in Latin America the reverse is true. This is yet another example in which it's important to take a gendered approach that doesn't lump both boys and girls together, but seeks instead to understand what different challenges they face and to help them overcome those challenges.

Remember all those great benefits of girls being in school—later marriage, fewer births, better earnings, higher child survival rates, and the rest? All those beneficial effects, which some call the "girl effect," don't come from girls sitting in class, they derive from girls *learning*. If there's one thing I've learned from 15 years of managing people, it's that what gets measured gets done. This learning crisis is a result of choosing to measure only one thing. The world said, "Get all children registered for school," so that's what people focused on doing. Classes swelled from a manageable number of kids to a hundred or more per teacher. Countries didn't necessarily add new teachers or support their educators with training and materials to effectively engage more pupils. Teachers don't get paid enough to justify being in the classroom every day; lots of good teachers have to work other jobs to make ends meet. Government education ministries got parents to put their children's names on the register but didn't necessarily work with parents to make sure kids actually showed up in class.

Why don't they measure how much kids are actually learning? There are many reasons, from technical testing challenges to cost, but one powerful deterrent is that the results too often stink. If teachers are going to be evaluated or compensated based on these scores, a method called high stakes testing, then there is little incentive to test. And if policy makers in developing countries have to stack their country's results up against the rest of the world, why would they want to risk that kind of global humiliation? The best solution is to give teachers the training and tools they need to help kids learn and encourage countries to include learning in their education goals in whatever way makes sense for them.

The world is watching an epic tragedy in the making, like seeing a train wreck in slow motion. You've already read about the mothers who are working themselves to the bone to earn money to send their kids to school. Take their stories and multiply them by a hundred million. If children aren't learning, then their moms are wasting all that incredibly precious cash, which could buy more food or better shelter instead. Not only that, those families are sacrificing the earnings those children could be providing. If kids come home with poor scores, have to repeat grades, and still don't learn, then it doesn't make sense for parents to invest in education. I have heard this sentiment expressed by more than a few parents in villages in Africa and Asia. It's not hard to see how, in less than a generation, schooling could become a low priority for people with few resources. Without basic skills, another generation will watch oppor-tunities fly over their heads and find themselves stuck in the quicksand of poverty.

# 42

## RED DIRT

It's not hard to see what keeps Burkina Faso, a forgotten country in the western part of Africa that's about the size of Colorado, in poverty. Unlike Sri Lanka, Honduras, and Nicaragua, there is not much here to work with. Parched red dirt, scattered scrubby bushes, and an occasional mango or baobab tree are all you can see in any direction. Mud brick huts rise out of the desiccated ground like same-color skin tags on a reddened membrane of earth that absorbs the full force of the African sun.

In other places on the continent, dirt can hide valuable mineral deposits. Though gold has been found in Burkina by panning the soil, pretty much what you see here is what you get: red dirt. Only about 20 percent of the land can grow anything edible.[9] The summer rains wash away the soil to form miniature canyons like small versions of Georgia O'Keeffe's paintings of the New Mexican desert. They remind me a lot of the arroyos (dry stream beds) I used to explore for hours as a kid in Arizona.

You might remember Burkina Faso from your grade school geography classes as Upper Volta, the "lower" Volta being what is now Ghana. The French colonized the country, but I'm not sure why. Perhaps after they got Algeria and Mali to the north they just kept moving south because there were no natural barriers to stop them except for dehydration. Have water, will conquer. In 1960, the country threw the French out and went through the obligatory spasms of military coups and then settled on the quasi-military, quasi-democratically elected leader they've had since 1987: President Blaise Compaore. In 2000, he changed the constitution to allow the president to serve three consecutive five-year presidential terms, so he is up in 2015, but I wouldn't hold my breath that the limit will stick after that. The Burkinabé (bur-KEEN-ah-bay) people are a deep, mesmerizing black; every bit of melanin is used to its full biochemical potential. Unlike the dry and withered land they have inhabited since their ancestors walked upon it, the people are like the mangos that grow abundantly in this desert: richly sweet, brightly colorful, unbelievably generous, and patiently ripening.

I say patient because they have been waiting for a long, long time for development to arrive. Most of the country does not have access to clean water or basic sanitation. I don't mean running water inside their homes. I mean being able to walk to a well with clean groundwater within three hours or less. Only a third of men and 15 percent of women can read and write. The risks of waterborne and vector-borne (for example, from mosquitoes and flies) diseases are still extremely high. One bright spot for Burkina: less than 3 percent of the population suffers from obesity.

Ninety percent of the people are subsistence farmers, scratching on the land to coax up enough grains and vegetables to eat. They also raise chicken, pigs, goats, and sheep, which graze on whatever specks of green dare appear on the red soil. Cotton is the primary export of Burkina and sucks up most of the arable land and water. However, you can't eat cotton. So more good land for cotton means less good land for food.

The total population is about 18 million people, 45 percent of whom are under fifteen years old. Women each have six babies on average, but also on average 8 out of 100 kids die as infants.[10] If you are having trouble imagining what that statistic means, picture a kindergarten classroom of 25 kids with two empty seats representing the children who have died. Now multiply that by all the kindergarten classrooms across the country and you begin to understand that a lot of babies needlessly die in Burkina. (By comparison, in the United States 0.6 newborns die out of 100.)[11] One out of every four children is underweight in Burkina because they don't get enough to eat.

Now we come to what might be the most important statistics for Burkina: 60 percent of the people are moderate Muslims. Of those, 47 percent are poor or extremely poor, and 77 percent are unemployed. The top 10 percent of Burkinabé consume more than 30 percent of the resources.

If you add it all up you get the perfect recipe for radical Islamists to make Burkina their next home: a large population of Muslims who lose their children to hunger and curable diseases and who don't have the opportunity to get an education and escape poverty because the government doesn't prioritize basic health care, education, or development. Imagine if you were a parent in Burkina and someone came along and said, "Hey, we'll give you free health care, educate your boys, and help feed your family. But the deal is you have to repress your women, loathe America, and don't ask any questions about what we're doing here." What would you do?

Mali, which shares half of Burkina's border to the north, casts an ominous shadow. In March 2013, the military overthrew Mali's democratically elected government. Al-Qaeda took advantage of the coup and lawlessness in the country's northern territory, seized control, and began enforcing harshly conservative sharia law. When al-Qaeda began moving southward toward the capital of Mali, the French came to the rescue and pushed the insurgents out of the country completely, at least for now.

Burkina could easily go the same way, and we are almost too late to make a difference. Education, health care, and economic development cannot be spawned in a day, especially by a government that is encumbered by complicated administrative rules inherited from the French system. Terrorists don't have to deal with all that paperwork, multiple signatures, or government infighting. They are fast, efficient, and flush with cash. They can meet the needs of Burkina's 90 percent rural poor population.

So what's the solution to this mess? Pay

attention now. Invest in development now. Push hard for good governance that is responsive to people *now.* Or possibly pay dearly later in deaths and dollars, like we have in Iraq and Afghanistan.

# 43

# A BRIGHT IDEA

There was a time when our government invested in Burkina Faso's children. In 2004, shortly after Congress passed the legislation creating the Millennium Challenge Account (MCA), the Millennium Challenge Corporation (MCC) released its seventeen eligibility criteria to select which countries were going to receive its massive grants. These criteria looked at how well governments were doing in three major areas: good governance, human development, and economic openness. As you might remember, Women Thrive got Congress to include a few key phrases in the original MCA legislation to urge consideration of gender in their eligibility criteria. But when they unveiled those highly anticipated yardsticks, not a single indicator of seventeen looked at males and females separately.

Women Thrive, working very closely with the International Center for Research on Women,

World Vision, and other aid organizations, upped the pressure on the MCC to adopt at least one gendered criterion the next year. We made the case that because there was a huge gap between girls' and boys' primary school completion rates, it should be used as an indicator of how well countries were meeting girls' education needs. In August 2004, the Bush administration announced that it would replace the primary education completion rate indicator with the *girls'* primary education completion rate indicator to signal that the MCC viewed women's empowerment—and specifically girls' education—as a key ingredient of economic growth and poverty alleviation.

A few countries were about to qualify for MCA funding under the former metric of overall primary school completions rates. When the MCC introduced this new indicator, however, they failed. It was a major disappointment for those nations; they had been sharpening their pencils and getting ready to draft their projects. It was also a loud and clear signal to all countries with their eyes on the MCA checkbook that, like in the case of Lesotho (see Chapter 29), the United States meant business on women's rights and development.

One of the countries on the cusp of qualification was Burkina Faso. It fell behind when the indicator changed. Even though Burkina Faso had been making progress in getting children into school, in 2003 only 29 percent of girls in the country were registered in school compared to 42 percent of boys.[12] Instead of kicking Burkina to the curb, the MCC decided to make a $12 million grant to the country to help them boost girls' primary school enrollment and completion.

The Burkinabé Response to Improve Girls' Chances to Succeed (with the fudged acronym of BRIGHT) project was born. The ambitious project was funded by MCC, managed by USAID, and implemented by a consortium of top-notch organizations including Plan International, Catholic Relief Services, the Forum for African Women Educationalists, and a local organization called Tin Tua. The goal was to build new, well-equipped schools in 132 villages and put 16,076 girls—and 11,134 boys—in school for the first time in their lives.[13] The consortium had a holistic method for creating girl-friendly schools, which has the following components:

- **Integrating preschools with the primary schools.** One big reason girls don't go to school is because they need to take care of their younger siblings. In addition, the early years are the most important for cognitive and emotional development. The BRIGHT project solved two challenges at the same time with this approach. They were so successful that the Burkina Faso government has begun doing the same for the whole country.

- **Engaging parents and communities in changing social norms around girls' education.** Even before school construction began, Plan International and their local partners engaged parents in a discussion to understand why families were not sending their girls to school. Through conversation, community education, and directly addressing parents' concerns, families felt more comfortable sending their girls to school for the first time.

- **Making sure every child mattered.** Plan International trained some mothers of the students to follow the girls' school attendance closely. When a girl did not go to school, one of the women would go to her home to find out what was wrong. This boosted girls' regular attendance dramatically.

- **Recruiting skilled teachers, in particular women teachers.** Girls' parents prefer female teachers, given cultural issues and the commonality of violence against girls in school. The BRIGHT project focused on getting qualified and dedicated female teachers into their classrooms.

- **Providing housing and training to teachers.** In many developing countries, teachers get little training to take on complicated classrooms with too many kids, of all different ages, and more than a few challenges. Teacher training is extremely important in helping kids to learn. In addition, the BRIGHT schools provided safe and convenient housing for teachers to attract and keep the most qualified.

- **Building separate bathrooms for girls and boys.** It seems like it would be obvious, but parents keep their girls home when they have to use the same toilets as boys. This simple change can make a big difference for girls.
- **Providing desks, books, and school kits for children.** Most schools in Africa lack the very basics of chalkboards, desks, pencils, and materials, making teaching and learning almost impossible tasks. The BRIGHT schools provided simple sturdy desks, chalkboards, and chalk, as well as pencils, papers, and basic learning tools for children.
- **Adding a water well that the entire community could access.** One task that normally takes girls hours each day is fetching water for their families. Each BRIGHT school had a water well on site so that girls could bring water home after school.

- **Feeding hungry minds (and bodies).**
Probably the most valuable thing that the
BRIGHT program did was provide meals
for children who came to school and sent
home rations for families when girls had 90
percent or better attendance each month.
Most of the children and parents I interviewed stated that food was the strongest
incentive for girls being in school regularly.

The BRIGHT formula removed obstacles to
education by listening to the parents, educators,
and children and meeting their needs. Two years
later Burkina did qualify for the MCA money, in
part because of the country's commitment to girls'
education through the BRIGHT program.

There's nothing like seeing the results of a
strategy for social change that is smartly grounded
in the realities of the people it's meant to help. I
had witnessed the very beginnings of BRIGHT,
and now, in the summer of 2013, I returned to see
how it had blossomed. As we turned the bend on
the dusty, bumpy road into the Pissila schoolyard,
the first thing I noticed was something I had never
seen at any African school before: a playground.
They added a playground! How simple and how
profoundly important. What it communicates to
children is subtle but critical: "Play matters" and
"You are worth it." The entire BRIGHT school—
its solid, well-constructed buildings, good paint,

and neat grounds—sent the message to kids that their future is important enough to warrant a good investment. I think all children are deeply affected by the environments in which they live, play, and learn. A beat-up school with no chalkboard or chairs reinforces for children that they are poor and that nice schools are for other children, not for them. It puts prison bars around their dreams. A school that is lovely to look at, comfortable to sit in, and easy for teachers to teach in can put wings on children's dreams.

And fly they did. The children who swung and jumped on that playground were getting a better education than their brothers or sisters that may have attended other schools. "There is a big difference between the BRIGHT school and the other schools around here," one mother told me. "The BRIGHT teachers are better trained and more motivated to teach the children. Here the children are so busy and well supervised that they don't take needless risks by playing in the bush. At other schools, there are no classes on Thursdays and Saturdays, so the children have more time to get into trouble." A rigorous evaluation of the program published in 2013 proved numerically that kids did indeed perform better at BRIGHT schools.[14]

Things are changing for the whole community. Parents are seeing for themselves the benefits of girls' education. One father said, "For me, girls' education is very important and I'm going to give you an example that impressed me. One of the girls in this village was sent to school. She worked hard in school and got a job. Now she's taking good care of her parents, even more so than she takes care of her in-laws." One reason parents don't send their girls to school is because they feel the resources they sacrifice will only end up benefiting her husband's family. Happily, this father has seen how everyone can win. "I'm hopeful that sending my daughter to school will contribute to her and my betterment," he said.

# 44

# FOOD FIRST

The holistic approach certainly had a lot to do with the BRIGHT schools' success. However, when I talked with girls who had graduated from the BRIGHT primary schools and parents of current students, there was one surprising theme that kept popping up: Kids go to school for the food.

Aicha and Yasmine, who both attended BRIGHT primary schools and were now in secondary school, were so incredibly shy. They would look at me with their gorgeous brown eyes, and when I'd look back their eyes would dart to the floor. Their teachers said they were very excited to meet us, but I think the enthusiasm turned to stage fright when the time came for our interview. So we kept our questions very basic and light.

Aicha was fourteen years old, Yasmine fifteen. They sat with their arms touching, supporting one another during the conversation. They attended different BRIGHT primary schools but shared similar experiences.

"What did you think about primary school," I asked them. "Did you like it?"

Aicha looked at Yasmine to see who should go first. Yasmine nudged Aicha's arm as if to say, "You jump off the diving board first." "I really enjoyed my primary school because we were given rice every month and we had excellent teachers in our classrooms every day," Aicha offered. She started at a BRIGHT primary school when she was six years old. "In my village there was no school, so I had no chance of getting an education until the BRIGHT school came. My parents didn't want to send us to school, but thanks to BRIGHT, our families had food to eat, and that motivated our parents to let us complete our primary school studies."

Yasmine followed. "I really enjoyed primary school because we got some food every month to take to our families, and there were trees in the school yard where we could learn our lessons.

Also, we had light at nighttime to study." Most families living in poverty don't have electricity, so sundown also means the end of the productive day, including the end of homework. My boys would be thrilled with that lifestyle, but for girls in Africa who have to do chores until the sun sets, it means there is a hard and early stop to their study time. So Plan International provided battery-powered lamps to families, with the understanding that their children should have priority access to the light to do their homework.

"What else did you like about school?" I inquired, hoping for more academic insights.

"Something else I thought was great," said Aicha, "was that we got food every midday. And when we took the primary school certificate exam, we got to eat before it and we didn't have to move to another school to take it. We felt very at home." These things, however small they may seem, make a critical difference to children's success in learning.

Aicha's and Yasmine's words about food stuck with me. We've all had days when we're too busy to eat breakfast or lunch, and then realize a few hours later that we're too exhausted to think straight. If you have children, you know that keeping them fed is key to avoiding meltdowns and setting them up to learn. We know from our own experience that a famished child will have a hard time sitting still and listening, let alone retaining information, taking tests, and participating in classroom discussion when all they can think about is how hungry they are. BRIGHT's excellent teachers and careful consideration of cultural concerns were central to its success, but an essential element was that they ensured children's bodies were nourished enough to free their minds to learn.

All in all—whether we were talking to the children, their parents, or were looking at the data—we saw that the BRIGHT schools were a great success, and cost-effective too. Putting one child through the primary program costs between about $62 and $70 per year.[15] Just to put that in context, in the United States, the cost per pupil for primary or secondary school is about $10,700 per year. I'm not advocating for less money for US public education (I support the opposite, in fact), but I'd say the BRIGHT schools are a bargain and give us a great return on investment.[16]

So is there a bright future for the BRIGHT schools? No one knows. When Burkina's MCA program came to an end, so did funding for the highly effective program. Congress has lowered poverty and humanitarian assistance levels for the last five years, and there's little room left to help school kids in Burkina. The US Department of Agriculture is using some of America's international food aid, which I talked about in relation to Honduras and Nicaragua, to keep up the school food programs in four provinces of Burkina. The World Food Programme is also providing foodstuff for schools in Burkina's Sahel region. At schools that aren't covered by these programs, parents are putting their heads, and the little resources they have, together to at least keep providing lunch to the pupils. They know how critical that is for getting children to school and for learning once they are in class. Plan International is trying to find funding to support teacher training and to provide the materials they need to teach. No one from the United States is working on improving the whole education system in Burkina so that being in a public school there doesn't have to mean a bad education. How sad it will be to see the great strides BRIGHT had made slip away, when it would take so few resources to see it thrive.

# 45

## PENNY WISE AND TON FOOLISH

A lot of people say we just can't help the rest of the world right now—not while we're dealing with our own problems with education, health care, and budget deficits that will sink our grandchildren into inescapable debt. "Home first is what I hear a lot. This might shock you, but I agree that home should come first. No question. We've got to get our own house in order. The question really is: How much is appropriate to spend on helping people in poverty worldwide to have a prosperous and, more self-interestedly, a peaceful future? Well, we Americans were asked that very question. More than a thousand people in the United States were asked, "Just by your best guess, what percentage of the federal budget is spent on foreign aid?" On average, people replied that the government spends 27 percent of the federal budget on aid to other countries.[17] When asked, "What percentage do you think we *should* spend on international aid?" the median response was 10 percent of the federal budget.[18]

So how much of the federal budget is *really* spent on foreign aid? *Less than 1 percent.* Yes, it's true. We spend about 99.3 percent of the federal budget at "home." Of the 0.7 percent that we spend on aid, about $14 billion of that is military assistance to foreign armies, something that many antipoverty advocates oppose.

*Less than half of 1 percent* of the US budget is spent to help children learn, immunize babies, save mothers' lives, assist subsistence farmers in growing more food, and all the things that will make this world one that we'll feel good about leaving to our great-grandchildren.

Figure 45.1 shows how the US budget was sliced up for fiscal year 2012. You'll notice the little sliver that is international aid. The big hunks of pie are for three things: Social Security, Medicaid, and defense.[19] Those who say that we can deal with our debt or our budget imbalances by eliminating 0.7 percent of the budget are playing games, games that cost the lives of hundreds of thousands of children who won't get the help they need.

As a country, we have to deal with Social Security and the Medicaid/Medicare programs. I don't pretend to know how to fix these particular complex issues, but plenty of smart people in

FIGURE 45.1 US FEDERAL SPENDING, FISCAL YEAR 2012

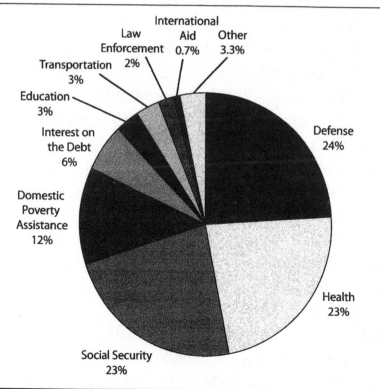

Washington, DC, have excellent ideas about that. I can, however, do basic math, so I do know that tinkering around the edges with 1 percent of the budget this way or that isn't going to solve our bigger budget problems. All of US global poverty assistance amounts to a rounding error for the defense budget. In fact, our nation's military leaders are begging Congress not to cut international aid spending. Robert Gates, the former secretary of defense, spent many days on Capitol Hill trying to explain to members of Congress that, as he put it, "Economic development is a lot cheaper than sending soldiers."[20] General Colin Powell, another former defense secretary and former secretary of state, said, "We live in a dangerous world and a world of opportunity. Increasing our diplomatic and development resources is absolutely critical, and money well spent to deal with the dangers and seize the opportunities."[21]

Members of Congress know all this. They know the public has an outsized view of how much is spent on aid overseas. They know the military wants more money to help people in poverty create stable nations. They know educating girls is important. They know it's the moral and the smart thing to do.

The *real* reason they keep cutting poverty and humanitarian aid is because they think people don't care. They can do it and then brag about it to voters back home. While folks will say in a telephone interview that 10 percent of the budget should go to help children and families abroad, the truth is that they don't write, call, or visit their member of Congress to say that. These simple acts may be all it takes to keep the BRIGHT schools shining brightly for girls and boys.

# 46

# KAYA GIRLS CENTER

The BRIGHT program succeeded in getting thousands of girls into school and in helping them successfully complete their primary education. Like many successes in life, however, it opened new frontiers of challenges. The biggest of those problems was that many of those girls could not continue their education because there are precious few secondary schools in Burkina. The "college," as they refer to secondary school in West Africa, is likely too far away for a girl to commute each day. And secondary education is not necessarily tuition-free like primary school, putting it out of reach for a large portion of the BRIGHT girls, as well as many others.

The consequences of girls staying home after they finish elementary school are significant, and not just for them. The lack of educational advancement opportunities can create a negative feedback loop that discourages parents from even starting their daughters in school. Girls who only complete primary school get a small boost in their long-term economic outlook, but the big gains come from attending secondary school where critical (and marketable) skills are taught. The small benefits of primary education are sometimes not enough to outweigh the significant costs to parents. It basically boils down to this: If a girl can't get enough education to earn good money, it might not make sense for her to get an education at all. The team at Plan International in Burkina understood this all too well.

When it became clear that the United States was not going to support the BRIGHT schools anymore, much less help build secondary schools for the BRIGHT graduates, Plan International staff decided they would not sit still and do nothing. "When the door was closed to continuing the BRIGHT program, we had to react and show the communities that even without US funding things are still moving ahead," Monsieur Francois Yonli, head of the Sanmatenga office for Plan International in Burkina, explained to me during one of our breaks from the baking sun. "We were not just sitting and waiting for other people to come. We got in touch with different community leaders, gathered our resources, and built a secondary boarding school for the BRIGHT girls and others. That resulted in the Kaya Girls Center, where some of the BRIGHT girls who passed their secondary entrance exam attend school now. If we did not create the center, there was no hope for these girls to pursue their studies in the future. What would girls that benefited from BRIGHT do? If they were not able to do anything, that would contribute to the failure of the project."

A colleague of Monsieur Yonli's added, "The skills a child acquires in primary school can slip away if they don't keep up their studies. But when we ensure that education goes through secondary school, the knowledge sticks with them and is worth something. They can use it for vocational work and can pass public exams to qualify for various professions."

The Kaya Girls Center is a beautiful place with two main school buildings, a large veranda, a rose garden, and a dormitory just off the main campus area. Plan International built the facility with some of the materials and labor coming from the community. A group of nuns from the Order of the Immaculate Conception, affiliated with the Catholic charity Caritas, support the operations of the school and the dormitory day-to-day. Fifty girls were selected to attend their first year of secondary schooling at the center based on their grades, their secondary school entrance exams, the distance that their families lived from a secondary school, and/or if their family could afford secondary schooling.

A flock of fathers waited under the shade of a lone, scrawny tree to take their daughters home for the summer break. Some had gray beards and deep smile lines in their cheeks, displaying a long life of both hard work and laughter. Others looked young, fresh, and ready to take on the world. I wanted to hug them all and thank them for sending their daughters to school, but that would have been a cultural cataclysm. Instead, my translator in Burkina, Paul Kinda, went over to talk to them while we were waiting to meet the girls and shared my gratitude in their local language with the appropriate cultural courtesy. I watched them nod their heads and occasionally laugh as Paul talked. Paul was so good at taking whatever it was I wanted to communicate and translating it into just the right words to ensure that the listener received my true meaning. He often made people smile, laugh, and feel at ease with a strange woman from America. I know people would have never told me many of the things they did if Paul hadn't made them feel so comfortable. He came from the same circumstances as they did; his parents were farmers and then workers on coffee and cocoa plantations who had no opportunity to get an education. The familiarity helped people open up.

The classroom was filled with 50 girls between

thirteen and fifteen in matching uniforms of white shirts, blue pleated skirts, white socks, and black shoes. I introduced myself and explained the reason for my visit—I had come a long way to see and learn more about the BRIGHT schools. Paul asked how many of them attended BRIGHT schools, and more than half of them raised their hands.

We broke the ice talking about their most and least favorite subjects. Some interesting patterns emerged. Ellen stood up first and said math was her favorite subject and her least favorite was, no question, physical education. That elicited a burst of laughter from all the girls; clearly Ellen wasn't the only one who disliked exercising in 100-plus degree weather. I told them, through Paul, that I didn't blame them and I'd be right there with them sitting in the shade under a tree rather than doing jumping jacks and running laps under the sun. Martha loved biology and hated English. I couldn't blame her for that either. English is a really hard language with all its irregular verbs, exceptions to rules, and idioms. Kadi got up next and said she actually liked English, but also hated PE. Esther, Aminata, and Nadege all liked math too. Maybe their math teacher was particularly good, but whatever the reason, I was thrilled to see so many girls excited about math.

I like to give kids a chance to ask me questions whenever I visit a school. It uncovers the things that are on the tops of their minds, which is usually pretty hilarious, very powerful, or both. Aminata stood up and asked, "How old are children in the United States when they start school?" I responded that children are usually five years old when they must start school by law, but they often attend preschool as early as one and a half. The girls were surprised to hear that we have a law that says all children must go to school. I told them it was the truth and that if I didn't send my kids to school "the police would come and take me away." Their eyes got really big when Paul translated that. I could imagine how strange it sounded to them in their context, where it's a privilege to go to school—a gift that half the children in their country don't have.

Another girl asked, "What kinds of animals do you raise in the United States?" I said that unlike in Africa, where every family has chickens, pigs, and maybe even goats around their homes, Americans only have dogs, cats, fish, and sometimes snakes and lizards as pets. We don't raise the animals we eat. The snakes and lizards part made them laugh, because to them it would be absurd to have pests like that around their house. I reassured them that it, too, was true, and that my little son has wanted a lizard since he was seven (he still doesn't have one).

The last question was a really good one that gave me an opportunity to encourage the girls to let themselves dream, even if just a little. A very sweet, and astute, girl stood up and asked, "What do people in the United States do for their professions and who makes the most money?" That's just the right question for an ambitious young woman to ask. I replied that the richest people in the United States are those who lend money to other people and then get paid back that money with interest or profit—we call them investors—as well as business people, lawyers, doctors, and celebrities. But I wanted to convey there is something very unique about the United States, which is that people can choose to do all kinds of different work that suits them and make money at it. "Many people in America can decide what they are passionate about and what they love doing and then find (or make) a job doing that," I said. "I love to work on women's and girls' rights, so I made that my job. Our photographer, Julie, loves to take pictures, so she decided to make that her work. So let yourself dream a little bit; maybe you don't have to be a doctor, lawyer, or businesswoman if you don't want to. Whatever you love to do, the world probably needs it."

I asked them if they liked to dance and they erupted with "*Oui!*" in unison. So there was only one thing left to do: get up and dance. A few girls had prepared a special dance of gratitude for our visit that had lots of quick footwork and upbeat, syncopated rhythms. There was no way I was going to join in with them. The second dance had everyone up out of their seats with deep African beats and a call and response melody that even I could manage. We didn't want to overstay our welcome since their fathers were patiently waiting for the girls under that unforgiving sun. They joyfully ran out when the headmaster released them for the summer.

Meeting the Kaya girls made me feel optimistic about Burkina's future. If these 50 could finish and even half of them could go to college, that would be 25 more women leaders for the country. I have no doubt they would have an impact. If only we could multiply that by a thousand, Burkina could fly.

# 47

# THE GIRL IN THE RED SHIRT

We were at the end of our lively visit to the Kaya Girls Center, and most of the students had left to start their rainy season holiday. The girls had completed their first year in secondary school and they were happy to be going home. The sisters brought us some more cold water while we waited inside for our chaperones from Plan International. I held the bottle to my face and let the condensation drip down my arm;

it was way too hot to care how I looked. Monsieur Yonli, the head sister, and the school director were outside engaged in an urgent conversation, while a beautiful girl in a bright red shirt quietly stood on the edge of the porch looking down at the ground. It was clear they were talking about her. After about 30 minutes of tense conversation, Monsieur Yonli came back inside to retrieve us.

"Do you mind if I ask what the commotion was about?" I tentatively asked, expecting him to say it was nothing. Monsieur Yonli sighed, shook his head, and said, "We have a student whose family wants to marry her off while she's still just a child. She's only thirteen."

It was the first time the Kaya Girls Center had this problem on their hands since it was their first year in operation. But the faculty and administrators were familiar with the issue since 61 percent of rural girls in Burkina are married before they reach seventeen, the age when they would finish secondary school if they're lucky enough to be in school.[22] In the developing world generally, one in three girls will be married before she turns eighteen.[23] Rural girls are twice as likely as urban girls to get married young, and girls from families in poverty are married as children at three times the rate of their higher income peers.[24]

The Plan International team and Kaya Girls Center teachers had done their best to talk with the girls and their families about early marriage. When the school opened, Monsieur Yonli came to visit often, and before the first holiday chatted with the girls about the issue of child marriage. He told them that they should—and could—refuse to marry anyone they didn't want to marry. They could even say no to their parents if they suggested it. Later that school year, the female governor of the province also talked to the girls and advised them not to get married young. She told them that marriage before age seventeen was illegal and she didn't want to see it happening in her part of the country.

The girl in the red shirt came forward a few days before our visit and told the director about her problem. The director enlisted Monsieur Yonli's help in deciding what to do. They thought the best course of action would be for the girl to stay at the school that night with the sisters; they did not want to risk someone hiding her from them before they could reach the family. Plan International would send a social worker and a child marriage specialist to the girl's home to try to comprehend the circumstances and know what the parents were thinking. "We need to first understand the family's perspectives and issues before we can take any action," Monsieur Yonli said wisely. "We don't know what agreements they may have made with another family, perhaps even before the girl was born."

Intervening to stop a child marriage is a delicate affair. If you report the impending marriage to the authorities, the police may come and take the parents away, which will only create more problems for the girl. If the parents are aware that outsiders might intercede, they may send the child away to another village or rush ahead with the marriage. Most often, there is no time to help. Discussion of early marriage is taboo, so no one is aware until after it happens. Girls are often just taken against their will, dressed up as brides, and made into wives in a single day.

Child marriage is another incredibly widespread, but ignored, form of violence. Marriage usually means the end of schooling and the beginning of childbearing. Pregnancies in early adolescence are very risky. Miscarriage, obstructed labor, postpartum hemorrhage, and pregnancy-related high blood pressure are much more common for girls whose bodies are not ready for babies. Obstetric fistulas are an awful result when babies become stuck in the slim hips of a young mother during labor. The extended pressure kills the pelvic tissue, which then atrophies, leaving these young women with no bladder or bowel control. They are rejected by their husbands and families and become destitute castoffs.

"This work is hard," Monsieur Yonli stated flatly. "You have to try your best to fix the individual situations you can. But if you can't change it, you really have to let it go and move on. For every girl that we find out about, there's a hundred more that we don't. There's just no shortcut—you've got to do the public education and social norm change. We have to fix the problem at the systemic level. It's not easy."

My last update from Plan International Burkina in the winter of 2013 was that something had been worked out with the family and the girl in the red shirt was in school, working hard on her studies, and probably praying each day that she'll be allowed to grow up before her wedding day.

# 48

## MCA 3.0

I walked behind Madame Maryam Sirima along the dirty street curb, dodging buzzing motorbikes and hawkers selling cigarettes and phone cards, to the steps of the Millennium Challenge Account building in Ouagadougou. The ubiquitous small, black plastic bags that shops used were strewn about the ground along with bottle caps, dried mango pits, used paper napkins, flattened cigarette boxes, and all kinds of other detritus in a salad of street trash. Madame Sirima wore a long, sparkling white dress, custom cut with detailed gold embroidery, and a matching headscarf. As she walked in front of me, the hem of her dress swayed just above the street salad without picking up a speck of dirt; she seemed to float above the filthy mishmash as if she was above it all.

Madame Sirima is the secretary general of the Coalition Burkinabé pour les Droits de la Femme (CBDF), which translates to the Burkina Coalition for Women's Rights. She cut her teeth as a lawyer working for the basic rights of women in her country. When she became involved in the early days of the coalition, her dynamism and energy quickly propelled her into the primary leadership position.

Since 2002, CBDF has worked to increase women's capacities to understand and exercise their human rights, as well as ensure that legal equality is enshrined in Burkinabé law at the provincial and national levels. As Madame Sirima put it, their mission is simple, but big: "Our goal is to eradicate violence against women and girls and see them exercise their rights like any male citizen of our country."

We were headed to the MCA Burkina Faso office to catch up with Madame Irene Kabré, the senior gender specialist for Burkina's entire MCA program. I had been to that office four years before when it was brand spanking new, built on Ouagadougou's John F. Kennedy Avenue just to house the MCA Burkina Faso and a few American MCC staff. Somehow the structure did not possess the same untouchable superiority as Madame Sirima and looked 50 years older than it should. The fresh paint had dulled to the same red dust color as everything else outside. The plaster was chipped away from the corners and I hoped the deteriorated skin of the building did not reflect the program's progress.

Burkina's $481 million MCA program includes three major projects. The first is improvements in 422 kilometers of small rural roads and major transportation routes to help farmers (and others) get their products to market centers. The second is a massive expansion in irrigated land for small-scale farmers in two provinces. The last is a revamp of Burkina's overall rural land tenure and management systems to assist the 90 percent of the population that depends on subsistence agriculture. This includes an important step toward improved productivity: land security. The program started in July 2009 and ends July 2014 unless the MCC grants it an extension. Each of the projects within Burkina's MCA program has the potential to benefit or harm hundreds of thousands of women depending on how the gender aspects of the work are handled.

I have to admit that the first time I met Madame Kabré four years before I felt a little worried about how gender was going to fare. She was quite experienced with gender issues in her country, but she was much younger than her equals in the program and did not have a track record in maneuvering government bureaucracies. What was most concerning to me was her shyness. She did not seem to have the "you-will-do-it" attitude of Sylvia from Nicaragua or the quiet iron will of Irangani from Sri Lanka. Based on my experience, an effective gender specialist needs to have exquisitely sensitive political antennae, plus body armor, to get things done. On that first visit, Madame Kabré took me around to each project director and introduced me by explaining that I was with an independent advocacy organization in Washington, DC, that held the MCA program accountable on gender. Essentially, she was saying to them, "There are people watching us on gender."

The person I met the second time I entered Madame Kabré's office four years later was entirely different. Her hair was no longer in a demure bob; it was shorter and spunkier, with a rebellious streak of red flashing through the right side. Her stance was solid as she hugged me and took my shoulders in her hands to kiss me on both cheeks. She commanded the room, which she now shared with other project officers. She was happy to see me, but chastised me for taking so long to come back to Burkina. I apologized and explained that I came back as soon as I could find a way. I wished I could have witnessed some of her transformation. I wanted to hear as much of what I had missed as possible.

Burkina's MCA story began in 2008 when they began conceptualizing their proposal to the US government. A Women Thrive team traveled to Burkina that year to find a local women's organization that wanted to influence their country's program. Out of several very strong women's groups, we decided to partner with CBDF, largely because of the ties they had with grassroots women in villages, similar to the National Women's Collective of Sri Lanka. CBDF empowered women to act, rather than studying women and then acting for them. Madame Sirima and the team at CBDF were all sophisticated and experienced advocates; we simply added our knowledge about the ins and outs of the MCA program, as well as the cultural peculiarities of working with Americans, of which there are many. For example, one of the biggest problems that trips up many developing country advocates is the American penchant to just get to the point. In other cultures it would be very rude to walk into a meeting and say, "Look, here's what we want. Yes or no?" One must first express thanks for the audience, inquire about the decision maker's family and community well-being, fully describe one's qualifications, gently introduce the problem, and then even more sensitively propose the solution. If you do that with an American who only has fifteen minutes to listen, you'll get to the end of the meeting before you've said why you're there. With Americans, you have to start with the point and work backward.

By the time that Burkina's program came around, the MCC Washington had much more experience in getting governments to take gender seriously. The strides were evident even before the Compact was signed. Women's perspectives were actively ignored in Sri Lanka. In Honduras, women were included only when it was forced to do so at the very end. The Nicaraguans resisted at the beginning, but acquiesced when they realized that no gender meant no money. By contrast, the Burkinabé government created a new National Gender Policy to ready itself for the MCA program. The United States doesn't have a domestic gender policy or anything close to it; not even equal rights for men and women in the Constitution. This was an impressive arc of progress on gender within the MCA program in only five years.

Between Burkina's National Gender Policy and the MCC Gender Policy, Madame Kabré had two strong legs on which to stand, something that few of her counterparts in other MCA countries possessed. Working closely with all the important stakeholders, she drew up an excellent action plan for how gender differences would be handled in each of the projects, complete with people's roles and accountability mechanisms. For example, the rural land tenure gender plan indicated that

**Burkina Faso's National Gender Policy**
Burkina Faso's National Gender Policy, created in July 2009, outlines the following seven strategic objectives:

1. Improve men and women's equal and equitable access to and control of basic social services.
2. Promote equal opportunities and rights for men and women to access and control the means of production and an equitable subdivision of the resulting income.
3. Promote men and women's equal access to the decision-making process.
4. Promote the institutionalization of gender by ensuring gender integration in the planning, budgeting, and execution of public policies at all levels.
5. Promote respect for human rights and the elimination of violence.
6. Encourage behaviors that promote equality between men and women.
7. Develop partnerships at all levels (i.e., between government, NGOs, and CBOs [Community-Based Organizations]) to promote gender equity in Burkina Faso.

specifically training women on their new property rights was essential to success. General raising of public awareness, which is how it's usually done, would not be enough.[25] This plan was not another heap of paper on a shelf. Madame Kabré has used it to effectively leverage changes from the implementing contractors. "It's still hard to get people to consider gender differences, but with the support of the MCC and this document [the action plan], it's a bit easier," she said. "Take the training targets. We had been talking about it since the beginning of the program, but no one was really paying attention to it. But we got the contractors to include a target of training 45 percent women on land governance." Sometimes government plans amount to less than the paper upon which they are printed. And sometimes a plan that everyone had agreed to is an incredibly effective tool to leverage action.

Beyond the action plan, the MCA Burkina Faso has a more substantial team thinking about gender every day than I've seen in any other MCA country so far. Each major project has an overall gender strategist, and each contractor is required to have a gender focal point on their team. The gender person is no longer just a lone voice pushing the rock up a hill. While these individuals are swimming against a strong cultural current in the opposite direction, they have one another to learn from, lean on, and reinforce. That's a huge step forward.

# 49

# LAW ZERO-THREE-FOUR

Until 2009, the government officially owned all the rural land in Burkina Faso. Farmers had been growing on that land, communities had developed upon it, and villages with their own kings thrived all around the countryside for generations. These rural Burkinabé considered the land theirs by customary right. However, at any time, the government could take the land away without providing compensation. More problematically, government approval was necessary to make any major changes to the land, like building proper irrigation systems or establishing commercial centers. In essence, the rural poor had no land security, and women had no land rights under customary law.

Here it is again—a systemic barrier to people in poverty who are trying to get themselves out. Without the ability or incentive to invest in the land, rural people in poverty were sentenced to a subsistence life. This is also a perfect example of why government assistance is necessary. Land rights are not something that corporate or nonprofit charities can (or should) fix. This is a legitimate role for government; staunch conservatives and hard-core liberals agree that one thing a government should do is enforce people's property rights. This kind of systemic change happens best when government donors work with recipient country governments. I am not saying that NGOs, traditional leaders, citizen groups, and businesses should stay out of it. Quite the contrary: These critical stakeholders should be deeply consulted and listened to. But at the end of the day, it is the government that makes the laws. In fact, CBDF played an important role, as did other women's organizations, in ensuring the passage of a new law that enshrined equal rights for women.

Law 0-3-4 (people in Burkina call it Law Zero-Three-Four) turned Burkina into a very progressive nation for women's land rights. The law contained the following important provisions:

- Individuals, corporations, communes, and the government may hold title to land.
- There is no discrimination in ownership of land by ethnicity, sex, or other characteristics. There are new safeguards to protect access to land for women, and the poor in particular.
- Communal property rights are recognized and can be formalized.
- Local governments take the lead on managing land rights, including conflicts,

partially through local land rights committees, which must each have at least two women.

The right words were there, but then came the hard work of changing ingrained attitudes about gender roles. Madame Sirima told me about a radio show she was on soon after the new law was passed. "This land law is the greatest opportunity for women to be real land owners, but only if they can exercise their rights. I was on a radio program with the president of a village development committee. The host gave him the floor and he encouraged everybody to make land accessible to women. The journalist wanted to check if he really meant what he said, so she asked him, 'If you legally shared your land with your wife and it happened that she left you, she wouldn't have to return the land to you and she could still work it if she wanted. What do you think about that?' He reacted angrily and said, 'I'll be waiting for her to give her a beating if she comes back to my land! That's what I think!'" Madame Sirima cracked up laughing and said, "You can never rely only on words."

# 50

## DEVILISH DETAILS

A dear friend of mine always says to me when I'm going through yet another change in circumstances: "Change is good, it's the transitions that suck." Transitioning from informal communal land management to formalized legal land ownership is not pretty. When combined with traditional beliefs about gender roles, the transition is more like a perfect storm.

In the Sourou province of Burkina, the MCA has undertaken a massive and ambitious project to transform 2,033 hectares (about eight square miles) of land from low-output subsistence farming to irrigated, high-output, and small-scale agricultural microbusiness. The MCA Burkina Faso selected a vast tract of land and built a state-of-the-art irrigation system with huge cement canals, two-story pumping stations, and a web of arteries and capillaries ending in fields of 500 square meters. Everyone had to move off the land—homes, fields, and all—to do the construction work. It wasn't an easy sell. "We were first very afraid when we first heard about the MCA project because we knew that our lands would be taken," a woman in the small village of Oue told me. "But later on we understood that the lands would be taken, developed, and then given back to us to farm with better results. Then we were happy to welcome the project."

Once the construction is done, people will go back to farming, but who goes back, how much land they get, and how that will get figured out in a fair and transparent manner are complicated considerations. This is where it gets really messy, and where women need advocates every single step of the way so they aren't left standing on the outside. The MCA Burkina Faso came up with a set of criteria to allocate the improved land, but it did not work well for women. Women weren't left out by design, but cultural norms wouldn't allow women to take advantage of this rare opportunity.

Traveling with Madame Sirima, I was able to visit with about 80 women in three different villages across Sourou province. I thought Kaya was hot when I spent a few days there with the BRIGHT girls, but Sourou is Death Valley hot. Just for fun, I left a thermometer in the sun for a few minutes to see how hot it really was. Our photographer guessed it would be about 120 degrees and I wagered 140 degrees; Paul, my translator, laughed at us and shook his head. It was 150 degrees in the sun. That's hot enough to bake cookies outside. I wondered how on earth people could farm there.

When I sat down in a circle with the first group

of women in the village of Oue, the first thing I noticed was their clothing. They were covered from head to toe by long dresses and head wraps since they were Muslim, but they were wearing several layers of clothing. Almost every woman had an underskirt beneath her dress and a tightly-wound head covering below her flowing outer headscarf. While I was experiencing something akin to an inferno, they were accustomed to it. And like them, their crops managed to survive in one of the bleakest and hottest places on earth.

I ceased my internal whining about the heat and asked if any of them had been able to get some land registered in their own name. No one raised a hand. I asked them if they would have any access to irrigated land to farm. Almost all of them raised their hands. "Some of us will be given a place to farm by our husbands if they were allocated a plot," a beautiful young woman explained to me. "All of us will have access because, thanks to CBDF, we formed associations and were able to secure land for women's farming in that way." After much conversation with the group, I understood that the association was a work-around to help women get something because the original idea of women having land in their own name didn't materialize as planned.

When the MCA began work in Sourou and moved people off their fields, they set up a registry for Program Affected Persons (PAPs) to capture the population that would need compensation for two to three years of lost growing seasons, as well as new plots in the irrigated area. Women were allowed to enter themselves separately from their husbands if they were working some land, even if they didn't own it, because PAPs included people who lost the *use* of land, not just land they owned by customary practice. But women didn't put themselves on the list. What I gleaned from my conversations across the three villages was that neither men nor women felt that it was appropriate for women to register themselves separately from their husbands. As women previously could not possess land by custom, they still didn't see themselves as being affected by the project. Moreover, women referred again and again to "not wanting to make problems within the family" as a reason to stand invisible behind their husbands. Given their circumstances, I certainly could not blame them. What it meant, however, was that women missed the first and most critical opportunity to get into the system to benefit from the project.

The second, and very logical, reason women didn't claim their own land was because larger households (with more people to work the soil) got larger plots to farm. A person cannot be part of a household farm group *and* apply for their own land at the same time—it's one or the other. Families didn't realize that the program was trying to boost women's land ownership and that they would actually get more land in total if a woman claimed her own parcel, rather than being counted as one more worker on her husband's farm. Not knowing that, they made the logical choice to list all wives (remember this is a polygamous society) as household workers in order to get the largest piece of land they could.

CBDF had conducted several training workshops for women in the community to help them understand these complexities. But the time was short, the rules were confusing, and cultural norms were hard to change. Madame Kabré, with the encouragement and support of the MCC team, did her best to organize educational outreach to communities, but it was a battle every step of the way. I've seen this before in other countries from Central America to Central Asia. Often, empowering women to understand and exercise their rights takes longer than the couple of years a project allows. Of course, working with men is critical and would have been incredibly useful to the women in Sourou; they may have been much more willing to step out and put their name on a list if they knew their husbands saw it to their own advantage. But in the zeal to have quantifiable results in a short time, the essential actions for success are habitually shortchanged. The MCA program in Burkina ends in July 2014. I am worried that the education of women and men in relation to land rights won't happen fast enough. As land gets divided up and titled, women might be systematically and irreparably sidelined. Rather than removing a principal barrier to women's advancement, the MCA will institutionalize another systemic roadblock for women.

When I returned from Sourou to Ouagadougou, I went to meet with Kateri Clement, the resident country director of the MCC in Burkina Faso. If you could meet Kateri, it would make you feel proud about the people representing the United States around the world. She seemed grounded in the values we hold dear—fairness, freedom, and free enterprise—and was still culturally astute and committed to Burkina taking the lead role in the MCA project, as they should be the leaders of their own country's development. My impression was that her considerable intellect and social grace were being well utilized each day as she balanced the need for Burkina to deliver on its goals, including the objectives it set on women, against the need to not be culturally imperialistic. Doing that is like dancing on the edge of a blade.

I gave Kateri a full download of what the Sourou women shared with me. She was not surprised in the slightest. She also pointed out, "Before this project, Burkina had issued only 28 land titles to individuals; everything else was titled to the state or commercial interests. These are first titles given to *anybody,* and the first ever for rural women here." Kateri heard the same things I did during her visits with women, and she actively pursued other options to see that women got a piece of the pie. She strongly supported the women's association pathway but didn't feel that was sufficient. There were still 1,300 more hectares to allocate, plus an additional 140 hectares for 99-year leases. The MCA Burkina Faso has agreed to give women an advantage if they apply for that land, with the goal of women getting 10 percent of the surface area that is left. But women still have to apply for it on their own.

Kateri thought it would be a good idea for me to meet with the head of the MCA Burkina Faso before I left the country to share what I learned as well as my concern that if gender activities were not ratcheted up, Burkina was not going to hit its benchmarks for women. I wasn't sure I could get a meeting with him that quickly. "Sure you can," Kateri said while she picked up the phone and called his direct line. Five minutes later, I had a meeting for the next day. I asked Madame Kabré to join me, since this was her boss.

Monsieur Joseph Bissiri Sirima (no relation to Madame Sirima) was a large man with an authoritative look about him. He was wearing traditional clothes that day, and I noticed four or five rings on his wedding finger. I assumed he must have that number of wives. Paul told me later those were charms to ward off bad spirits. "Like me," I said. Paul smiled, not disagreeing with me.

Monsieur Sirima seemed particularly uninterested in meeting with us; he kept us waiting for almost an hour and when he finally granted us an audience, we had only fifteen minutes. So I introduced myself and got right to the point in the typical American way. "Monsieur Sirima, Burkina has the chance to be a model among MCA countries on gender. You've done so much already, more than I've seen done in some other MCA countries," I said. "But failure is also a distinct possibility if there isn't more focus on this in your last year of the program." He seemed indifferent. He said they were working really hard on implementing the gender action plan that Madame Kabré put together, they paid for a woman lawyer to make sure gender was reflected in the new land law, and the MCA Burkina Faso "made it clear" to beneficiaries that women working the land should be listed and become land owners. I thanked him for giving us his time and ended by saying that I hoped to return in a few years to find women proudly showing their land titles.

# 51

## MARRY ME

There was one more work-around to help women secure their land rights: marriage. Law 0-3-4 and the MCA Burkina Faso land allocation guidelines stated that women in legally recognized marriages had rights to their husband's land. The problem was, as one village woman put it, "In most villages it is not normal to get married legally. We get married in the traditional way, which is not recognized by the law. If there is no paper, nothing proves this man is really mine." That last part made the entire circle of women chuckle. Perhaps it was especially funny because for many of these women, even if they have marriage papers, a husband isn't theirs because they share him with other wives.

CBDF organized couples across Sourou to have mass legal marriages in local town halls. Each man had to choose one wife to legally marry, however, as Burkina doesn't legally recognize polygamy. But at least one wife, perhaps the first wife or the favorite wife, would have some claim to the family's land.

As a special treat, Madame Sirima arranged to have a marriage ceremony while we were in

Sourou. I pictured a mundane office, with a quiet group of people approaching the mayor's desk in pairs, silently signing their names, or leaving their fingerprints, on pieces of paper. I couldn't have been more wrong. It was a riotous scene and a great excuse to have a hopping big party.

We arrived at the mayor's office in the town of Di to find men standing by the front of the building. Women and children were around the other side, in the morning shade. Most of the women had the tips of their fingers and soles of their feet dipped in black dye, decorated for the special occasion. Some didn't have their hair in the traditional plaits; instead they wrapped their hair tightly in black plastic cords to make locks. The locks were then woven together like a basket. It was very beautiful. Some of the men and women were there in worn clothes and old foam flip-flops; others came in lovely dresses with wonderful head wraps and heels, and men arrived in spiffy suits.

The festivities began with an announcer—a cross between DJ, town caller, and storyteller—bantering over the loud speaker and getting everyone hyped up. He put on some music with an African calypso beat, marimbas, and steel guitars. I love this music. Even though I'm a really bad dancer, I could not hold my feet still. The volume was so high there was nothing else in my brain except the vibration of the notes. I was completely lost in it; nothing before each note and nothing after, just the now of the beat. It didn't matter what just happened or what would happen next. I wished I could float like that all the time. For a little while, I forgot about how darn hot, sweaty, and tired I was, and how much I missed my boys.

I asked Paul when the wedding would start and he said, "Soon on G-M-T." I looked at him, puzzled, and he said, "Gonna-Maybe-Time." After about an hour and a half the mayor entered the room where couples, their families, and friends squeezed together. Children looked in from the open windows, the little ones hopping up and down or standing on someone's knee to get their eyes above the threshold to see their parents get married.

The mayor talked a little about what legal marriage meant and read out of a book about the rights of women and men in legal marriage. The first couple, a pair in their sixties, approached the mayor's desk and he asked them for their consent in marriage. The woman said, "Yes, I agree with my whole heart," and the mayor announced them "*mari* and *femme*." The mayor teased them to kiss and they did; the crowd erupted in claps and laughter. That kind of public display of affection didn't happen around here. The next wife declared that she would love her husband until she "passed on." A heckler in the audience shouted out, "But what if he dies before you do.

Will you love him then?" The mayor naughtily went on to tell every couple to kiss, but the next pair embraced one another in the traditional way—a light hug barely touching opposite cheeks four times. The man in the next couple covered his bases by saying, "I love my wife so much, I will love her even after death—hers or mine." Bidding in the love auction was open—to the mayor's delight.

After all the couples had declared their affections and signed their names, the mayor gave them advice on how to live together in marital peace. "In case the husband is angry," he said, "the wife should avoid getting angry as well. She should try to cool him down. The husband should do the same when the wife is angry. They should make decisions when everybody is calm and ready to come to an agreement, not when angry." That is sound advice for marriage in any culture. He went on to say that husbands who don't want to assume their responsibilities and give their wife enough money for the family food when the woman asks for it are going to "get themselves into trouble." I liked the mayor very much.

# 52

# USAID FORWARD

On March 1, 2012, the first day of Women's History Month, I was in the Eisenhower Executive Office Building auditorium for an event that I thought would never happen. By 2007, when the MCC adopted its gender policy, we had all but given up on USAID doing the same thing. The right leadership was not in place at the agency. President Bush was nearing the end of his second term and there was no appetite to go in bold new directions.

So we waited until there was a new president, and even then, we waited some more. After being elected, it took President Obama nearly two years to put someone in place to lead USAID. The agency had been in suspended animation all that time with a capable and seasoned acting administrator, but he did not have the legal authority to make big changes. Acting Administrator Alonzo Fulgham did everything he could to help push gender along within the confines of his job description.

Finally, in December 2009, a fresh new face arrived with the drive and brains to shake things up and—importantly—without any institutional inertia to weigh him down. Rajiv Shah, a young man who at only 24 years old had advised Vice President Al Gore on health issues during his 2000 presidential bid, took the helm at USAID just days before the massive earthquake in Haiti in January 2010. It was clear to everyone in the development community that he immediately ran up against walls of bureaucratic habit as he tried to oversee a swift and modern response to Haiti's worst disaster ever. Administrator Shah was not at USAID long before he announced his "Forward" program to renovate how the agency does business, hire more than a thousand new aid professionals, invest more in local country systems and organizations, focus evaluation on outcomes that matter, and put assessments in the public space so people can see for themselves how US assistance is working. In three years, USAID has made enormous strides in all of these areas.

One of the biggest and best changes is USAID's Gender Integration and Female Empowerment Policy, released at the event I thought would never happen. I know it seems boring and obtuse with a name like that, but the new policy fundamentally changed the way billions of dollars in aid are designed, delivered, and judged. For many years, people have asked me, "Don't you think 50 percent of aid should go to women?" And I have always said, "No, 50 percent of aid shouldn't go to women; 100 percent of aid should benefit women and girls at least as much as it benefits men and boys." We have always wanted it all and nothing less. The USAID policy gave it all.

This policy goes beyond just looking at different gender roles to make sure that US projects in developing countries don't make needless mistakes and leave people out. The policy makes women's and girls' advancement an *explicit end goal* of every single US assistance project where it makes sense. The US government is putting a stake in the ground and saying that, in addition to advancing democracy, economic growth, and health, empowering women and girls is an important goal in and of itself and a mission that it will put serious money behind. So now, agriculture programs will be created to not just increase the productivity of subsistence farmers but also make sure that in doing so women farmers get more control over their crops, get more say in how things get done, and get to keep more of their own money. It means that disaster aid must help women and girls move forward after devastation, not send them reeling backward because they are destroyed by violence. Even infrastructure projects must look at how roads are designed to ensure women's safety and consider where women want the road to go (e.g., to the water well and the doctor, as opposed to the town gathering spot). The gender policy is one of those things where the name completely belies the revolutionary potential.

So are there any teeth to this policy? Women Thrive and our coalition partners made sure that there are plenty. Now, it is the responsibility of many people in the chain of command to ensure that women's and girls' unique challenges are addressed (that's the minimum) and also that US aid effectively *advances* equality for women and girls. Everyone in USAID, not just a handful of gender advisers, is being trained to design projects through a "gender lens" so they don't inadvertently leave out women—or men for that matter. Every project that involves people must report on its outcomes for males and females separately; there is no way to cover up bias toward men anymore. And if someone wants to hold on to outdated thinking about gender issues, their failure to consider it will block their chances for promotion. Even better, no contractor can get money from USAID unless they adequately address gender issues in every aspect of their project *and* demonstrate that they really know how to deliver on women's empowerment.

Administrator Shah is a stalwart supporter of women's advancement and the gender policy. "If you really care about ending conflict, you have to care about equality for women and girls," he told me. "Afghanistan is a good example. The big success story in Afghanistan, the one you don't hear about in the news, is the National Solidarity Program." The National Solidarity Program

(NSP) was started by the Afghan government in 2003 to help communities identify, plan, manage, and monitor their own development projects (what a concept!). Villages elect their own representatives to form a Community Development Council. The council looks at the village's needs and decides what project they will propose for government support. Almost all of the councils include good representation of women—overall, women compose 36 percent of the councils—with a number of them now being led by women. Through the Afghan government, the United States has supported about 22,000 villages all over the mountainous country. "Including the rural, hard-to-reach, and super-inaccessible parts of Afghanistan," Administrator Shah added.

"Almost every community asks for a school or a health clinic," he continued. "Once they build it, the women run the facilities themselves, even if they have to do it less visibly than in other places. Women have told me how they face resistance at first to forming a group. Men start to offer their support when they see resources come into the community. It's clear that women are being successful, standing on their own, and their image of themselves—as well as their standing in the community—is evolving.

"Afghanistan has no chance if women are repressed throughout their lives. Once people see a future where more than half of the population contributes to the country's potential (and, by the way, we know that they contribute more effectively than the other half), they will not allow themselves to go back to Taliban-like cultural and operational norms. They will not allow the suppression of women who have become a completely integral part of providing economic welfare, educational opportunities, and health care services to their communities. I have visited these mountain villages and their leaders, and it's very hard to imagine them wanting to go back to the Taliban, who will completely reverse the nation's hard-won gains. These villages are choosing something different for their future."

I am incredibly proud of the role Women Thrive Worldwide played in bringing this new policy forward. We brought women leaders from the developing world every year to Washington to speak directly with policy makers. We organized countless coalition meetings; garnered support from hundreds of organizations; got Congress to mandate that USAID integrate gender; pressed every key leader at USAID and the State Department over fourteen years; petitioned the president and the secretary of state; brought to light examples of how aid fails without gender integration, and how it succeeds with it; and provided specific ideas for what to include in USAID's policy, even how to staff it. I honestly don't think we could have done anything more than we did.

Still, the work is not done yet. Just as we did for the MCC, we need to look at how USAID puts these words into action, examine how it's playing out in countries, and point out the places that are getting stuck. I know from our work in Sri Lanka, Honduras, Nicaragua, and Burkina Faso that this is the part that really matters. In fact, this is the part where we get to see what we've fought for come to life and change the lives of real women and girls who deserve to be heard, included, and empowered. We're not done with our work until *they* say so.

# 53

# LIVING ON A DOLLAR A DAY IN BURKINA FASO

The longest and hardest dollar-a-day that I've done was in Doulougou, Burkina Faso, in 2010 (before my stays in Sri Lanka and Nicaragua). I was really nervous about this one. It was going to be over 100 degrees in the sun and I was planning on staying for a 72-hour, full-immersion experience. But I thought that if more than a billion women can do this every single day of their lives, I could probably do it for just three days and two nights. Besides, I had my mandatory emergency medical evacuation insurance in my pocket, so if I keeled over, I wasn't going to die.

After hours of planes through several West African capitals, many taxis, and head-bobbingly rough dirt roads, I arrived in the kingdom of Doulougou. Yes, feudalism still lives, and in Burkina Faso it is married to French-style bureaucracy and African-style polygamy. Each village has a king, a mayor, a prefect, a royal council, and a civic council. And most married men have at least two wives, with some "rich" men having up to ten. (For the life of me, I cannot figure out what happens to the other nine men who can't find a wife.)

My host, Mariam Ouadraogo, and her family greeted our little Women Thrive delegation under the family mango tree. Her family is large—one husband, two wives, and seven children—living in one compound. Would she like me? What would she think of me, the crazy American that wants to live with her for a few days? Would she let me really do all the things that she does, like fetching water and fuel wood, planting crops, and cooking?

I immediately saw that Mariam was a rock. From behind her eyes I caught a glint of steel. Her hands were wide and calloused. Her neck was thick and strong. But she smiled at me as though I was a daughter coming home for the first time after being married off to another village; she was giddy with delight. We greeted one another in broken French, a little English, and the few words of Moré (the local dialect in that part of Burkina Faso) I learned in the car on the way there:

*Barka*, which means thank you.

*Neh-ee beyogo*, which means good morning, and *neh-ee zabré*, which means good evening.

If someone asks, *Beyogo kibaré?* (How is your morning?) I should answer with *laafi bala* (fine, thank you).

After our welcome under the mango tree, Mariam turned all business. We were losing light quickly this close to the equator and she was anxious to begin cooking a dinner of *toh*, ground sorghum and a vinegar-like broth made from soaking the leaves of the baobab tree in water. Her daughter had taken the sorghum to the mill to grind but had not yet returned. Mariam invited me to join her on a short bike ride to investigate what the delay was. The miller, a whisper of a man, peered out from the darkened interior of the small structure and, not quite believing his eyes, stepped out into the dusk. Mariam introduced me as the American who had come to stay with her for a few days. Her daughter skipped back home and Mariam's sorghum was ground in two minutes flat.

The water was already boiling when we returned and Mariam asked me to sift the flour through a sieve made from an old window screen and a bent cut of wood. She only had to correct me three times before I got it right. She and her daughters giggled at the sight of me awkwardly sitting bent low to the ground on a wooden stool as I shook sorghum into the basin. No one in Doulougou had seen a "white" person in maybe ten years, which is funny because I'm not white. But they don't usually see cinnamon-brown people walking around, either. Here in Doulougou you're either black or white—end of story.

The girls were washing dishes and, wanting to be the gracious guest, I offered to finish for them. They couldn't believe their ears; their eyes grew as wide as the coins they rarely got to hold. I assured them I was not insane. They giggled and happily went to rest.

Mariam then invited me to stir the thickening porridge with a three-foot-long wooden spoon. Easier said than done: This stuff did not move. Imagine a vat full of Elmer's Glue left by forgetful children on their craft table for a week. I gave it my all, but I was afraid I was either going to tip the whole pot onto the ground (it was barely suspended over an open flame by three or four rocks) or catch my skirt on fire. I handed the spoon to the expert. What followed was an incredible rhythmic dance of muscle, spoon, pot, and bubbling glue. Mariam started to sweat hard from the exertion and the heat. All this after she had worked in the fields since 5 a.m. I was in awe. I was also really hungry.

Mariam insisted that I take a bath before eating dinner. A bath? I didn't see a bathroom, much less a bathtub. She pointed to a wall to the side of the courtyard, where there was a bucket full of cloudy well water, a bar of white soap, and a piece of two-by-four wood on which to stand. I peeled off my sticky clothes and stood under the almost-full moon. It was a moment of peaceful disbelief: Am I really here? Bathing under a silvery African moon? As poor as it is here, there was an earthy sensuality to the place, pulsing right alongside the glaringly hot reality.

At about 8:30 we settled down to dinner in the dark. Mariam's husband was served first, and separately. I ate with Paul. I accidently washed my hands in the calabash bowl meant for drinking and Paul laughed at me (only the first of about a thousand gaffes and laughs). Since everyone ate with their hands, I dipped mine into the bowl of hot porridge and got burned. Not wanting to be ridiculed again, I lifted it up to taste and nearly gagged. It tasted like warm, fermented pancake batter, only crunchier. But this was all there was on the menu, and if it was good enough for Mariam, it was good enough for me. By nightfall I had a million questions for Paul. He very patiently explained why Burkinabé compounds are arranged as they are—a set of small mud huts, the largest for the husband and smaller ones for each of his wives and their children. All set in a circle, with a courtyard in the middle, and surrounded by a wall. The arrangement defined and protected the family unit. Most interestingly, Paul told me how Mariam is much more than just one wife in this family of ten. She's a community leader and a role model to young women throughout this village. She's a local rock star.

It was getting much too late. Mariam begins work at 5 a.m., and so would I. It was about 85 degrees outside and over 90 degrees inside, so I opted to sleep outside with the rest of the family. The father and boys constructed a "bed" by jury-rigging mosquito nets, plastic mats, and a bedsheet on a flat piece of concrete.

I lay down and felt the heat of the day radiate up from the concrete through the plastic mat, the sheet, my skin, my muscles, and into my bones. I was sweating and fidgeting. I was anxious about the next day and startled by every unfamiliar noise. Then the moon rose over the small hut and I watched it pull a graceful arc across the sky. It calmed me down and I finally fell asleep.

It felt like my eyes had just closed when Mariam clapped me awake. I woke to a purple, sunless dawn. It was about 5 a.m. *I can't believe I asked to do this,* I thought. I cracked myself loose and took apart my bedtime pallet.

Our first task was to collect the nuts of a shea tree that stood about fifteen minutes away on foot.

We had to beat the pigs to them. As we walked, I asked Mariam to tell me about the women's farmer association she leads. The association has about 2.2 hectares of land on which it grows vegetables during the dry season. The well in the center of the plot has barely enough water to irrigate the crops, bucket by slow bucket. The members of the association are organic farmers, but not by choice, like the women farmers in Honduras and Nicaragua. In a kind of twisted irony given the high price of organic products in the United States, these African women are too poor to farm any other way. They can't afford the basic fertilizers that would help them grow more food from soil that has been depleted from generations of farming.

Once we got to the tree, I picked up shea nuts like little brown Easter eggs, excited to find each one hidden in the grass. Mariam chuckled at me. In less than ten minutes, we filled a tin bucket to the rim. Later, Mariam would shell the nuts, boil them for about an hour, and make a buttery paste to sell in the market.

I peppered her with more questions as we walked back to her compound. About 25 years ago, Mariam heard about another village where the women organized themselves into an association and pooled their resources, land, and brainpower to grow more food, sell some of it, create a joint kitty of savings, and lend funds to one another. She thought she'd give it a try and went to each household in the village to gather up women. She only corralled a few; women were skeptical, the men suspicious. The women worried they'd just end up with extra work, and they were busy from dawn to dusk as it was.

The little clutch of women Mariam gathered together each contributed one bowl of shea nuts to sell; they managed to raise a few dollars. It was enough to go to the village elders and ask for a tiny piece of land to farm together. They were given a plot the size of an average kitchen. They started with black beans, rice, and millet.

There are no secrets in a village this size, so when Mariam's family started eating better and buying a few things with profits from the women's farm, more and more women came forward. Their association grew to 65 women strong. They have a pool of money in the bank from which they give each other loans for major family events like weddings and funerals, and every member gets 2,500 CFAs (pronounced SAY-fahs, it is the monetary unit of formerly French colonies; this is about $5.50) each year to put into a small business. For her part, Mariam has a small stand in the Friday market where she sells rice and African curry.

The women's association members farm together, sharing the planting, weeding, de-bugging, and harvesting—all by hand. The village families eat these vegetables. The basic staples—rice, sorghum, and millet—come partially from this land, but mostly from their husbands' farms.

I asked Mariam where she'd like the association to go from there. She replied that she'd like to access a lot more land, to buy the association a donkey to plow more efficiently, and to purchase a gas-powered grain mill. These improvements, she told me, would really help grow food, even in bad seasons, and also create a surplus when the rains are good, which they could then sell. Plus, the grain mill would break the monopoly the miller holds on the village, which would save them lots of money and increase their profit margin in the market.

More land, a donkey, and a gas-powered mill? That's it? We're talking about maybe $10,000 to transform the life of a whole village. I wished I had that kind of money to spare. I've felt this way so many times before: Women living in poverty are really clear about what they need to improve their lives. Once again, all we need to do is ask them.

By the time we returned to the compound, I was all fired up. Our next task was to go see the women's association farm and to collect greens for lunch and dinner. Mariam looked at me with concern and asked through Paul, "Are you too tired?" Though I was exhausted from only having three hours of sleep, I answered, "Let's go!" This type of experience was what I'd been looking forward to for months! Finally getting out there to talk to women farmers and experience a little of what their daily lives are like. Besides, if we didn't harvest the greens there wouldn't be lunch or dinner. Amazing how simple that fact makes decision making.

The women work on the association plot more intensively in the dry season, when they grow eggplant, beans, spinach-like greens, and squash. These vegetables are a critical part of their families' diets; without them they would eat only plain grains. In the rainy season of May and June, their focus shifts to growing the staples—millet, sorghum, and rice.

As soon as we arrived, Mariam handed me a short-handled hoe and I got to work weeding one of the beds. There was no comfortable way to lean over and scrape the earth clean. After ten minutes, I slowed down and Mariam jokingly asked if I wanted a chair. I couldn't imagine doing this for hours and hours in the hot sun with a baby strapped to my back. I was totally embarrassed that I couldn't keep up. She released me to go pick greens, which was so much easier.

We trekked back again to the compound to have breakfast. Yes, breakfast. It was only 8 a.m. and I had already put in three hours. I was drenched in sweat and was beat, and the temperature had only begun to rise. How was I going to make it through the rest of the day? I fell into a chair under the mango tree, grateful to be still. Mariam reappeared in a few minutes with last night's leftovers. I hoped the hunger would make the meal more flavorful this time around, but it actually tasted worse cold. I forced down something, knowing I'd need the energy.

Mariam reviewed our to-do list. Time was running out to plant seeds, but there hadn't been enough rain to soften the soil to receive them. She needed to get firewood, but she feared that as the day got hotter the snakes would hide beneath the leaves of the fallen branches and bite us as we gathered wood. Honestly, I thought she was just taking pity on me. I was so tired and hot that I felt nauseated. I knew darn well that she would be out there with her back to the sun inserting hopeful seeds into the earth if I weren't there to slow her down.

I put my pride aside, spread my plastic mat under the tree, lay down, and passed out.

A few hours later, I woke up to a commotion. There were at least fifteen women hovering around the house furtively watching me. I looked at Paul with a question mark on my face. "They came to welcome you," he stated as if it was obvious. "These are the women who couldn't come to the farm to see you there. They will be so pleased that you have woken up."

Were they ever! They broke into a traditional

welcome dance that I've seen before. I call it the "bumper-bum" dance. One woman jumps into the circle and invites another to join her. They spin, they stomp, and they bump their hips together. Then the second woman invites another and on and on it goes around the circle. I can't think of a better way to welcome a sister home. Although I'm pathetic at getting a rhythm, I could swing my hips well enough to delight them. I love this place, I decided.

We settled down to lunch under the mango tree. In Africa anything worth doing seems to take place under a tree. Mariam and I continued our conversation about the women's association. Here land is power, she explained. It's all about who has it, who can access it, who inherits it, who cares for it, and what you grow on it. It's unusual for women in Africa to own land like the association does. Normally, women are allowed to use some marginal piece of property that nobody else wants, but as soon as they improve it with trees, nutrients, and tender loving care, the owner (normally a man) will take it away to use for himself. Mariam proudly told me that they have ownership papers. This made me very happy.

Procuring more land would involve navigating a maze of traditional and bureaucratic twists. The women would have to raise enough money to prove that they could pay the fees to get the land title (about three months' worth of income!) and that they were able to get crops started. They must then get approval from all their husbands in order to go to the village elders to formally make the request for the land. If the elders agree, they would select a parcel and bequeath it to the women in a ceremony (under a tree, of course). Once that happened, they could apply for "papers" from the municipal government and pay the extortion-like titling fees. Eventually, the papers would come and they would own the land until they pass it to their daughters under the ceremonial tree.

Mariam's husband must have overheard us talking about land and he sauntered over to join the conversation. He declared that there was "no problem with women getting more land here, that they can have as much land as they want, they just have to ask for it." Mariam fell silent and stared at the ground. I smiled and reassured my host that I was impressed by the support the women receive from their husbands here, and that I didn't always see that in other places I have traveled. I emphasized how remarkable it is and how the men of Doulougou could be models for the rest of the world. I could see the corners of Mariam's mouth sneak into a smile. Of course, I didn't know if that's entirely true, but I think that if treating women well can be a source of pride for men, it can help them let go of the false sense of security they may derive from controlling or abusing women.

. . .

Fetching water is a daily ritual for almost a third of the world's women and girls. At any given moment, millions of them are walking on dirt paths through deserts or forests or fields to get a few gallons of cloudy water with which to bathe, cook, and quench their babies' thirst. If you're lucky and the pond or well is close, it might only take you an hour. If you're not, it might take you two or three hours to get to the source and then wait your turn. (And if you're me, you might start back with a full basin of water but arrive with only half.) Placing a clean water source within fifteen minutes of every rural household would save women up to six full months a year of productive time, according to the World Bank.[26] Imagine what women could do with that time. They could learn to read and write, they could grow more food, they could start making handicrafts to sell, or they could—imagine this—not work for seventeen straight hours a day. God forbid that women actually sit down to rest and gaze at their growing children and really take in the wonder of what they've created.

The well Mariam goes to was only ten minutes away, but it was almost empty because the rains have been light and infrequent. The water level was more than 50 feet down and made me slightly dizzy to look into it. Mariam pulled me back by my shirt, like a mother rescuing an errant toddler, and handed me a bucket made from old tires. She motioned for me to quit well-gazing and get to work. It took many dips to fill my water pot because the bucket was seriously leaking. Half the water escaped before I could yank the tire bucket to the top, so I started pulling up faster to see if I could beat the force of gravity. My best time yielded a three-quarters full vessel and a wicked cramp between my shoulders.

Mariam planted a rolled piece of fabric atop my head and then a two-gallon basin of water. She put some leaves in the pot, which helped the water stay in: water-fetching training wheels. I took two steps and the momentum of the water rocked the basin forward. A waterfall passed in front of my face onto my feet. Mariam looked back at me, bemused. I couldn't walk in her elegant, posture-perfect, no-hands footsteps as she carried her water in front of me. I had to give in and hold the basin with both hands. When we arrived home, I was wearing most of my catch. Mariam said, with a straight face, "If you wanted a bath, you only had to ask."

Once again it was getting late. I slowed her routine too much. She hustled me into the kitchen to make *babenda*, literally meaning "the dog's underwear." I kept repeating *ba-ben-da* to make the kids laugh, as if my mere presence wasn't funny enough already. This dish is made from ground millet with leafy greens cooked directly into the porridge. Salt and oil are sprinkled on top. Mariam told me it's very nutritious. And it's good. I felt grounded having a stomach full of food gathered from the fields around us.

Mariam and her girls were busy cleaning up and her husband retired to his own private hut for the evening, so I went ahead and rebuilt my bed myself. There was a breeze and I was hoping to have a long dreamless sleep. But that was not in the cards. About a half hour after falling asleep, Mariam grew upset about something. She told me to get up and I panicked, worried that I'd done something gravely wrong. She motioned for me to get out of my bed; I did so obediently, but with a sinking stomach. Had I slept in the wrong place? Did I need to cover myself up more? Then she took her only blanket and spread it over the plastic mat, and I got it. She was horrified her guest was sleeping on a bare "mattress." I thanked her ten times in Moré, "Barka, Mariam, barka, barka." She scolded her daughters for being so rude to the guest; she had asked them to make up my bed properly, but they had been too busy watching me and giggling with their friends. Moms and daughters are the same the world over.

A little while later, the rains had come at last. *"Why now?"* I asked the sky. *"Couldn't you just wait until morning?"* Everyone scooped up my mat and blanket and rushed me into the hut. It's made of mud bricks with a corrugated tin roof and one *very* small window. I'm short and I couldn't even stand up in it. I re-created my bed, as Mariam would like it, shuffling and squatting around the tiny space. I settled and listened to the wind whisk the dirt around and scratch it against the tin roof. No rain, just wind. I could feel everyone's anxiety that the rain would not come soon enough. The growing season would be short. The harvests would be small. And hunger would return. I lay there, willing it to rain. Dawn was only a few hours away.

Clap, clap, clap. *This must be the African alarm clock,* I thought. Clap, clap, clap. *God help me, it's still dark.* But I had wanted to collect shea nuts again this morning and here was Mariam to rouse me. The romance was already gone, but we got the work done twice as fast.

The cool night and wind had probably shuffled the snakes back to their quarters, so Mariam thought it'd be safe to go fetch wood. Mariam, her co-wife, and I started out along the dirt road, without Paul (he had another errand to attend to), and Mariam attempted to teach me some Moré:

"*Yaam,*" she said.

"*Yam,*" I replied.

"*YAAHHMM,*" she tried, loudly this time.

"*YAAAAM,*" I said and she smiled her gorgeous smile.

It means "me" or "I." About 30 minutes later

when we reached the eucalyptus grove, I could say: "*Yaam banga Moré. Tanda banga Moré. Taam fua banga Moré.*" I speak Moré, you speak Moré, we speak Moré.

The eucalyptus trees belong to the men, and every year they cut some of the straight limbs and sell them for a dollar each. This is Africa's Home Depot; it's the skeletal structure of huts, verandas, chicken coops, pig fences, and just about anything else standing up. The men leave the smaller bent or broken branches for the women to collect as kitchen firewood.

Mariam apparently had no fear of snakes, and she crunched over the floor of dead leaves to pull out a couple of twenty-foot-long branches by their base. It reminded me of those cartoons where a Neanderthal pulls his woman along by her hair. Here, the men rule the women and the women rule the firewood. Without words, Mariam used her machete to slice the small twigs off the body of the tree and then placed them in a growing pile. *No problem, I can do this,* I thought. There were not enough machetes to go around, so I used my bare hands. I was feeling rather proud of myself.

My barehanded, branch-breaking pride was short-lived. After about two hours of whacking, twisting, bending, breaking, and leveraging twigs and branches apart with my knee, I made a five-foot-high pile of wood and had multiple cuts on my hands and legs to show for it. Mariam took pity on me and we started the walk back home to breakfast. She and her co-wife would come back later with some rope to tie the wood together and carry it home—on their heads, of course.

I kept repeating *"Yaam banga Moré, tanda banga Moré, taam fua banga Moré "* and it started to take on its own rhythm, and then turned into an African dance tune with clapping and hip swinging. Mariam couldn't stop laughing at me. It kept us entertained all the way home.

Breakfast never tasted so good. Add a little oil and salt to ground millet porridge and it's actually pretty good. Luckily, both oil and salt were quite cheap so I was okay dosing up my plate. Mariam wanted to make sure I'd eaten enough so I rubbed my belly in "yum" circles to signal that I was happily full. She must have thought I meant something else because she pulled up her shirt to reveal her baby belly. I laughed and proudly displayed my jiggly, stretchy middle. The shared experience of carrying and bearing babies is the most common denominator for women everywhere. Mariam's is a champion belly. She has seven living children and probably bore more who did not survive, but that is a painful subject in a place where losing children to birth defects, easily preventable diseases, or accidents is all too common. Just in the few days I had been here, we had given condolences to two families who had just lost small children.

I wondered if knowing that many of your children will die lessens the grief when it actually happens. I couldn't imagine looking at my newborn baby boy, knowing in my heart that there was a one in five chance I would lose him before his fifth birthday. But that's the reality for billions of mothers.

Friday is the most important day of the week: market day. Mariam changed into her Friday best—a very pretty light blue shirt with a matching skirt and head wrap. She looked regal and proud. The market would be my first brush with the cash economy. I had been living on far less than a dollar a day since I had only eaten the food that Mariam and her family have grown or gathered, with the noted exception of the salt and oil (about 2 cents worth). I had not changed my clothing (yes, I was ripe and salt stained) or purchased anything. I was tempted by a cold Coke the day before, but it would have cost an entire dollar. I didn't see Mariam kick one back, so neither did I.

There was an electric energy in the market. A combination of anticipation and hope radiated from each seller's stall. Even in this small outback of humanity, you could buy just about everything a person needed: soap, clothing, pigs, donkeys, hair clips, cigarettes, underwear, and on and on. My task in the market was to see how far I could stretch a dollar for a basket of typical items Mariam would buy (one dollar is 450 CFAs). After an hour of walking around, a dollar bought me a bowl of cooked spiced rice to eat as a market day treat, cooking oil for a few days, some spices, bar soap, matches, detergent, and small amounts of dried fish and dried okra. That's way further than I thought it would go, but certainly not enough to feed even one person if they don't have access to a plot of land. I was deeply relieved that I wouldn't have to pay for food for the rest of the day.

I was curious to know what Mariam's family survives on—is it a dollar a day or less? When we found a quiet moment, she walked me through her annual expenditures:

Her family hovers around surviving on a dollar a day. If they have a bad season and have to buy grain to eat, that would add another 50,000 CFAs ($111) and pretty much break the bank. If someone gets really sick, medicine could cost up to 50,000 CFAs, pushing them into a deep hole of debt. The older children earn their own money from cultivating small scraps of land to pay for their own high school fees, which generally run about 40,000 CFAs ($89).

The most interesting thing about this list was that the two things that consume most of our

## MIRIAM'S ANNUAL FAMILY BUDGET

| Item | CFA | USD |
|------|-----|-----|
| Medicines (doctors are free) | 15,000 | $33.33 |
| Immunizations | 8,000 | $17.78 |
| Bus rides to Ouaga (1,000 CFAs each way) to visit her son, 10x per year | 20,000 | $44.44 |
| Clothing | 12,000 | $26.67 |
| Primary schooling for 4 children (20,000 CFAs each) | 80,000 | $177.78 |
| Various household items | 25,000 | $55.56 |
| Personal items | 3,000 | $6.67 |
| TOTAL | 163,000 | $362.23 |

money as Americans—food and housing—didn't even show up on Mariam's list. Housing is made from sticks, mud bricks, and leafy, thatched roofs—all plentiful in Burkina Faso. No one can afford much else. And there is no money to spend on food. It struck me again how high-stakes farming is for African families, and I could feel in my chest Mariam's worry about the rain. There is no money to buy food if the sky withholds its liquid generosity and the ground refuses to release the seeds into daylight. Keeping track of my spending against a dollar became irrelevant quickly. There was nothing to buy. I simply ate what Mariam gave me. Since she didn't pay for that food, I didn't need to count it toward my allotment.

We wound our way through the labyrinthine market stalls to a huge tree surrounded by a clearing of pounded dirt. The women's association had invited us to another dance, this time a proper one with full market-day regalia and empty-bucket drums. They began with my (and their) favorite: the bumper-bum welcome dance and then moved into several other dances that I couldn't feign very well. As hard as these women's lives were, they still found joy, exuberant joy, in life and in each other. It reminded me of the sign on top of my piano at home: *The best thing to hold on to is each other.* That's how we survive. Their dancing energy carried me away from the heat, the dirt, and the hunger in my belly, and the pounding plastic drums beat every other thought out of my head. What a wonderful escape, however fleeting it was.

My visit would not have been complete or proper without a visit to the king of Doulougou. I met him about this time the year before on my first trip to Burkina in 2009. That year, he was completely taken with one of my younger team members from Rwanda and actually asked, in all seriousness, if she would marry him and become his umpteenth wife. She declined, but we never stopped teasing her about it. The king remembered her clearly as the "woman who would not have him" and admitted that she might find him too old, but generously offered to find her a younger man so she could stay in Burkina. He broke a smile, and we realized this time he was just playing with us.

We thanked him for the generosity of his village, and I told him how impressed I was with his people's strength, creativity, intelligence, and hopefulness, especially the women of Doulougou. He agreed that women hold the community and the family together and then said, "Women have the power to end all war." Pardon? There wasn't time to explain further, so I just assumed it got lost in translation. In honor of the visit, he presented me with a male sheep and a rooster. A *live* sheep and rooster. I had to take them or he would have been deeply offended. After twenty minutes of angst, creative thinking, and a clear cultural clash between the animal-loving Americans and the puzzled Burkinabé, we figured out how to transport the gifts back to Ouagadougou along with a car full of luggage. The sheep rode strapped down to the metal roof rack next to a bicycle that took up most of the rack. Every time we hit a bump we all groaned in unison for the poor thing. The chicken got scrunched under the video camera tripod, which gave it only marginal protection from the luggage stacked up to the van's ceiling. I asked what would become of the poor animals. "We are going to enjoy them for dinner," Paul said with a naughty grin.

• • •

I have thought about Mariam every day since I met her. When I feel like I've had a bad day, I ask myself, "So how was Mariam's day today?" And I return to feeling blessed and lucky to be in a country where I can have a job, don't have to grow my own food, and have more than one pair of shoes. Those three days showed me that women who can't even read, women who often move us to pity, have the grit, creativity, and mental and physical strength to raise a whole family from what they grow or make. They are strong and capable. They may be living in poverty, but they are not poor.

When I got back to the States, some friends and I raised about a thousand dollars to send to her women's association. At least it was a start. I hoped I'd go back some day to see what she had created with this seed capital. Given what she had done with nothing, I had no doubt it would be something incredible.

# 54

# CELEBRATION

Just like I did with the girls in Sri Lanka, I fell in love with Mariam and her children. I worried every time I heard about drought in West Africa or fighting in Mali. I prayed she and her women's association were prospering. I had told her I would return someday, but I had no idea how that would come to pass. I'm deeply grateful that it did.

I arrived back in Doulougou on a Friday evening in 2013 and, per the custom, first went to greet the king. It was our third meeting and he treated me like an old friend. He dropped the formal ceremonial greetings, which last time involved my companions and me getting down on our knees and offering gifts. I did, of course, bring him a small token of respect and appreciation: a gold colored coin with President Obama's face on one side and the presidential seal on the other side. The king loved it. "An African king for an African king," he said, and I smiled.

Dusk was gently flowing in from the pink and gold edges of the horizon as we sat on the king's living room furniture, which had been rearranged outside so we could enjoy the evening's cool breeze. One of his wives brought out crystal glasses and a bottle of a Cabernet/Syrah to share. A little girl of about three sat on one of his knees; she clearly had him under her spell. When I visited last, the king's youngest wife, who was about fifteen years old at the time, was ready-to-pop pregnant. I wondered if she had this little princess in her belly.

The evening was an unexpectedly relaxing experience. The king opened up more than he had before and told us about his travels through France and across much of the African continent. I had no idea he'd ever been outside of his native village. As a young man he worked for a French trucking company. They brought him to France for a few weeks of intense truck training and then he crisscrossed Africa for a few years. He was very grateful for the chance to see the world outside of Burkina. "It prepared me to be a better leader," he said. "I could see that the world was changing quickly and that change would come to see us in Burkina Faso someday. I could help my people adjust and take best advantage of it when it arrived." That explained a lot for me, particularly his openness to women's empowerment and welcoming spirit toward outsiders. I said my good-bye to the king because I knew that Mariam and all the women were waiting for me.

I leapt out of the truck as soon as I saw Mariam and ran to embrace her. We hugged for a long time. I couldn't believe I was really there again, and I know she could hardly believe that I came back. The women immediately began dancing the welcome-sister dance; the hip bumping went on for a good hour. I had the bruises to prove it. After many embraces and big, cheek-tiring smiles we went to Mariam's house.

It was hard to see who was there in the dark. I recognized two of her younger sons, but the other children had changed so much. We sat outside the compound wall using the truck's headlights to see, and I gave them the presents I had brought with me from home: clothes, shoes, purses, and solar flashlights. Each item looked larger than life with its big shadow cast on the wall.

Mariam had prepared a special dinner for me, so we went right to it. Paul let me spoon my pieces from the chicken stew first, and I ladled out some unrecognizable parts. I held my plate to the headlight and yelped when I saw what I had chosen: the chicken's head with cloudy eyeballs, yellow beak, and gray skin covered in red palm oil. Paul laughed his distinctive I-love-making-fun-of-Ritu chortle. I lost my appetite after that, but ate a little of the plain spaghetti that I believe Mariam had prepared for my bland palette.

The stars were beautiful, just as they were last time, and the moon had a broad, misty band around it, which Mariam said meant that something good was going to happen soon. I was looking forward to falling asleep outside with the family. Mariam led Paul and me into the family enclosure and to a fresh new mud hut. The cement floor was still cool and wet from being laid down. "This is your house," Mariam said. I must have looked shocked because she followed that with, "Really, I made this hut just for you. When I heard you were coming I wanted to have a proper place for you to stay. It took me three weeks to make the bricks and eleven days to build it." Too many feelings rushed into me at once. I felt horrible that she thought I needed a "proper" place to sleep and went through so much trouble for me. At the same time, she was clearly so pleased with it and I was thrilled that she could afford the materials to make it. It would give her some nice new quarters or perhaps a separate place for her teenage daughters. Tears came to my eyes as I said to her in the little Moré I recalled, "Barka, Mariam, barka soh." That night, I stared at the circles of moist cement on the walls and the corrugated tin roof for a long time. *Yes, I* thought, *something good is just about to happen.*

Mariam did not wake me up at 5 a.m. this time to go pick shea nuts, and for that I was grateful. I initially thought I'd try to live on a dollar a day again and shadow Mariam in her work, but it was clear from the get-go that she was having none of it this time. I was going to be an honored guest regardless of how I felt about it. When I stepped out of "my" hut into the morning, I was astonished by what I saw. Chickens were picking at the ground. Guinea hens and their little chicks ran in strands across the yard. Several goats were tied to a tree. Two cows grazed in the field just in front of the compound. And Thunder, the donkey that Jessica Kizorek, the videographer from my last trip, bought for Mariam's women's association in 2010, looked healthy as he swished his tail against his chubby belly. There was a motorbike and several bicycles under a makeshift veranda. It was a significant accumulation of wealth from three years prior.

"Since you left us last time, I can't say that we've become very rich, but we haven't become poorer. We have built a house, and acquired some animals, and that is very good," Mariam explained. "We have three cows, the donkey, four sheep, and each one has got a lamb. We had six goats but three were killed. I got a motorbike and so did my husband. We've got fifteen hens." Certainly I would agree that Mariam's family is not rich, but the assets they now had were significantly more than what they had during my first visit to their farm.

I was very happy to hear what she said next. "We have been working on the farm. So far, even with the shortage of rains this year, we've been eating from the harvest of our fields. We've never been to the market to buy cereals." That was a very positive development. "My husband has his rice farm," Mariam continued, "and when we harvest the rice, we sell it and save the money. We didn't acquire everything you see here in one year. Each year we get a little more to buy animals or things like the motorbikes."

I asked how they managed to do better these last years. "Thunder," said Mariam. The word thunder has very negative connotations in Burkina. "Thunder means lightning and lightning kills people here," Paul explained. But the donor gave the donkey that name and they've stuck with it. Clearly it hasn't harmed them. "We use our three cows in the morning to plow, but they are not as strong as Thunder. When they get tired we send them out to the bush to graze. We take Thunder in the afternoon to substitute. Without him, we couldn't work all day long. He has made our farm activities easier and faster. We can do twice as much now that we have him." I was amazed. It was so little. One donkey made such a big difference for them.

We stopped by the local market center on our way to check out what Mariam's association had done with the funds we had raised for them after my last visit: they launched a soap business. Everyone wanted to welcome me as I walked past. I guess I was a local celebrity now. A very old gentleman—the oldest person in the village, in fact—held both of my hands, looked me deeply in the eyes, and said, "We never expected you to come back. You have come again and you can consider this your home." I was overcome by his statement. I knew enough to know that the community elder welcoming me in this way was significant, yet I felt unworthy. I had done so little for them—just a modest contribution to the women's association. But when I saw what the association had done with that investment, I started to understand.

We arrived at a lovely building with a high ceiling. It was open on all sides except for a large storage room. The members of Mariam's association were ready to get going with the soap-making demonstration. I had no idea how easy it was to make soap. With the funds we had sent them, the association bought potash, coconut oil, perfume, and lye from Ouagadougou. The primary ingredient in their soap—shea butter—came from a sister women's association. I loved it. They were "vertically integrating their value chain," as the economists like to say. The important trick was to mix the ingredients in just the right order in the right proportions. "From the beginning, we stir it slowly, very slowly, taking turns; in one direction and in the right way," one of the younger members told me. I asked if I could try and she very politely said no because I would probably mess it up. It was a wise choice. "After an hour of continuous stirring, toward the end, we add perfume and the lye to harden the liquid," the young woman continued.

I asked why they decided to make soap, of all the products they could have chosen. Another member replied, "In our village we need soap to do anything—wash hands, clean dishes, bathe children, and launder our clothes. People are more interested in soap than any other product. We used to get our soap from the traders who brought it from Ouagadougou, and it was very expensive. Soap costs 250 CFAs [about 50 cents] per bar. We sell ours at the same price, but it's better quality. It smells nice and gets the clothes cleaner than other soaps." They were definitely on to something because, as she added proudly, "Even when we make it in big quantities, people buy so much that you rarely find any left." Such good quality at an affordable price? I bought a bunch of their soap to bring home to my sweaty and usually dirt-encrusted boys.

I was curious about how the whole association was going. I remember how hard it was for Mariam to start it in the beginning. "Since your last visit many women have joined us," Mariam answered with a smile. "We registered fifteen right after you left, and just today three women were asking to join us. This was possible thanks to the money that you gave us," she continued. "Instead of spending it all on soap-making supplies, we opened an account at the local savings bank, and that account gave us a lot of opportunities. For example, in the past if you needed a small amount of money to start a little business, it wasn't possible because you had no bank account. So our association got a loan of 200,000 CFAs [$420] to buy the soap equipment and ingredients. We were able to pay it back in six months. Now, we can have loans payable in eight months." It was brilliant! Instead of spending it all on the soap business, they made it their collateral and then borrowed against it. "Any person who benefited from the loan had to pay an extra 500 CFAs [$1] for every 5,000 CFAs [$10] borrowed as a contribution to our joint account. This helps us increase the amount of the savings." This was basically the same model Karuna and the Tsunami Women's Network used in Sri Lanka. Great women think alike.

"We didn't want to invest all the funds in the soap enterprise because it could have failed," Mariam said in a lowered voice. "Investing all the money was quite risky. Putting the money in the bank helped us gain some security, and it united us." I asked if the profits from the soap business were divided among the members of the association like a cooperative. They were not. "We take the profits and keep them to solve social problems. For example, this morning, some of the women didn't come to see you because a relative passed away. And sometimes if we need money at night or on weekends it's not easy to get to the bank. We go to the association accountant and she can give us some until we can get to the bank." This was really impressive. They had taken the thousand dollars we gave and turned it into a profitable business, a revolving loan fund, an emergency assistance account, and an ATM. Lots of people take an opportunity and do some good with it, but few do something as smart and transformative as Mariam had done.

"I always knew you were one of the smartest people I've ever met," I told Mariam. Even without an education, her natural intelligence shined through.

I could now understand why the whole community was grateful. However, their gratitude was misplaced in me. Their deepest thanks should go to Mariam and the women of her association. I hoped they were getting the accolades they deserved.

Later in the afternoon, Mariam shared a little more about the realities of leadership in her community. I could relate to everything she was saying though our contexts were worlds apart. "I have been president of the association for twenty years," she said with a sigh, "and I must confess that it hasn't been easy. People tire me, insult me, and accuse me of things I have not done. Some of what they say gets to me, but usually I don't care about that, otherwise I couldn't be the leader of the group. I don't react to what people say and I try to keep unity among the group. I think that is the best way of being a good leader." She struck a chord in me. I find that one of the toughest things about being a leader is listening deeply to people without taking it personally. I made a mental note that next time I start to bristle in the face of feedback to ask myself, "What would Mariam do?"

"Even if I wanted them to find another person to run the association, they insist on keeping me," Mariam concluded. I saw Mariam coaching some very spunky younger members of the group that morning. I had confidence that, being such an exquisite leader, she will surely mentor several young women to take her place.

Paul and I retreated back to the mango tree at Mariam's house to take a little break before the big celebration in the afternoon. A pack of kids came over to take a closer look at the "White Lady," as they called me. I started by asking their names.

"My name is Bintu," said the first little one. "I have no idea about my age." The other kids laughed, but I gave them a stern look and they covered their mouths. It was not unusual here to be without a birth certificate or even a recorded birth date. Birthdays are not celebrated the way we do in the West. Lots of kids didn't know when they were born. "You look to be about five or six," I said. "What class are you in?"

"Primary school," Bintu responded, "second form."

"So that makes you about six or seven," I calculated. "How lovely it is to meet you, Miss Bintu," I said and shook her petite hand.

"My name is Julienne and I am ten. I am attending school, third form," the next girl said in a more assertive way.

"My name is Sakeena. I'm twelve, and in primary school fourth form," added the next girl. "Mariam is my aunt. My mother is Mariam's younger sister." Mariam had mentioned to me the night before that Sakeena was there with them because she was struggling in school in her home village; they thought a change of location and schools could make a difference.

A sweet little whisper of a girl was next and said, "My name is Florence. I am one month and a half old." I couldn't stop the giggling that time. And I have to admit, I love the sound of little-kid laughs freely bubbling up. They were so delightful.

One of the boys said, "She is two." He continued, "I'm Augustine, I'm five, and I'm not going to school yet."

Françoise, eight, spoke up next and said proudly, "I'm attending primary school second form."

Finally, the eldest of the bunch introduced herself. "My name is Nasiratu. I am sixteen and in secondary school first form." Nasiratu was Mariam's daughter. She didn't really need to introduce herself, I remembered her well from last time, but I think she wanted to stay in form with the little kids.

I was really pleased that all the kids were in school, though I have no idea if they attended regularly or had any extra amenities like the BRIGHT kids did.

"What is your favorite game to play?" I asked the kid caucus.

Françoise immediately came to life and said, "There is a game called 'The Fox Is Passing,' that's my favorite game."

"And how do you play this game?" I asked, and he answered. "You need many children, sitting in a circle. One child is holding a shoe and he is on the outside of the circle. All the kids sing, 'The fox is passing, passing, passing. Everybody will do it in turn.' While they're singing the boy with the shoe runs around the circle and leaves the shoe behind someone." So far it sounded like a cross between musical chairs and tag. "If you don't realize the shoe is there behind you, when the boy gets to you again, he will beat you with the shoe." Yikes. "Then you get in the middle of the circle and you become a prisoner. The same boy goes around again. If you check for the shoe and it isn't behind you, you immediately become a prisoner."

"How do you know if the shoe is behind you?" I asked, not wanting to get beaten up if they asked me to play it.

"The fox is going around holding the shoe; if you realize he's not holding the shoe anymore, you can get up and start chasing him."

"And what if you're wrong and the shoe wasn't behind you?" I needed more guidance on this.

"Then he will beat you and you will become a prisoner too." Okay, then. I'm certain it was a lot of fun for them, but I thought a change of topic would be good before I had to play this get-beat-up-with-a-shoe game.

"So, do you help your parents on the farm to grow your food?" I ventured.

"Yes," they all said almost in unison.

"We get to spread the seeds," said little Bintu.

"Do you have to carry the heavy water to the plants?" I asked. They all nodded. I know how hard that work is for an adult; it must be really difficult for children. "Do you like doing the farming?" I asked, expecting booing and hissing in response.

"Yes! A lot!" several of the children said, mostly the younger ones. That was surprising.

I released them to go play and asked Nasiratu, the eldest, to stay with me a bit longer. "Last time we talked, you were studying hard in school.

You wanted to become an office worker, a professional, and work in the big city," I reminded her.

"Yes, I still want to do that," Nasiratu said.

"Is school going okay?" I inquired. "Last time we talked about it, you said it was hard to find time to study because you had chores. Has that changed at all?"

"Things have improved. I can have a little time to learn my lessons at home," she responded.

"Are you still farming too?" I asked.

"Yes," Nasiratu said, "and I still don't like it." She shares that sentiment with a whole generation of young Africans who want to get as far as possible from the farms where they grew up. The office jobs might not be there for them in the big city, though. It's a big problem across the continent. Somehow kids need to be inspired to stay home, learn about the land, and turn their parents' farms into profitable businesses. But the lure of a nine-to-five schedule, no manual labor, and daily air conditioning are pretty hard to beat. In twenty years, Africa may face the same crises as we see growing in the Middle East: millions of smart and educated, but jobless, young people feeling hopeless about their prospects.

The women were gathering up again, this time wearing matching headscarves and skirts in red and black with doves printed all over. They began singing a call-and-response melody that sounded to me like, "KAY-lah wash-AHM-bah," which meant "The sun says, 'Welcome foreigner.'" This dance only involved foot stamping to the rhythm of the jerry-can drums; I mostly managed it all right. Then they revved it up with the bumper-bum dance again, and I decided it would be better for me to sit and watch since my hips were still tender from the night before.

The homemade beer came next, and as the guest of honor, I was the first to imbibe. Paul had instructed me during previous visits to just dip my upper lip into the foamy yellow liquid without taking any into my mouth to avoid the risk of picking up an amoeba or parasite from the water. But this was the end of my trip and I figured that if I picked up something really nasty I'd be home before it really hit me. So I went ahead and took a swig. It was shockingly smooth and flavorful. Then the gourd was passed around, first to all the men in order of seniority. They all wanted me to take their picture drinking the beer. Over the course of fifteen minutes I must have snapped 50 beer portraits. I asked Paul to make prints and take them to Doulougou next time he returned.

The mayor of Doulougou stepped forward to make a speech, which took me by surprise. I was not expecting (or wanting) any ceremony for my visit. But I had no choice in the matter. "We are grateful you've been able to come back to our village, especially after your hard experience three years ago," he said.

*Goodness,* I thought, *I guess they remember how badly I failed to keep up with Mariam during my last stay.*

"We hope it will start raining soon," the mayor continued, "so that we can have food and stay alive until your next visit." I hoped it sounded less morbid than the literal translation Paul gave me. "We are happy that you have started speaking Moré in the right way," he went on, which made Paul laugh, of course. "We would like you to make it possible for one of your daughters to become my son's wife," the mayor declared. I wasn't sure if I had heard him correctly or if he was just kidding. Paul explained that I have only two sons, to which the mayor retorted, "Then my daughters can be given to your sons."

I bowed my head in thanks and said, "I'll let them know." My boys were still at the age when they think girls are gross. I could just imagine their horror when I told them that when they're old enough I'm packing them off to Africa to get married.

"You are really integrated now," Paul said, knocking me in the shoulder to be funny.

"The men of Doulougou thank you for your support to our women and we offer you this rooster in gratitude," the mayor concluded. After he translated, Paul added that a male chicken was a particularly generous gift. There was no way I could cook the poor thing, so I gave it to our driver as a special gift for his wife, who had just had a baby girl a few days before.

The day was coming to a close and we needed to hit the road back to Ouagadougou before darkness fell. I thanked everyone with my whole heart and saluted Mariam and all the women in her association. "You are the heroines," I added. "I am just your friend and your witness."

Mariam, and all the women in these pages, are the portrait of those living in poverty. Brave beyond imagination. Smart beyond expectation. Strong beyond reason. Dedicated beyond belief. They seek a friend, not a patron, and a witness to their achievements, not an assessor of their worth. Within them and through them a new and better world is being born for all of us.

# 55

# WHAT YOU CAN DO FOR BURKINA FASO

Someone who cared animated every story of change and triumph that you've read about in this book. I believe that caring for one another is exactly what we are here to do, and that belief enlivens my actions. I hope you are as inspired as I am by these remarkable women to care—not only about them but also for the world of women and girls who are waiting for you to stand with them in friendship.

## SHARE AND DARE

Please share this book with others in your family, neighborhood, school, and faith community. Add it to your book club's reading list or host a special evening of discussion (and writing!) around any of the topics in it. You can find reading guides and discussion questions at www.teachawomanto fish.org.

If you have an urge to do something, do it. Don't dismiss it or put it off until later. I know that when I let the inspiration get away from me, it dissipates away into the busyness of life. Let yourself get involved. Take whatever action appealed to you, or find others on the website. Just as for the other countries you've read about, you can make a contribution to support local organizations in Africa at www.teach awomantofish.org. I promise that you'll receive more satisfaction and fulfillment from being part of the most important movement of the twenty-first century than you could ever imagine.

## PLEASE DON'T AND PLEASE DO

You may want to help or get to know some of the individual women whose lives I've shared with you. That's natural. However, many of their names have been changed to protect their privacy. While they agreed to share their stories with the world, they were not comfortable with being contacted. If you would like to visit with grass-roots women living in poverty, meet with local organizations that serve them, or try something similar to my Dollar-a-Day experiences, there are several ways to do that. You can use the Internet to find local women's organizations in a country you want to visit or travel with groups that organize tours of this type (Global Exchange and the Global Fund for Women are two such organizations).

Most importantly, please do what only you can

uniquely do—tell your elected leaders that helping women and girls around the world is important to you.

I look forward to your joining me on this journey.

# NOTES

## INTRODUCTION

1. Organization for Economic Cooperation and Development, "DAC Guiding Principles for Aid Effectiveness, Gender Equality, and Women's Empowerment," December 2008, http://www.oecd.org/dataoecd/14/27/423101 24.pdf.

## PART 1: SRI LANKA

1. Sunila Abeysekera, *Tsunami Aftermath: Violations of Women's Human Rights, Sri Lanka* (Chiang Mai, Thailand: Asia Pacific Forum on Women, Law and Development, 2006), 1.
2. Ibid., 8.
3. Irangani Magedaragamage (Chair, National Women's Collective of Sri Lanka), Responses to an electronic questionnaire from Women Thrive Worldwide, January 2005.
4. Ibid.
5. Ibid.
6. Ibid.
7. "Internally Displaced People Figures," United Nations High Commissioner for Refugees, accessed March 30, 2013, http://www.unhcr .org/pages/49c3646c23.html; "Facts and

497

Figures about Refugees," United Nations High Commissioner for Refugees, accessed March 30, 2013, http://www.unhcr.org.uk /about-us/key-facts-and-figures.html.

8. Wikipedia,"List of US States and Territories by Population," accessed March 15, 2013, http://en.wikipedia.org/wiki/List_of_U.S._states_and_territories_by_population.

9. Inter-Agency Standing Committee Task Force on Gender in Humanitarian Assistance, "Guidelines for Gender-Based Violence Interventions in Humanitarian Settings," September 2005, http://www.unfpa.org /women/docs/gbv-glns-eng091305.pdf.

10. United States Agency for International Development, Office of Foreign Disaster Assistance, "Indian Ocean—Earthquake and Tsunamis Sheet 10 for Fiscal Year 2005."

11. Ibid.

12. House Report 109-16–Making Emergency Supplemental Appropriations for the Fiscal Year Ending September 30, 2005, and for Other Purposes, 109th Congress, March 11, 2005.

13. Abeysekera, *Tsunami Aftermath*, 23.

14. Women in Informal Employment: Globalizing and Organizing (WIEGO), *Informal Workers in Focus: Home-Based Workers*, accessed April 15, 2013, http://wiego.org/sites/wiego

.org/files/resources/files/WIEGO_HomeBased _Workers-English.pdf.

15. Zoe Elena Horn, "No Cushion to Fall Back On," Inclusive Cities Project, accessed March 14, 2013, wiego.org/sites/wiego.org/files/ . . . /files/Horn_GEC_Study_2009.pdf.

16. Sri Lanka Bureau of Foreign Employment, *Annual Statistical Report of Foreign Employment 2011* (Colombo, Sri Lanka: Sri Lanka Bureau of Foreign Employment, 2012), 194.

17. Ibid., vi.

18. Ibid., 183.

19. Ibid., 91.

20. International Finance Corporation, "Market Movers: Lessons from a Frontier of Innovation," 2007, http://www.ifc.org/wps /wcm/connect/14488d0048855cc28cc4de6a6 515bb18/Market%2BMovers_Final.pdf?MOD =AJPERES&CACHEID=14488d0048855cc 28cc4de6a6515bb18.

21. MAS Holdings, *Inspired Women Change the World* (Colombo, Sri Lanka: MAS Holdings, 2007), 22.

22. Ibid., 32.

23. Melanne Verveer, "Women as Economic Drivers," *AARP International Journal*, June 11, 2013, accessed October 7, 2013, http://journal.aarpinternational.org/a/b/2012 /02/Women-as-Economic-Drivers.

24. "Women's Empowerment Principles: Equality

Means Business," 2011, UN Women and UN Global Compact.

25. Office of the United States Trade Representative, "GSP by the Numbers Fact Sheet," September 27, 2013, http://www.ustr.gov/sites /default/files/GSP-by-the-numbers2013.pdf.

26. Ibid.

27. Michael J. Hiscox and Nicholas Smyth, "Is There Consumer Demand for Fair Labor Standards? Evidence from a Field Experiment," Social Science Research Network, April 22, 2011, accessed April 28, 2013, http://dx.doi.org/10.2139/ssrn.1820642.

28. Jens Hainmueller and Michael J. Hiscox, "The Socially Conscious Consumer? Field Experimental Tests of Consumer Support for Fair Labor Standards," Social Science Research Network, MIT Political Science Department Research Paper No. 2012-15, May 18, 2012, available at SSRN: http://ssrn .com/abstract=2062435 or http:// dx.doi.org /10.2139/ssrn.2062435.

29. Steven Lee Myers, "Foreign Aid Set to Take a Hit in US Budget Crisis," *New York Times*, October 3, 2011, http://www.nytimes.com /2011/10/04/us/politics/foreign-aid-set-to-take-hit-in-united-states-budget-crisis.html.

30. Intelligence Reform and Terrorism Prevention Act of 2004, Pub. L. No.108-458, 118 Stat. 3638 (2004).

31. Millennium Challenge Corporation, "MCC and the Consultative Process: Sri Lanka."

32. Derek Thompson, "These 4 Charts Explain Exactly How Americans Spend $52 Billion on Our Pets Each Year," *Atlantic*, February 23, 2013, http://www.theatlantic.com/business/archive/2013/02/these-4-charts-explain-exactly-how-americans-spend-52-billion-on-our-pets-in-a-year/273446/.

33. Freedom House, "MCC Should Withhold Funding from Sri Lankan Government," April 6, 2007, http://www.freedomhouse.org/article/mcc-should-withhold-funding-sri-lankan-government.

34. "US Deselects Sri Lanka from 2008 Funding," *Daily Mirror* (Colombo, Sri Lanka), December 19, 2007, http://www.lankanewspapers.com/news/2007/12/22789.html.

35. United Nations Human Rights Council, Resolution A/HRC/19/L.2, "2012 Resolution on Promoting Reconciliation and Accountability in Sri Lanka," adopted March 22, 2012, http://ap.ohchr.org/documents/dpage_e.aspx?si=A/HRC/19/L.2.

36. United Nations Human Rights Council, "2013 Resolution on Promoting Reconciliation and Accountability in Sri Lanka," Resolution A/HRC/22/L.1/Rev1, adopted March 21, 2013, http://ap.ohchr.org/documents/dpage_e.aspx?si=A/HRC/22/L.1/Rev.1.

37. "Exhibit B to Registration Statement Pursuant to the Foreign Agents Registration Act of 1938 as amended, Registration Number 6159," March 25, 2013 (Washington, DC: US Department of Justice).

PART 2: HONDURAS AND NICARAGUA
1. International Coffee Organization, "The Story of Coffee," accessed October 1, 2013, http://www.ico.org/coffee_story.asp.
2. Eduardo Galeano, *Open Veins of Latin America* (New York: Monthly Review Press, 1997), 38.
3. Fair Trade International, "The History of Fair Trade," accessed August 25, 2013, http://www.fairtrade.net/history-of-fairtrade.html.
4. Fair Trade USA, "The Real Impact of Fair Trade," infographic, accessed August 25, 2013, http://fairtradeusa.org/blog/infographic-real-impact-of-fair-trade.
5. Fair Trade USA, "What Is Fair Trade," accessed August 25, 2013, http://fairtradeusa.org/what-is-fair-trade/faq.
6. US Federation of Worker Owned Cooperatives, "Frequently Asked Questions about Worker Cooperatives," accessed October 1, 2013, http://www.usworker.coop/frequently-asked-questions-about-worker-cooperatives.
7. Greenpeace USA, "Small Farmers Are Feeding the World," accessed October 4,

2013, http://www.greenpeace.org/usa/en/campaigns/genetic-engineering/our-vision/small-scale-farming/.

8. Howard G. Buffett Foundation, *The Hungry Continent: African Agriculture and Food Insecurity* (Decatur, IL: The Howard G. Buffett Foundation, 2011), 17.

9. Food and Agriculture Organization of the United Nations, "FAO Statistical Yearbook 2013: World Food and Agriculture," 2013, http://www.fao.org/docrep/018/i3107e/i3107e00.htm; "Who Are the Hungry?," Why Hunger, accessed October 3, 2013, http://whyhunger.org/portfolio?topicId=15.

10. Howard G. Buffett Foundation, *The Hungry Continent*, 100.

11. Robert Bailey, *Growing a Better Future: Food Justice in a Resource-Constrained World*, (London: Oxfam International, 2011), http://www.oxfam.org/sites/www.oxfam.org/files/cr-growing-better-future-170611-en.pdf.

12. Ibid.

13. United States Agency for International Development, "The Future of Food Assistance: US Food Aid Reform Fact Sheet," http://www.usaid.gov/sites/default/files/documents/1869/TheFutureofFoodAssistance-USFoodAidReform.pdf.

14. Adam Vaughan, "Elimination of Food Waste Could Lift 1bn out of Hunger, Say

Campaigners," *Guardian*, September 8, 2009, http://www.theguardian.com/environment /2009/sep/08/food-waste.

15. Millennium Challenge Corporation, "Promoting Gender Equality in Lesotho: Maleribe's Story," April 5, 2011, http://www.mcc.gov /documents/press/action-2011002056901- maleribe.pdf.

16. Millennium Challenge Corporation, "MCC, Lesotho and Gender," http://www.mcc.gov /documents/press/results-2012002131601- lesotho-gender-wpas.pdf.

17. Cuenta Reto del Milenio Nicaragua, "Considerando sólo los Planes de Negocio Activos (excluyendo los cancelados)."

18. World Health Organization, London School of Hygiene and Tropical Medicine, and the South African Medical Research Council, "Global and Regional Estimates of Violence against Women: Prevalence and Health Effects of Intimate Partner Violence and Non-Partner Sexual Violence," 2013, http:// apps.who.int/iris/bitstream/10665/85239/1 /9789241564625_eng.pdf.

19. Ruth Levine, Cynthia Lloyd, Margaret Greene, and Caren Grown, *Girls Count: A Global Investment and Action Agenda* (Washington, DC: Center for Global Development, 2009), 53, Figure 4.3.

20. C. Garcia-Moreno, H. Jansen, M. Ellsberg, L.

Heise, and C. Watts, "WHO Multi-country Study on Women's Health and Domestic Violence against Women: Initial Results on Prevalence, Health Outcomes, and Women's Responses," 2005, http:// www.who.int/gender /violence/who_multicountry_study/en/.

21. Valerie M. Hudson and Patricia Leidl, "The U.S. Is Abandoning Afghanistan's Women," *Foreign Policy*, May 10, 2010, http:// www.foreignpolicy.com/articles/2010/05/07 /the_us_is_abandoning_afghanistan_s_ womentoiii.

22. Faith Karimi, "Congolese Women Graduate from Inaugural Rape Survival Class," CNN.com, January 29, 2012, http://www.cnn .com/2012/01/28/world/africa/congo-survivors-graduation/index.html.

23. Barbara Burton, Nata Duvvury, Anuradha Rajan, and Nisha Varia, *A Summary Report for a Multi-Site Household Survey: Domestic Violence in India* (Washington, DC: International Center for Research on Women, 2000), 25.

24. Rocio Ribero and Fabio Sanchez, *Determinantes, Efectos, y Costos de la Violencia Intrafamiliar en Colombia* (Bogota, Colombia: Centro de Estudios para el Desarollo Economico [CEDE] de la Universidad de los Andes, November 2004), 1, http://economia .uniandes.edu.co/documentocede2004-44.htm.

25. United Nations, "Ending Violence against Women: From Words to Action—Study of the Secretary-General," 2006, http://www.un.org/womenwatch/daw/public/VAW_Study/VAW studyE.pdf.
26. Kajsa Asling-Monemi, Ruchira Tabassum Naved, and Lars Ake Persson, "Violence against Women and Increases in the Risk of Diarrheal Disease and Respiratory Tract Infections in Infancy," *Archives of Pediatrics and Adolescent Medicine* 163, no. 10 (2009): 931–36.
27. Garcia-Moreno, Jansen, Ellsberg, Heise, and Watts, "WHO Multi-country Study on Women's Health and Domestic Violence against Women."
28. Aslihan Kes, Krista Jacobs, and Sophie Namy, *Gender Differences in Asset Rights in Central Uganda* (Washington, DC: International Center for Research on Women, 2011), 15.
29. Congressional Research Service, "CRS Report to Congress: International Violence Against Women: US Response and Policy Issues," 2008, https://www.fas.org/sgp/crs/misc/RL34438.pdf.
30. United Nations, "United Nations Trust Fund to End Violence Against Women: Annual Report 2012," 2013, http://www.unwomen.org/en/trust-funds/~/media/B1720435450D42 FFB553FA43A0D6C59E.ashx.

31. Hearing before the Subcommittee on International Organizations, Human Rights, and Oversight of the Committee on Foreign Affairs of the House of Representatives, *International Violence Against Women: Stories and Solutions*, 111th Congress (October 21, 2009) (statement of Nicole Kidman, actor, UNIFEM Goodwill Ambassador).

32. InterAmerican Development Bank, "Educational Failure: Pregnancies to Skip School," accessed October 3, 2013, http://www.iadb.org /en/news/webstories/2011-12-05/teenage-pregnancy-in-latin-america-and-the-caribbean ,9721.html#.Uk1_JCR57v2.

33. Levine, Lloyd, Greene, and Grown, *Girls Count*, 3.

34. Andrew Woodbury, "Booming Babies: Prevalent Teen Pregnancy in Latin America and Caribbean," The Canal, blog of the *Pan American Post*, July 18, 2013, http://blog .panampost.com/andrew-woodbury/2013/07 /18/booming-babies-prevalent-teen-pregnancy -in-latin-america-and-caribbean/.

PART 3: BURKINA FASO

1. Jad Chaaban and Wendy Cunningham, "Measuring the Economic Gain of Investing in Girls: The Girl Effect Dividend," (policy Research working paper no. WPS 5753, 1, Washington DC: The World Bank, 2011),

http://elibrary.worldbank.org/doi/book/10.15
96/1813-9450-5753.

2. Ruth Levine, Cynthia B. Lloyd, Margaret
Greene, and Caren Grown, *Girls Count: A
Global Investment and Action Agenda*,
(Washington, DC: Center for Global
Development, 2009), 3.

3. Chaaban and Cunningham, *Measuring the
Economic Gain of Investing in Girls*, 2.

4. Ibid., 2.

5. Brookings Institution, Center for Universal
Education, *A Global Compact on Learning:
Action on Education in Developing Countries*
(Washington, DC: Brookings Institution,
2011), 9, http://www.brookings.edu/research
/reports/2011/06/09-global-compact.

6. Ibid., 9.

7. Ibid., 2.

8. Ibid., 10.

9. CIA World Fact Book, Burkina Faso,
accessed June 15, 2013, https://www.cia.gov
/library/publications//the-world-factbook/geos
/print/country/countrypdf_uv.pdf.

10. Ibid.

11. The World Bank, "World Development
Indicators: Mortality rate, infant (per 1,000
live births)," accessed October 12, 2013,
http://data.worldbank.org/indicator/SP.DYN
.IMRT.IN.

12. Harounan Kazianga, Dan Levy, Leigh L.

Linden, and Matt Sloan, "The Effects of 'Girl-Friendly' Schools: Evidence from the BRIGHT School Construction Program in Burkina Faso," *American Economic Journal: Applied Economics* 5, no. 3 (2013): 41–62, http://dx.doi.org/10.1257/app.5.3.41.

13. Plan International, "BRIGHT II Indicator Tracking Table (ITT)," Burkina Faso, July 2012.

14. Kazianga, Levy, Linden, and Sloan, "The Effects of 'Girl-Friendly' Schools."

15. Ibid., 61.

16. US Department of Education, *Digest of Education Statistics, 2011* (NCES 2012-001): Table 191 and Chapter 2, National Center for Education Statistics, accessed October 22, 2013, http://nces.ed.gov/fastfacts/display.asp?id=66.

17. Kaiser Family Foundation, "2012 Survey of Americans on the U.S. Role in Global Health," conducted February 2–12, 2012, 3, http://kff.org/global-health-policy/report/2012-survey-of-americans-on-the-u-s-role-in-global-health/.

18. University of Maryland, Program on International Policy Attitudes, "American Public Opinion on Foreign Aid," World Public Opinion.org, conducted November 30, 2010, accessed October 22, 2013, http://www.worldpublicopinion.org/pipa/articles

/brunitedstatescanadara/670.php?nid=&id=
&pnt=670&lb.

19. "Federal Budget Spending Actuals, Fiscal Years
2008–2012," USgovernmentspending.com,
accessed October 22, 2013, http://www.us
governmentspending.com/federal_budget_
detail_2013bs12012n_50#usgs302.

20. US Global Leadership Coalition, "In the
Spotlight," accessed October 22, 2013,
http://www.usglc.org.

21. US Global Leadership Coalition, "Quotes,"
accessed October 22, 2013, http://www.usglc
.org/budget-center/on-the-record/.

22. Anthony Davis, Claire Postles, and Giorgiana
Rosa, *A Girl's Right to Say No to Marriage*
(Woking, UK: Plan International, 2013),
19, http://plan-international.org/girls/child
marriagereport/.

23. Ibid., 2.

24. Ibid., 3.

25. Millennium Challenge Account—Burkina
Faso, "Gender Integration Action Plan, Table
4, Linkages between the PNG (National
Gender Policy) Strategic Axes and Objectives,
the Compact Projects, and the PAIG (Gender
Integration Action Plan) in Burkina Faso,"
May 2010.

26. I. Barwell, "Transport and the Village:
Findings from African Village-Level Travel
and Transport Surveys and Related Studies,"

World Bank Discussion Paper no. 344, Africa Region Series, 1996, http://siteresources .worldbank.org/EXTROADSHIGHWAYS /Resources/tr_village_en.pdf.

**Center Point Large Print**
600 Brooks Road / PO Box 1
Thorndike ME 04986-0001 USA

(207) 568-3717

US & Canada:
1 800 929-9108
www.centerpointlargeprint.com